The Very Rich Hours of Jacques Maritain

The Very Rich Hours of JACQUES MARITAIN

A Spiritual Life

R ALPH M c I NERNY

University of Notre Dame Press

Notre Dame, Indiana

The University of Notre Dame Press and the Jaques Maritain Center
appreciate the support of the Robert T. Rolfs Foundation.

Library of Congress Cataloging-in-Publication Data
McInerny, Ralph M.
The very rich hours of Jacques Maritain : a spiritual life / Ralph
McInerny.
p.   cm.
Includes index.
ISBN 0-268-04359-0 (cloth : alk. paper)
1. Maritain, Jacques, 1882–1973.   I. Title.
B2430.M34 .M35   2003
194—dc21

2003012371

∞ *This book is printed on acid-free paper.*

FOR CONNIE

May she rest in peace

CONTENTS

Invitatory

Meeting at Meudon

Aperi, Domine, os meum. . . .

Four Germans who were in Paris for a meeting devoted to phenomenology visited the Maritain home in Meudon on September 14, 1932. Jacques Maritain had opened the conference and, at the age of fifty, was already enjoying a global reputation as a Christian philosopher and Thomist. Here is how Maritain recorded the visit in his journal. "Wednesday 24. Exaltation of the Holy Cross. Visit of Edith Stein, Dom Feuling, Rosenmoeller and Soehngen." It was more than gallantry that led him to mention the woman before the men. Edith Stein, Jewish like Raïssa Maritain, had become a Catholic and would soon enter the Carmelite Order and eventually be put to death at Auschwitz. It was their shared sense of the nature of Christian philosophy and a love of Thomas Aquinas that created immediately a special relation between the Maritains and Edith Stein.

The meeting to which Edith Stein had been invited was the first sponsored by the French Thomist Society. The second had as its theme the notion of Christian philosophy. A reading of the papers presented and the lively discussion of them that followed makes it clear that a common faith did not produce anything like unanimity on the question of the relation of faith to philosophy. Significantly, it was two laymen, Jacques Maritain and Etienne Gilson, whose views were subjected to prolonged and severe criticism as well as defense and celebration by clerical philosophers and theologians.

In his Gifford Lectures, *The Spirit of Medieval Philosophy*, Gilson had made the historical point that any number of philosophical concepts had first come to the fore while Christian thinkers were engaged in theology, that is, in sophisticated reflection on truths revealed by God. Gilson was understood by his critics to have a feeble sense of the distinction between theology and philosophy because he insisted that philosophy too was carried on by Christian thinkers in the light of their faith. Maritain's conception of "moral philosophy adequately considered" also was attacked as involving a fundamental confusion of philosophy and faith.

Quite apart from the niceties of the dispute, it serves to call attention to a central fact about Jacques Maritain. He and his wife had been rescued from an intellectual and spiritual wasteland by their conversion. Listening to lectures at the Sorbonne, they had seen no point in devoting the few decades of their lives to such academic activity if it were to be followed only by annihilation. The absurdity of such a view of life all but overwhelmed them. Charles Péguy urged them to attend the lectures of Henri Bergson, and, like so many of their generation, they got from the lectures an intimation of something more, of the metaphysical. But it was the white-maned, fiery eyed, unclubbable Léon Bloy who first made Catholicism a living reality for them and was the occasion for the conversion of both Jacques and Raïssa. Bloy was their godfather, and they retained a loyal affection for him throughout their lives, making him known to a wider audience.

All that had happened many years before the time that Edith Stein visited the Maritains in their house at Meudon. One is tempted to work a variation on Newman's motto and suggest that, on such occasions with such people, *spiritus ad spiritum loquitur*. The young German philosopher, whose academic career had been thwarted by her gender and even more by the Nazi racial laws, had converted to Catholicism more recently than the Maritains. Having lost her Jewish faith while at the university, she later was impressed by the way her Christian friends accepted the death of a loved one because of their faith that souls survive and their hope in the resurrection. But it was reading the autobiography of Saint Teresa of Avila that prompted the simple and decisive judgment, "This is the truth."

Unlike Jacques Maritain at the time of his conversion, when Edith Stein came into the Church she was already an established philosopher, trained in a single mode of philosophy, the phenomenology of her mentor Edmund Husserl. After she received her doctorate, she was employed by Husserl as his assistant and aided him in the preparation of several of his publications, put order into his notes, and generally became his good right hand. She was a confirmed phenomenologist but resisted Husserl's drift toward idealism. Once she had become a Catholic, she felt a duty to begin a serious study of Saint Thomas Aquinas. Her remarkable comparison of Husserl and Thomas appeared in the phenomenological *Jahrbuch*. Then she undertook a tremendous task, the translation of Thomas's *Disputed Question on Truth*, a collection of some twenty-nine disputed questions, which takes its title from the initial one. Perhaps nothing brings one into closer contact with a thinker than translating him into one's mother tongue. It was Thomas who enabled her to see the connection between her two major interests, philosophy and the spiritual life. "It became clear to me, in reading Saint Thomas," she wrote in 1928, "that it was possible to place knowledge at the service of God and it was then and only then that I could resolve to take up again my studies in a serious manner." No wonder she was attracted to the work of Jacques Maritain. She would already have been aware of his little book on Christian philosophy. After her visit to Meudon, the Maritains sent her their joint work, *De la vie d'oraison*, called *Prayer and Intelligence* in the English translation.

Edith Stein is a canonized saint of the Church. Jacques Maritain and his wife spent their lives in the pursuit of sanctity. In the eyes of many, they achieved it. Jacques's influence on hundreds of souls is recorded in a veritable mountain of letters. He was instrumental in the conversion of many, and he and Raïssa were godparents to dozens. Maritain was a philosopher who metamorphosed into a theologian in his last years. He filled a shelf with books that have formed the minds of many and provoked both allegiance and attack. He was a quintessential intellectual. But he was more.

The premise of this little book is that we can find in the person of Jacques Maritain a model of the intellectual life as lived by a Christian believer. Of course, there can be no question of talking of his life apart from his life's work. It is rather a matter of emphasis. If I can succeed in showing how Jacques Maritain has functioned, for friend and foe alike, as the model and ideal of the Catholic philosopher, this little book, however flawed, will have achieved its end.

Matins
(1881–1906)

Chronology

1882   November 8. Jacques Maritain born in Paris, son of Paul Maritain and Geneviève Favre, grandson of Jules Favre.

1883   September 12. Birth of Raïssa Oumansov at Rostov-on-the-Don.

1885   Divorce of Jacques's parents.
Religious instructions from Jean Reveille, pastor, liberal Protestant, who from 1907 occupied a chair at the Collège de France.

1898–1899   Jacques studies rhetoric at the Lycée Henri IV. Meets Ernest Psichari.
Declares himself a socialist.

1899   Jacques begins his studies at Sorbonne.
Dreyfus Affair. Meets Charles Péguy.

1901   Jacques enters Sorbonne. Meets Raïssa.
Péguy takes Jacques, Raïssa, and Psichari to hear Henri Bergson lecture at the Collège de France.

1902   Jacques and Raïssa secretly engaged.

1904   November 26. Marriage of Jacques and Raïssa.
             They begin to read Léon Bloy.
             Paul Maritain commits suicide.

1905   June 25. First visit to Bloy's home.
             Jacques passes his *agrégation en philosophie.*

1906   June 11. Baptism of Jacques, Raïssa, and her sister Vera in the
             church of Saint-Jean-l'Evangeliste. Léon Bloy is their god-
             father.
             Maritain, at his own expense, reissues Bloy's *Salvation by the Jews.*
             Departure for Heidelberg.

BEFORE RAÏSSA

Je serai socialiste et vivrai pour la revolution.

I

Jacques Maritain tells us so little of his antecedents and boyhood that one is tempted to agree with his biographer Barré that the philosopher made a concerted effort to cut himself loose from his roots, choosing to be an exile in his native land and elsewhere.[1] In many respects, one could scarcely blame him.

Although a remote ancestor was one of the first Jesuits, it was Maritain's grandfather Jules Favre whose memory brooded over Jacques's childhood, even though the great freethinker and politician had died in 1880, two years before Jacques's birth. There was something untoward even in this heritage. Jules was unable to marry the woman by whom he had Geneviève, Jacques's mother. Jeanne Charmont had a husband when she began her affair with Favre, and divorce was not yet legal in France. Apparently Jeanne Charmont was a fervent Catholic, and Geneviève remembered attending church with her as well as the fervor of her prayers. But after she died in 1870,

Geneviève repudiated her mother's faith. To her consternation, her father married a woman, Julie Velten, who drew him into Protestantism. Geneviève apparently saw her accomplished stepmother as a rival for her father's affections. In any event, she married Paul Maritain, a lawyer and lapsed Catholic who served as Favre's secretary. They had two children, Jeanne and Jacques. The father had the daughter baptized Catholic, whereas Geneviève had Jacques baptized as a Lutheran.

Paul Maritain is a hazy figure. He looks indolent in photographs, regarding the workaday world with the sleepy semi-interest of the sensualist. His libertine ways would not have contributed to domestic tranquillity and, in any case, the couple separated. Geneviève made an effort to heal the breach and restore the household, but Paul had had enough of her and the couple was divorced. Geneviève Favre—she resumed her father's name after the divorce—was one of the first divorcées in France. Paul Maritain, having published a collection of Jules Favre's papers in 1882, sank into comfortable obscurity and, before he committed suicide on February 20, 1904, composed a document that came into his son's possession. Having tried everything else, he had decided to try death. When Jacques looked over his father's papers, he got rid of those he called Rabelaisian; but the rest are to be found in his dossier at the Maritain Archives in Kolbsheim. The fact that Jacques chose to keep any of his father's papers tells, if only slightly, against Barré's thesis.

Jacques Maritain and his sister Jeanne were raised by their domineering mother, who was determined that her son would duplicate the political triumphs of her father. Boyhood photographs of Jacques reveal a delicate, almost feminine child, with long hair and a bewildered receptive look. The ménage à trois—in an innocent sense—that characterized his childhood— mother, sister, self—would be replicated soon after his marriage, when Raïssa's sister Vera would take up lifelong residence with the Maritains. Jacques broke free of the suffocating influence of his mother and found in his wife another self, a person whose moods and illnesses and tearful pursuit of the heights of mysticism and dedication to his career would define his life for sixty years.

Geneviève Favre turned against the Lutheranism into which her father had led her, just as earlier she had turned against her mother's Catholicism. Her household was one in which political and social affairs dominated and, in what seems a harbinger of later temptations to radical chic, Jacques tells us that he became a socialist as a child. What form did this take? It consisted of conversations with the husband of the Maritain cook, who was a socialist, and whom Jacques idolized. He tells us of evenings spent in the kitchen poring over the socialist paper with François Baton, but what this suggests is the need for masculine influence rather than any serious understanding of politics.

One of the surprises in Barré's book is the revelation that, at one point, Geneviève Favre enlisted the theologian Jean Reveille to instruct her children. Later Jacques would dedicate *Three Reformers*, with its severe treatment of Martin Luther, to his mother,

Jacques is little help in any effort to reconstruct his pre-school life. It has to be approached obliquely, by way of the ambience in which he was raised, what we know of his mother, and a few unreliable allusions of his own. But by and large those years are closed to us. Perhaps he did want to repudiate those fatherless years lived with a mother trying to be her father's daughter, with people like Charles Péguy dropping by to talk with her, and with the socialist in the kitchen to whom he might repair and mimic his mother's enthusiasms over the socialist newspaper. This household, in theory and action, sought to distinguish itself from the dreaded bourgeoisie, a distaste for whom Jacques retained throughout his long life. The only item from his pre-university days that he includes in his *Carnet de notes* is a letter written in his teens to François Baton, the cook's husband, in which he dedicates his life to socialism. The letter was preserved by Geneviève Favre.

Writing later in 1904, two years before his conversion, Jacques inveighs against communities, likening them to the family. "Communities. There is never a chance to be free! When three or four individuals are gathered together the same bonds of authority and the same servitudes appear. The smallest group becomes a little *family*. One becomes the father, the other the brother. . . . This community has all the vices of a bourgeois marriage."[2] Who can fail to see in this distaste for the most natural of human arrangements the influence of the unusual ménage in which Jacques was raised? On November 25 of that same year, he married Raïssa.

2

In 1898, Jacques entered the Lycée Henri IV at the age of sixteen and later remembered being caught up in the Dreyfus affair. He was under great pressure to succeed, to do well in class, to please his professors and his mother, presumably to prepare for a career like his famous grandfather's. This may have been the year when he felt a strong if fleeting impulse to commit suicide by hurling himself out the window of his room, thereby removing the frightening prospect of the years that lay ahead. His detestation of those "on the right" and a romantic desire to be "with the people" remained with him, as it would throughout his life; but these were the thoughts of a boy, as they would be those of a man, which were entertained while seated in a study. His later alliances as well as his political philosophy can scarcely be understood without this romantic radicalism. Late in his life, he would write that he had known only three truly radical men: Saul Alinsky, Eduardo Frei, and—himself! That he should think of himself in the same thought as a leftist agitator in Chicago and a Latin American politician gives the reader pause. But the identification of political, even revolutionary, action with thought began under the tutelage of Geneviève Favre. In these early stages his contempt for the army and the bourgeoisie extended to the Church as well.

It was at the lycée that he formed a friendship that would mark him for life. Ernest Psichari was the grandson of the famous apostate Ernest Renan, whose fatuous rationalism took the place of the religion he shuffled off while retaining a sentimental attachment to it. Like Jacques, Ernest lived in the shadow of his famous forebear, and the two boys became like brothers, inseparable. The socialist in the kitchen was not enough; Jacques needed male companionship, and not just the rough and tumble of boys in number, but someone who could give him respite from his mother's high hopes for him. Geneviève was delighted with Jacques's new friend, and Ernest became like a third child to her. Perhaps she imagined this friendship to be an alliance between two great families of liberal and republican France. In her memoir, Raïssa Maritain saw it in just that way. "On his mother's side, Jacques Maritain is the grandson of Jules Favre; Psichari, on his mother's side, was the grandson of Ernest Renan. In the nineteenth century, the Renans and Favres were among the most representative of the great intellectual and politically minded families of liberal and republican France."[3] The boys had been raised in the same atmosphere of free-thinking positivism. Ernest remembered his grandfather from summers by the sea, the old writer's eyes following his grandson with who knew what expectations? Ernest's father was Greek, his mother Dutch, and from his namesake he was Breton, so that he represented three rejected faiths: Catholicism, Protestantism, and Orthodoxy. Ernest had been baptized into the last.

The optimism of the Psichari household struck Jacques. It was as if they all believed the progressive slogans that for them replaced religious faith. There was something prelapsarian about it, and later Jacques would write, "I see now that it was a milieu in which original sin and even metaphysical misery were really nothing, not yet arrived." For all its supposed tolerance, the Psichari home was firmly anti-Christian, not antagonistically, but rather in the sense of having gone through all that and surpassed it.

Jacques and Ernest were both intellectually gifted and curious and, in their case, the lycée was a place in which they would discover everything for themselves, not receive it from the professors. It was a time of voracious reading. And they carried on an active correspondence, as if being together during the day was insufficient for all they had to say to one another. Baudelaire, Zola, Voltaire, Rousseau—they devoured and discussed these and other writers. The two boys saw themselves as opposed to the very milieu in which they found themselves, in which they had been raised, and from which they drew their companions. Jacques conceived a deep contempt for the society that had condemned Captain Dreyfus, and he would blame it later for the debacle of 1940.

Ernest fell in love with Jacques's sister Jeanne when she was twenty-five and he but eighteen. Jeanne Maritain did not take her young admirer seriously, soon married another and left Ernest crushed and in despair. He tried to take his own life twice and then sought oblivion in sensual excess, as Raïssa delicately puts it.[4] Ernest, in *Le voyage du Centurion*, was equally oblique. "Maxence wandered without conviction in the poisonous gardens of vice, pursued by vague remorse, troubled at the hatefulness of deceit, burdened with the dreadful mockery of a light caught in the trap of disorderly thinking and feeling."[5] Eventually, he sought redemption by joining the army, and the discipline of military life turned out to be precisely what he needed.

There is far more to the story of Ernest Psichari as it impinged on that of Jacques Maritain, but for now let us savor the irony of a passionate Dreyfusard seeking and finding salvation in the army, which, along with the Church and the bourgeoisie, had been an object of contempt for Ernest as well as Jacques. Somewhat similarly, Jacques would come to see in the faith he thought he had dismissed forever the only answer to the inner tumult that made him, too, think of suicide.

Raïssa

Dimidium animae meae.

I

When the Maritains were in exile in New York during World War II, Raïssa published two volumes of memoirs. The first, written in 1940, was an almost desperate effort to recall better days before the fall of France and to conjure from memory the presence of old friends, some of them already casualties of World War I. *We Have Been Friends Together* introduced American readers to a woman and her husband and their friends. It recalled forgotten figures and introduced others previously unknown. It was the story of the religious conversion of Raïssa, whose Jewish family had come from Russia to France when she was a child, and of Jacques, whose early years we have just considered. Nothing enthralls a cradle Catholic more than an account of conversion to the faith, a mature adult's deliberate choice of Catholicism. When there is added to this the éclat of cosmopolitan France, when the account of the conversion places it within the cultural developments of Paris, the result is heady indeed. Raïssa's book enjoyed a vast readership among American Catholics—and others as well, of course—but for American Catholics it was a first installment on what became an almost tribal legend.

The second volume of Raïssa's memoirs, *Adventures in Grace*, was written in 1944 when the liberation of France and the victory of the Allies were assured. In many respects, the second volume covers the same ground as the first, but there is an expansion of themes and episodes. Raïssa's memoirs were certainly read by many more Americans than had ever read her husband, but it is to Jacques that the reader's attention is directed.

Raïssa's memoirs; Jacques's *Carnet de notes*, published in 1965; and Raïssa's journal, which Jacques published first privately, then commercially, are the main elements in a problem that faces one seeking to trace the spiritual life of Jacques Maritain. Both Maritain and his wife have made it virtually impossible to deal separately with either of them. Raïssa was fiercely loyal to Jacques and jealous of his reputation; Jacques insisted that his wife was an accomplished poet, art critic, and, more importantly, mystic. Her journal is put before the reader as if it were equivalent to Saint Thérèse de Lisieux's *Story of a Soul*. There were some, however, who had a different view of Raïssa and of her literary accomplishments. Etienne Gilson, for example, disliked Raïssa and her influence on Jacques. Conflicting images arise from her journal. Must a biographer of Jacques address the enigma of Raïssa as well?[6]

My decision is this. I will by and large adopt Jacques Maritain's view of his wife, since it is his view of her that is an integral part of his own spiritual life. He deferred to her in aesthetic matters because she was the poet; his estimate of her inner life is clear both in deed and, in the case of the *Journal*, in word. Increasingly after her death he adopted a self-effacing attitude toward her, as if she had been the important unit in the dyad of their life. They lie buried in the same plot in Kolbsheim under a single stone that bears her name and dates in large letters and then, in a lower corner in small letters: *And Jacques*. Quite apart from the difficulties posed for such a book as this, the story of their meeting and their marriage and their conversion is fascinating.

2

Before the world of Jacques and Raïssa, there was the world of Raïssa and her sister Vera. Jacques did not so much replace Vera as to make way for a triad: Jacques/Raïssa/Vera. The three were to form one household shortly after the marriage of the young couple; eventually, the three came into the Church together. One could say that Vera played the role of Martha and Raïssa that of Mary, except this would assign too exalted a role to Jacques. Or would he be Lazarus?

Raïssa Oumansov was born in Rostov-on-Don on September 12, 1883. (All dates are according to the Gregorian calendar.) She spent her first decade in Russia. Her father was a tailor and hers was an extended family in which both her maternal and her paternal grandfathers were integral parts of the household. The family moved to Mariupol on the Sea of Azov in 1886 just before the birth of Vera. The two sisters were to be very close and, early on, despite the fact that Raïssa was the older, in their games Vera took the role of mother and Raïssa that of child, thus establishing a rapport that would remain for life. Unusually for a girl, Raïssa was admitted to school in Russia and, over the course of three years, did very well. In part to enable her to develop her talents, the family decided to emigrate. Their original destination was New York, but they stopped, then stayed, in Paris. At the age of nine Raïssa was sent to school in a strange land where a strange language was spoken, but soon she was excelling as she had in Russia. French came easily to her, and she fell in love with the language and France as well.

Raïssa was born into a religiously observant family but with adolescence she began to draw away and to entertain doubts about the existence of God and about the family's religious practices. Having completed the lycée at sixteen, Raïssa entered the Sorbonne shortly after her seventeenth birthday and devoted herself to the natural sciences, hoping to find in them the answers to the large questions of life. This expectation was derided by the one professor in whom she confided it. One day after class, she was approached by a young man who was soliciting signatures for a protest against the treatment of socialist students in Russia. His name was Jacques Maritain. It was the beginning of a relationship that would soon ripen into love, be consummated in marriage, and, sublimated, would continue until they were parted by her death in 1960.

3

I would have accepted a sad life, but not one that was absurd.
—Raïssa

Although both Raïssa and Jacques were preparing for a *licence en sciences,* they were dissatisfied with the broader picture of human life their courses suggested. She felt that a *malaise infinie* was created by a myopic concentration on structure alone. Felix Le Dantec, the professor the two young people were most struck by, maintained a "calm and resolute" materialism according to which life came down to a chemical combination, with thought a mere epiphenomenon. Could they turn from the sciences to philosophy for an intimation of transcendence? Young philosophers were deflected into the sociology of Durkheim and Lévy-Bruhl.

Written many years later, the pages that Raïssa Maritain devoted to the cultural and intellectual milieu in which she and Jacques found themselves at the age of twenty fill the reader with melancholy, a melancholy all the more sad because she might be describing the beginnings of a malaise that is only deeper now. A century later the materialism that so oppressed Raïssa Oumansov and Jacques Maritain has developed into what John Paul II has characterized as the "culture of death." This makes their response all the more relevant. In those poignant pages of *We Have Been Friends Together* that bear the subtitle "In the *Jardin des Plantes*," Raïssa gives us an indelible portrait of two lost souls. There are readers who lament the vagueness of her memoirs—it is not always clear exactly when things take place, and she even fails to mention her family name when speaking of her origins—but such complaints are churlish. The account we are about to examine is said to take place after "two or three years of study at the Sorbonne," yet they have "scarcely twenty years behind them." No matter. The vividness of the scene transcends such chronological vagueness.

"One summer afternoon Jacques and I were strolling about in the Jardin des Plantes. . . ." Thus begins the account of the two university students, very much in love, strolling home from classes, and on this occasion unhappy, very unhappy. Somewhat like the young Descartes in winter quarters, they reflect on what they have studied and realize that it has left them empty. "But this knowledge was undermined by the relativism of the scientists, by the skepticism of the philosophers." However incoherent and self-refuting skepticism might be, it was active and real and disruptive of life. The result is a "metaphysical anguish." Nor can Raïssa forgo drawing a parallel between the time recalled and the time in which she is writing, that of World War II. Despair is rampant and, with it, suicide. "On this particular day, then, we had just said to one another that if our nature was so unhappy as to possess only a pseudo-intelligence capable of everything but the truth, if, sitting in judgment on itself, it had to debase itself to such a point, then we could neither think nor act with any dignity. In that case everything became absurd—and impossible to accept—without our even knowing what it was in us that thus refused acceptance."[7] What is the measure of all things? She tells us that she had come to believe herself an atheist; she no longer put up any defense against atheism, not so much persuaded as devastated by the arguments on its behalf. "And the absence of God unpeopled the universe."

If there is no distinction between good and evil, how could they live humanly? "I wanted no part in such a comedy. I would have accepted a sad life, but not one that was absurd." Without the conviction that life had meaning, the prospect before them was indeed tragic. It was all the more tragic because their crisis was brought on by their studies, so they could not turn to science or philosophy. It was these that had caused the illness. How could they provide the remedy? The young couple did not want a false security. They were repelled by "epicureanism" as an alternative. Stoicism, estheticism—these were mere amusements, not answers to the problem that wracked them. For they had applied not only to the philosophers of the Sorbonne, but to Schopenhauer and Nietzsche, in each of whom, for different reasons, they found a temporary but finally unsatisfying respite from the sense of absurdity.

At an analogous point in his young life, Descartes had concluded that what was needed was a method that would turn opinion and falsehood into certainty and truth. But the intellectual morass in which Raïssa and Jacques found themselves was, in many ways, a logical development from what Descartes had set in train. For the moment, the young couple decided to have confidence in the unknown. They would "extend credit to existence," see the coming months as an experiment during which the meaning of life might reveal itself to them, unveiling a meaning to which they could give their total allegiance—something for which they could live and die. "But if the experiment should not be successful, the solution would be suicide; suicide before the years had accumulated their dust, before our youthful strength was spent. We wanted to die by a free act if it were impossible to live according to the truth."[8]

4

Their despair first began to lift and, with it, their self-imposed death sentence when they were induced by Charles Péguy to attend the lectures Henri Bergson was delivering to enthralled audiences in the Collège de France.

Bergson had already published *Essay on the Immediate Data of Consciousness* and *Matter and Memory*, although Jacques did not read them until later. But almost immediately he was hooked and became a devotee of Bergson. To the Friday lectures was added a course in Greek given by Bergson in which the young couple read the *Enneads* of Plotinus. It is not too much to say that this was first of all a mood, an intimation, rather than intellectual conviction on this or that point. Bergson proceeded on the assumption that the truth could be known, that the human mind was capable of knowing reality.

Nonphilosophers might regard the restoration of such convictions as small beer, but minds that had been subject to the assault of the dominant mood of the day—it too was initially a prejudice, the assumption under which one worked—had been taught to doubt the mind's ability to know with certainty and truth.

It is a paradox of the time that progress was read in terms of the inexorable advance of the sciences, while accounts of human knowledge seemed to undercut this confidence. Bergson's examination of what is given immediately to consciousness was meant to provide an alternative to skepticism. By contrast with the scientific method, his thinking appeared mystical; and indeed, no less an authority than Henry Bars felt that reading Plotinus with Bergson had played a role in opening up the minds of Raïssa and Jacques to the Christian mystics.[9]

The attendance at Bergson's lectures is a source of difficulties in establishing the chronology of Maritain's life prior to his conversion in 1906. Maritain entered the Sorbonne in 1900 and, during the first academic year, he met Raïssa. Presumably it was in the spring of that year, 1901, that the resolution was made in the Jardin des Plantes. The following autumn they began to follow the lectures of Bergson and their metaphysical gloom began to lift. In 1902 the couple became engaged, but this was kept a secret from their families. Raïssa's family had felt that she was drifting away from them and taking her sister Vera with her. Geneviève Favre could scarcely have regarded an immigrant Russian Jewess as a fitting wife for the son in whom she had invested such hope and ambition. Jacques married Raïssa on November 26, 1904, and in that same year they began to read Léon Bloy. This leaves a stretch of years about which we have minimal information in the published record. One thing that does emerge is the unstated resolution that their ambitions would merge into Jacques's career. Raïssa's intention to take a degree began to recede: it is Jacques who must carry the torch for both, but it will be fueled through the years by the constant inspiration of Raïssa.

Bergson had convinced them that life had meaning, and Jacques became known in the university as a disciple of Bergson. "He bore aloft through the classrooms the revolutionary torch of passionate socialism and of the philosophy of intuition."[10] Bergson liberated Jacques from the oppressive materialism of the Sorbonne. Students, intellectuals, fashionable Paris, came to the late afternoon lectures of Bergson at the Collège de France. Doubtless there was an element of chic in being there for some, but for Péguy, Maritain, Etienne Gilson, and many others, Bergson was a revelation. He became something of a darling of Catholics. It is ironic, given the role Bergson played in his intellectual and spiritual life, that Maritain, in his first book, should launch a sustained crtique of Bergsonism. By that time he had become a student of Thomas Aquinas, whose teaching he applied as a standard to the work of Bergson, to find it woefully wanting. Maritain himself would half regret this critique on the occasion of the twenty-fifth anniversary of *Bergsonian Philosophy*. He continued to think that the points he had made were just, but regretted the manner in which he had made them, since the book seemed an ungrateful response to a liberating and formative influence in his life.

Conversion

Il n'y a qu'une tristesse, c'est de n'être pas des saints.

I

The lectures of Henri Bergson had lifted the cloud of despair from Jacques Maritain and Raïssa Oumansov—she wrote, "I was rediscovering the lightheartedness and joy of my childhood, of those days when, with beating heart, I went to the lycée." They were experiencing a philosophical conversion, not unlike Augustine's first conversion. The instrument of this conversion, according to Raïssa, was as much Plotinus as the Bergsonian philosophy itself. Reading the *Enneads* with Bergson, the young couple were put into contact with a philosophical tradition that was sapiential and ultimately theological. God had been chased from the intellectual milieu of the Sorbonne, but a first antidote lay on the shelves of libraries and in the minds of such rare luminaries as Henri Bergson.

Since we must rely on Raïssa's account in which she virtually fuses herself and Jacques, it is not easy to separate her own enthusiasms from Jacques's state of mind and soul. On other occasions, she went first where he later followed, as in the reading of Thomas Aquinas. We do not know if Jacques reacted to Plotinus with the same intensity or whether he too went on to read the Rhenish mystics, but there can be no doubt that the lectures of Bergson opened his mind to a reality beyond the physical and restored his sense that the mind is capable of attaining the truth. And what we find in the few passages from this time that Jacques included in his *Carnet de notes* is that he and Raïssa were reading Maurice Maeterlinck. It is Maeterlinck who prompts Jacques to speak of silence and of the fear men have of what is great, profound, violent, and definitive. We do everything to avoid such things. And he speaks of the supreme intuition with which souls communicate with one another and finds in this the basis for a moral chastity that is the presupposition of physical chastity.

The single entry from 1903 concerns idealists in the philosophical sense, that is, those who say, "We know only what we know and we can only know what we know." Will they go beyond this tautology and say something of being? He suggests that such thinkers are imprisoned in their minds and have stopped up every exit. "If we wish to speak of being, we must have different postulates."[11] In 1904, there is the diatribe against communities and the attack on the family already mentioned, but it is followed by a poem that deals with the relationship between human freedom and God. The two pages devoted to 1904 end with this note: *26 novembre 1904.—Mariage de Jacques et Raïssa.*

The force and beauty of Raïssa's memoirs have persuaded many that there is an effective identity between the spiritual trajectories of the Maritains during these crucial years. She speaks of herself and Jacques as virtually inseparable; she moves easily between accounts of what *I* have done and what *we* did and thought and read. From Jacques's contemporary entries, which were not published until sixty years after the fact, a more cerebral period is suggested, a more philosophical one. But his mention of their common reading of Maeterlinck is crucial.

2

It was an effusive judgment written by Maeterlinck that opened Jacques and Raïssa to the next stage of their journey. They were already enthralled by the Belgian writer and thus, we can imagine, disposed to be guided by him in the enthusiasm he expressed for a novelist of whom they had never heard before, Léon Bloy. Maeterlinck was discussing *The Woman Who Was Poor,* and his remark was quoted in a literary column "we" happened to be reading in *Le Matin.* Forty years later, Raïssa set it down in her memoirs as if from memory. "If by genius," Maeterlinck said, "one understands certain *flashes in the depths, La Femme Pauvre* is the only work of the present day in which there are evident marks of genius."[12] This had been written in 1897 in a letter to Bloy, which the latter published in a volume of his journal. Later they were to see the full letter, and Raïssa quotes it in full. Since we have arrived at a crucial moment in Maritain's life, we will follow suit.

> Monsieur, I have just read *La Femme Pauvre.* It is, I believe, the only work of this day in which there are evident marks of genius, if by genius we understand certain *flashes in the depths* which link what is seen to what is not seen, and what is not yet understood to what will be understood one day. From the purely human point of view one is involuntarily re-minded of *King Lear,* and nothing else comparable can be found in literature. I beg you to believe, dear sir, in my very deep admiration.— Maurice Maeterlinck.

Here was heady praise indeed, and what author would not want it more widely known? For the Maritains, who were predisposed to Maeterlinck— though neither mentions any particular work of his—this praise was a powerful inducement to read the novel. How, at this stage, could they resist a story said to relate the seen to the unseen, the known to the not-yet-known? The novel was to put before them the reality of Christian faith.

The final line of this strange story burned itself into the consciousness of these young people and swept away all their prejudices and received opinions that saw in Christianity the political, the comfortable, the bourgeois. "There is only one sadness, not to be a saint."

3

Reading the novel led to writing the author and eventually to visiting him in his Paris home. It is Jacques who has described this moment in unforgettable words.

> It was in June 1905 that two children in their twenties mounted the sempiternal stairs that climb to Sacred Heart. They bore within them that distress which is the single serious product of modern culture and a sort of active despair that was somewhat lightened, they knew not how,

by an inner assurance that the Truth for which they hungered, and without which it was almost impossible for them to accept life, would one day be shown them. A kind of moral aestheticism sustained them weakly, in which the idea of suicide—after several attempts, doubtless too beautiful to succeed—seemed to offer the only outcome. While awaiting, they had cleansed their minds, thanks to Bergson, of the scientistic superstitions the Sorbonne entertained—but knowing still that Bergsonian intuition was a too inconsistent refuge against the skepticism logically entailed by all the modern philosophies. Meanwhile they regarded the Church, hidden from view by inept prejudices and by the sight of too many comfortable people, as the rampart of the powerful and rich, whose interest was to keep minds in the "darkness of the Middle Ages." They were going toward a strange beggar who, distrusting all philosophy, cried from the housetops the divine truth: a fully obedient Catholic who condemned the times and those who sought their consolation here below with more *liberty* than all the revolutionaries in the world. They had a terrible fear of what they were going to encounter—they were not familiar with literary geniuses, but it was something very different they were going to seek. There was not a shadow of curiosity in them, but a sense filling the soul with gravity: compassion for a greatness without refuge.

They went through a little old-fashioned garden and entered a humble house whose walls were filled with books and beautiful images and were first of all struck by a sort of great blank goodness whose peaceful nobility impressed itself: Mrs. Léon Bloy. Her two little girls, Veronica and Madeleine, regarded them with astonished eyes. Léon Bloy seemed almost timid; he spoke little and softly, trying to say something important to these two young visitors that would not deceive them. What they found cannot be expressed: the tenderness of Christian fraternity, and that tremor of mercy and fear that seizes one facing a soul marked with the love of God. Bloy seemed to us the opposite of other men who conceal their serious lack in matters of the spirit and so many unseen crimes beneath the whitewash of the social virtues. Instead of being a whited sepulchre like the pharisees of any time, he was a sooted and blackened cathedral. The white was within, in the depths of the tabernacle.

Once they crossed the threshold of that house, all values were displaced as by an invisible trigger. One knew, one sensed, *that there was only one sadness, not to be among the saints.* Everything else became twilit.[13]

This moving passage is taken from the preface Jacques Maritain wrote for a collection of letters from Bloy to his godchildren that was published in 1928. It therefore antedates Raïssa's account of their conversion in her wartime memoirs. The account conflates a number of things that were separated by years. The despair and the consequent attraction of suicide takes us back to 1901. The judgment of the Sorbonne was the basis of that despair, but it increased over the intervening years. The role of Bergson is acknowledged, but regarded critically: it was not a sufficient antidote to the skepticism of the Sorbonne. Maritain emphasizes that they were about to have swept away all the clichés about the Church that had been received opinion in the home in which he was raised. Hatred of the bourgeoisie and hatred of the Church were two sides of the same coin. In Bloy, they were to confront a ferocious believer, a man whose appraisal and condemnation of the times appealed to Maritain's radical side. Bloy is described as showing more freedom—underlined—than all the revolutionaries in the world. But he was also a man who held philosophy in contempt.

Here we confront one of the great puzzles in Maritain's relations with Bloy. Bloy was to be the doorway into the Church for Jacques and Raïssa; he would be their godfather when they became Catholics in June of 1906, a year after this memorable first visit to the Bloy household near Sacré Coeur. Maeterlinck had described Bloy as a literary genius, but it was not in this role that he influenced Jacques and Raïssa. It was the man himself, a man of faith who had suffered enormously for his principles and whose writings were anything but mere aesthetic exercises. Bloy was a man who personified the truth of the sentence Maritain quotes and which Raïssa will quote in *We Have Been Friends Together:* not to be a saint is the only sadness because failing to do so is to fail to achieve the very point of life.

What Bloy represented then was an answer to the question that had caused them such anguish in the episode in the *Jardin des Plantes*. Why am I alive? The answer: in order to become a saint. Learning what that meant defined Maritain's life from then on.

The little booklet in which this preface was reprinted in 1928 was called *Quelques pages sur Léon Bloy;* it contains two other items, a response to certain criticisms and an essay on Bloy's tomb. Maritain occupies a role that was conferred upon him by his friendship with and loyalty to Léon Bloy, that of defending his godfather against criticisms with which Maritain clearly has some sympathy. Bloy was no respecter of persons, and his ferocious attacks startled and dismayed many who pardonably wondered how his profession of religious faith was compatible with such cruelty. Perhaps what most did not understand was how such an intellectual as Maritain could have been so decisively influenced by such an anti-intellectual as Léon Bloy.

But it was precisely the inadequacies of the intellectual life as practiced within the ambience of the Sorbonne that had led Maritain himself to lose confidence in it. Nor was this merely an epistemological crisis, à la Descartes. He saw suicide as the only reasonable alternative to the view that life is radically absurd. Later on he would develop an intellectual response to the antimetaphysical materialism against which he revolted. But at the moment, he needed an existential response to despair. He found it in a man whose whole life was meaningless if this earthly life is all there is. This "Pilgrim of the Absolute" was a powerful personal argument for an alternative, and Maritain and his fiancée were captivated.

One of the first things they did for the impoverished writer was to finance the reprinting of his book *Salvation Through the Jews*. This was to come back to haunt them when the seemingly heterodox views of Bloy were bruited about by Maritain's enemies. Did Bloy think there would be a coming of the Holy Spirit similar to the coming of Christ and that the Spirit, like the Son, would be rejected by the pharisees of the day? Bloy's criticisms did not of course spare his coreligionists. Jacques Maritain always remained loyal to Bloy, defending him by suggesting benign interpretations, urging others to see Bloy as a prophet, more patristic than medieval. He would never repudiate his godfather. It is one example among many of his unshakable loyalty to friends.

Bloy's devotion to Our Lady of LaSalette was central to his life, and Jacques and Raïssa adopted his attitude toward the private revelations given to Melanie by Our Lady in the village of LaSalette. The young couple made a pilgrimage to LaSalette and, as we shall see, these private revelations were the reason for the first trip the Maritains took to Rome.

4

The visits to Bloy continued. Later Maritain would recall this period and a day he was moved to put to the test the promises of this unknown God. "My God, if You exist, and if You are the truth, make me know it." He apparently repeated this until the day when he knelt and recited the Lord's Prayer for the first time. When he described this later to Raïssa, he added that from that point everything had changed for him. In visiting Bloy, he was not concerned with hearing how difficulties raised against Catholic doctrine could be answered. "The difficulty was in entering into the mystery proper to this doctrine; in finding the center around which all the rest is organized and oriented." During the months that passed after the first visit, Bloy had them reading visionaries and mystics, Saint Angela of Foligno and Ruysbroeck. As they discussed books they would never have opened on their own, Bloy's heartfelt faith was ever manifest and spoke to them more directly than the text. They read the visions of Anne Catherine Emmerich to the transcription of which the Romantic poet Brentano had devoted a large portion of his life.[14] It was through these visions, recounted by Brentano, that the Maritains became steeped in Catholicism—its history, dogma, theology, literature, mysticism. The doctrine of the Communion of the Saints, of the way in which all believers are bound together in the Mystical Body of Christ that is the Church, animated by the Holy Spirit, altered their view of the Church as a gathering of the smug and comfortable.

But it was George Sorel who came into Péguy's shop from a meeting of the Philosophical Society, devoted to mysticism, declaring that none of the participants knew the real sources and mentioning *The Spiritual Catechism* of Surin. Jacques read this with a telling effect. He began to thirst for the kind of contemplation described by Surin.[15]

The meeting with Bloy took place in June. By the following February, 1906, the Maritains had become acquainted in a more or less theoretical way with the nature of the faith. But during these eight months, the reading, reflection, and new friendships with Catholics such as the painter Georges Rouault, enabled them to set aside objections to Catholicism and instilled in them a desire for the happiness and holiness of the saints. In February Raïssa fell ill. Her fragile health is a leitmotif of her memoirs and indeed of the Maritain marriage. On this occasion, she was bedridden for several weeks. It occurred to Jacques that the time for vacillation was over. This was when he fell on his knees and recited the Our Father. On February 15, Bloy made this entry in his journal. "The miracle is accomplished. Jacques and Raïssa want to be baptized! Great rejoicing in our hearts. Once more my books, the occasion of this miracle, are approved not by a bishop nor by a doctor, but by the Holy Ghost."[16]

The Maritains thought that Bloy could baptize them secretly and that would be it, but of course there was no emergency justifying baptism by a layperson. The wish by the Maritains for secrecy was prompted by the realization of what the consequences of conversion would be. Their families would be alienated, their friends would first mock and then drop them;

there was a heavy price to pay for baptism, something analogous in their lives to the demands his faith made on Léon Bloy. "To ask for baptism," Raïssa wrote, "was also to accept separation from the world that we knew in order to enter a world unknown: it was, we thought, to give up our simple and common liberty in order to undertake the conquest of spiritual liberty, so beautiful and so real among the saints, but placed too high, we thought, ever to be attained."[17]

Bloy sent them to a priest at Sacré Coeur, Father Durantel. Their proximate preparation for baptism began and it went on for months. Jacques was convinced that to go forward and accept the faith would be to turn forever from philosophy. He made himself ready to do that. If the choice was truth or philosophy, he knew which he would choose. Raïssa quotes his remark at this time: "If it has pleased God to hide His truth in a dunghill, that is where we shall go to find it."[18] Raïssa calls these cruel words, but they convey something of the human sacrifice that conversion required of them, and of the lingering human estimate of that which now so attracted them. "Our suffering and dryness grew greater every day. Finally we understood that God too was waiting, and that there would be no further light so long as we should not have obeyed the imperious voice of our consciences saying to us: you have no valid objection to the Church; she alone promises you the light of truth—prove her promises, put baptism to the test."[19]

Raïssa's account of Jacques Maritain's conversion is written nearly forty years later, after the couple had sought to live the spiritual ideal they accepted in baptism for most of their adult lives. Her retrospect is suffused with her faith at the time of writing, and her account all but suppresses the repugnance conversion had for them before it took place. No doubt they were drawn, if only on an aesthetic plane, to the accounts of mystical experience. No doubt too the living witness of believers like Bloy and Rouault ignited their minds and imaginations. But Péguy's unwillingness to make Bloy's acquaintance and his dismissal of the letter Bloy sent him, full of praise for something he had read of Péguy's, suggests how against the grain of their upbringing and ambiance the move Bloy urged on them must have seemed. What precisely brought about the transition from repugnance to acceptance?

Perhaps every account of conversion—or deconversion—must fail to convey the heart of the matter. An Ernest Renan or an Anthony Kenny can write of his departure from the faith and the transition sounds smooth enough. One seeks to ground the faith in a way that faith assures one it cannot be grounded, and the result is predictable. But what leads a believer to act so contrary to his belief in the first place? That the arguments are bad arguments cannot of course explain the disposition to treat them as cogent. And so it is with the movement in the opposite direction. What explains the deed the doing of which has for so long seemed beyond the realm of possibility? The removal of historical and theoretical objections to Catholicism is only that. Something else must intervene. In deconversion, it is the slipping away of the faith, turning away from grace. In conversion, it is the opposite. The Maritains were baptized on June 11, 1906, in the Church of St. John the Evangelist in Montmartre.

Raïssa put it this way: "I was in a state of absolute dryness, and could no longer remember any of the reasons for my being there. One single thing remained clear in my mind: either Baptism would give me Faith, and I would believe and I would belong to the Church altogether; or I would go away unchanged, an unbeliever forever. Jacques had almost the same thoughts."

"What do you ask of the Church of God?" they were asked when they stood before the baptismal font.

"Faith," they replied.

The gift was offered and received. This was the turning point of Jacques Maritain's life.

LAUDS
(1906–1918)

Chronology

1906   July 6. Confirmation at Grenoble after a short retreat at LaSalette.
December 11. Vera, Raïssa's sister, comes to live with the Maritains in Heidelberg. She will live with the Maritains for the rest of her life, Martha to Raïssa's Mary, secretary, research assistant, nurse. . . .

1907   January. Raïssa, seriously ill, receives last Sacraments. Recovers after intercession to Our Lady of LaSalette.
August 24. Jacques visits on behalf of Péguy the latter's old friend, Louis Baillet, monk in the exiled community of Solesmes on the Isle of Wight. Meets Dom Delatte, the abbot. Péguy advised to have his children baptized. Maritain carries the message. Return to Germany.
Bergson's *Creative Evolution.*
December 8. Pope Pius X issues *Pascendi,* condemnation of Modernism.

1908   Spring. Decision to break with Bergsonism.
June. Return from Germany; Péguy still waffling. Maritain adopts "dogmatic manner, naively and unbearably arrogant" in effort to move Péguy.
October. Apartment in Paris. Hack work.
November. First visit to Père Clérissac.

1909   Early in year Raïssa begins to read Thomas Aquinas at suggestion of Père Clérissac.
June 22. Unfortunate and unsuccessful visit to Péguy's wife in effort to persuade her to have children baptized.
October 14. Move to Versailles to be near Clérissac.

1910   June. Jacques's first publication, "Modern Science and Religion," appears in the *Revue de Philosophie.*
Sept. 15. Begins reading the *Summa theologiae.*
December. Refuses offer from Henri de Gaulle (father of Charles) to succeed him as professor at Ecole Sainte-Geneviève.

1911   Both Raïssa and Vera ill. Jacques suffers severe temptations against faith.

1912   February 21. Under pseudonym Jacques Favelle, at the painter's request, Maritain writes preface to the catalog of Georges Rouault's first exhibition.
September 29. Jacques, Raïssa, and Vera become oblates of Saint Benedict.
October. Jacques becomes professor of philosophy at Collège Stanislas.
October 2. Vow by Jacques and Raïssa to live as brother and sister.

1913   February. Conversion of Ernest Psichari, grandson of Ernest Renan.
Bergsonian Philosophy, Jacques's first book, published.
Meets Louis Massignon, Henri Massis. Dreams of a Catholic publication.

1914   Spring. Remarkable lectures on the spirit of modern philosophy at the Institut Catholique, to whose faculty Jacques is appointed in June.
August 3. World War I begins. The Maritains vacation on Isle of Wight. Geneviève Favre urges her son to recognize his duty to the fatherland. Jacques demurs, says he is a prisoner on the Isle where "democracy has exiled the monks for the crime of prayer." His mother tells him to stay in England. "In 1914, just as twenty-five years later in the context of another war, the Maritains were conscious of spiritual responsibilities demanded by their circumstances." (Jean-Luc Barré)
August 22. Psichari killed in action.

September 5. Péguy killed in action.
October. Jacques returns to France, his exemption confirmed, considered unfit for service.
November 6. Resumes teaching, lecturing on German philosophy.
November 15/16. Père Clérissac dies.
Père Dehau becomes their spiritual director.

1916   Jacques begins teaching a course at the Petit Seminaire of Versailles.

1917   Temporary mobilization.
April 16. First letter from Pierre Villard.
November 3. Death of Léon Bloy.

1918   March 26–April 10. Visit to Rome. Audience with Benedict XV. Jacques decides against publishing his manuscript on LaSalette.
June 30. Death of Pierre Villard. Jacques named joint heir with Charles Maurras, founder of Action Française.
Jacques goes on leave.
November 11. Armistice.

Spiritual Directions

I

In 1905, Jacques Maritain passed his *agrégation en philosophie*, and was thus qualified to teach in a lycée. The following year was the decisive one of their conversion. Then, thanks to a fellowship he had received, still not having informed their parents of their conversion, Jacques and Raïssa left for Heidelberg where they would spend the next two years, soon joined by Vera, who had also become a Catholic. There would be periodic visits to France.

Jacques and Raïssa had learned from their godfather their overriding purpose of life, to become holy even as their heavenly father was holy, to become saints. It was to this exalted goal that they committed themselves. Jacques tells us how their days in Heidelberg were regulated.

6:00	Rise.
7:15	Mass and Holy Communion.
	On return from Church, read a bit while their breakfast was prepared. Then, until 11:30 Jacques worked.
11:30–12:15	Prayer and then lunch.
After lunch	Work, Latin, German, various readings.
5:00	Visit to the Blessed Sacrament.

6:30 or 7:00	Dinner.
After dinner	Chatting, reading a conference of Father Faber or another spiritual writer.
8:00	Compline. Rosary.
	Finally, Jacques read dogmatic literature in the kitchen after the two sisters had gone to bed.
11:00	Retire.

I have taken this from a passage in which Jacques mixes up Raïssa's and Vera's day with his own. In the mornings, Vera shopped or played the harmonium while Raïssa read. Raïssa had become a passionate devotee of the writings of the English Oratorian, Father Faber. Their prayer was the liturgy of the hours. The passage is included in his notes for 1907, but from the time of his conversion it was clear that the change was not merely a superficial one occupying a special area of attention. Jacques, his wife, and her sister had embarked on a life that would enable them to avoid the single tragedy mentioned at the end of *The Woman Who Was Poor*. They were in quest of sanctity. How were they to go about it?

2

What did they learn from Léon Bloy about the way to become one of the saints? First of all, Scripture. Bloy was a constant reader of the Bible and derived a good deal of his literary inspiration from it. He became himself a prophetic writer who inveighed against the sins of the times with the authority of one sent by God. In the book that all but overwhelmed Raïssa, *Salvation by the Jews*, Bloy announced that he spoke the truth in Christ. "I suffer a great sorrow and in my heart I have unceasing grief. For I wished to be an anathema from Christ, on behalf of my brethren, my kinsmen according to the flesh, who are Israelites, whose is the adoption as the children and the glory and the convenants and the giving of the law and the liturgy and the promises, to whom the fathers belong, and from whom is Christ according to the flesh."[1] From Bloy, they learned that Christ was the key to the link between the Old and New Testaments. That Christianity represented the fulfillment of her Jewish patrimony understandably had a great attraction for Raïssa, and, just as understandably, she spent many pages defending Bloy against the charge of anti-Semitism, a charge based on certain intemperate remarks scattered through what is an all but unrestrained celebration of the role of the Jews in salvation. But the first blessing they received from Bloy was this reverence for the Word of God.

Was Bloy unique in this? What of the widespread view that Catholics eschewed the Bible? The liturgy is the main vehicle through which Scripture came to Catholics: the readings in the Mass, the ceaseless recitation of the psalms in religious houses throughout the world. But for Bloy, as for Paul Claudel, the Book itself was a constant companion, an inspiration; and eventually both Bloy and Claudel wrote commentaries on parts of it.

Another factor prior to conversion was a visit to the cathedral of Chartres where they "read this great book of Christianity." For three days, they studied the architecture, the sculpture, the windows. "But in its first aspect, in its plastic language, it was for us a master-teacher of theology, of sacred history and of exegesis. It repeated for us what *Le Salut par les Juifs* had just told us: that the two Testaments are united in the person of Christ; that the old prefigures the New and is its basis, just as the New is the fulfillment and crown of the Old."[2] For the Maritains, as it had for the illiterate of the Middle Ages, the cathedral served as a catechism in glass and stone.

Bloy did not address their intellectual doubts or fashion arguments to counter them. He would have been incapable of this in any case. Rather, he read to them from the lives of the saints, Saint Angela of Foligno, in the translation of Ernest Hello. Bloy also spoke of Ruysbroeck, citing sentences from the mystic that went to the hearts of the young couple. He also read to them from the visions of Anne Catherine Emmerich, a German nun whose visions recount the life of Christ in a detail that goes far beyond the gospels. In them Catherine speaks of what she is seeing, and the narrative functions as a kind of running commentary on and supplement to the Evangelists' accounts of the life of Jesus. Neither Jacques nor Raïssa knew anything of Catholic history, dogma, theology, liturgy, or mysticism; and Raïssa thought that if they had at this time been offered a sober catechetical account of it all, it would have been of little help. It was then they were given a copy of Father Surin's *Spiritual Catechism*. It was a gift of Georges Sorel who also put them onto Father Poulain's *The Graces of Prayer.*

They were thus given instruction in the Christian life in terms of which they would later understand the dogmatic and moral content of the faith. In this they might have been following the advice of Pascal, a favorite author at the time. In the famous passage in which Pascal commends Christian faith as a good bet, a win-win proposition (either it was true and you go to heaven or it was false, death is the end, and you were no longer around to be a loser—not the most edifying passage in apologetic literature), Pascal goes on to say something of enormous importance. How does one set out on the path that seems open before one? How have others gone down it? "By doing everything as if they already believed, in taking holy water, in having masses said." It is the practice, the imitation of the acts of the faithful person, that can be a prelude to the gift of faith. Is the reader displeased by the Pascalian gamble? Then he should know "that it was written by a man who knelt down before and after writing it, to pray to that infinite being without parts, to whom he submits all that he is" and hopes that the reader will also so submit. As Pascal famously remarked, "*Le coeur a ses raisons que la raison ne connait point,*" something clear in a thousand ways. "It is the heart that knows God, not reason. That's what faith is, God sensible to the heart, not to reason."[3]

This gives us some indication of the direction Jacques and Raïssa were given for the development of their spiritual lives. "We studied the Scriptures, we read the liturgy for each day, as our godfather had advised us, the lives of the saints, and the writings of the mystics."[4] But there was another feature of what Léon Bloy bequeathed them, his devotion to the Blessed Virgin.

3

For Bloy, Mary was "She who weeps" (*Celle qui pleure*), the Virgin who had appeared at LaSalette to two little shepherds on September 19, 1846, and revealed such dire predictions of what lay ahead for the world. He wrote a book on LaSalette with that title. Jacques's grandfather, Jules Favre, as a lawyer represented a woman who had been accused of deluding the young shepherds and had decided to sue her accusers. He won the case.

As for Bloy, he came to feel that he had a mission to write about the apparitions.

I was born in 1846, at the moment willed by God, seventy days before the apparition. I therefore belong to LaSalette, in a rather mysterious fashion, and you have been chosen to put me in a position to write what must be written—at last! Each day this book is growing within me, and I marvel that after so many years of gestation it is asked of me at the very hour when the terrible threats of LaSalette seem about to be accomplished. What do I think? you ask. It is simple. Happy and blessed are those who have learned to suffer. The hour of reckoning is coming, and there is much to be paid for, infinitely more than one thinks. . . . The continual expectation of divine catastrophes has become my reason for being, my destiny; if you wish, my art. I have all my roots in the Secret of LaSalette, and this is doubtless why the conspiracy of *Silence* has tried to assassinate me. I have spent my life in indignation at not seeing the deluge." (Letter to Pierre Tempier, Dec. 21, 1906)[5]

In her memoir, Raïssa made no secret of the fact that she regarded LaSalette as more extraordinary than Lourdes, despite all the cures there, and the importance lay in the apocalyptic messages given the two shepherds, Melanie Calvat and Maximin Giraud. These two children—Melanie, 15, Maximin, 11—were watching cows in a remote alpine pasture above the town of LaSalette in the area of Grenoble. Having eaten their lunch, they fell asleep and, when they awoke, their cows were gone. In a panic, they began to search and soon found them peacefully grazing. Melanie's eye was caught by an extremely bright light. The children approached, and from it emerged the vision of a woman, seated, weeping. She wept throughout the time she spoke to them, giving them a message to be addressed to all the people. Her son, she said, was angry at the misdeeds of people, and grievous punishments would befall them if they did not repent. Divine mercy was promised if sinners mended their ways. Special mention was made of blasphemy and not keeping holy the Lord's day. Such was the public message. But each of the children was given a private message that the other could not hear. The Bishop of Grenoble appointed a commission to look into the claims and the commission concluded that the reality of the apparition should be acknowledged. Several miraculous cures took place.

Great opposition to LaSalette sprang up, within and without the Church, and the miracles were derided. The two secrets were communicated to Pope Pius IX in 1851 by the seers, on the advice of the bishop of Grenoble. Much of the future controversy about LaSalette would relate to these secret communications and their apocalyptic contents. Melanie was authorized by Our Lady to make known the private communication in 1858. It was when a new bishop was appointed, the former having resigned, that the accusation was made against Madame Lamerlière, which led to her successful suit against her accusers, conducted by the grandfather of Jacques Maritain. Attention has focused on the secret of Melanie, since Maximin never authorized any of the several versions of his secret that circulated. According to *The Catholic Encyclopedia* (1913), a question has arisen as to whether the version published in 1879 is identical to that sent to the pope in 1851. An English translation of Melanie's secret has thirty-three numbered paragraphs. It is easy to see, first, why Léon Bloy took such relish in it, and, second, why it stirred up such indignant opposition. The coming chastisement in punishment for sins is described in terrifying terms. Priests are excoriated for their bad lives, irreverence, impiety in saying Mass, love of money, honor, and pleasure. "The priests have become cesspools of impurity" (#2). Prayer and penance have been neglected by the leaders of the people, with the result that the devil has darkened their minds. "Society is on the eve of the most terrible scourges and of the greatest events; one must be expected to be ruled with an iron rod and to drink the chalice of the wrath of God" (#6). The pope is urged to stand fast, to remain in Rome, and to be wary of Napoleon, who aspires to be pope as well as emperor (##7 and 8). The pope will have much to suffer, there will be persecutions of the Church, there will be a frightful crisis in the Church (#13). Religion will be set aside for materialism, atheism, spiritualism, and all kinds of vices (#17). Natural disasters, wars, earthquakes, and the coming of the Antichrist are predicted. "Rome will lose the faith and become the seat of the Antichrist" (#28).[6]

One can see that these prophesies—with their descriptions of the world in which Jacques and Raïssa found themselves, descriptions they accepted and which had brought them to the brink of despair—coupled with the living witness to holiness of Léon Bloy, would find ready acceptance by the Maritains. Raïssa notes that such private revelations are not, of course, binding on anyone, though she also cautions against imprudent dismissal of them. There is little doubt that Jacques and Raïssa embraced the apparitions of LaSalette and adopted their godfather's interpretation of them as well as the secret of Melanie. On June 24, 1907, returning from Heidelberg, they detoured to LaSalette, a journey that took them several days. The solitude and silence of the site captivated them. The three bronze statues of Mary, Melanie, and Maximin made vivid to them what had happened there. It was there that they prepared themselves for confirmation, which was conferred on them in Grenoble.

4

Marian devotion and spiritual direction would come together in a dramatic way some years later. Let us jump ahead, chronologically, to an episode

Jacques Maritain considered to be important enough to receive a chapter of its own in his *Carnet de notes*, a chapter he calls "Our First Trip to Rome." This occurred in 1918, while World War I was on, and it concerned a manuscript Jacques had written on LaSalette. He called this the first of the Marian apparitions of modern times and one that has disturbed people for more than a century. He intended, in this chapter, to add a few items from his personal experience to the dossier. These would have, he hoped, some historical interest, however small. He added that the manuscript that occasioned his wartime trip to Rome was never published and he did not want it to be published, not even after his death, "even if, against all probability, one day circumstances have so changed as to permit its publication." After this, the reader's appetite will have been sufficiently whetted. What can be the point of a chapter devoted to a manuscript that never has been and never will be published?

Maritain mentioned the many personal reasons for his attachment to LaSalette—his connection with Bloy, the novena at Heidelberg to Our Lady of LaSalette that seemed to have cured Raïssa, and his visit there with Raïssa prior to their confirmation. "The freshness of the impressions received up there, and, to employ a word of Ruysbroeck, 'the delicious taste of the Holy Spirit'" were unforgettable. The thought of the Mother of God weeping before those two young children over the offenses against her son, saying how much she has suffered for mankind, so much so that no amount of prayer could make up for it, overwhelmed Maritain. All the more so because the bloody reality of World War I seemed to fulfill the predictions made at LaSalette. All around him, Maritain heard people cursing God for permitting such a dreadful slaughter to take place. Few Frenchmen seemed even to know about LaSalette, let alone to see its relevance to the times. Those who did were either put off by its stinging remarks on the clergy or embraced the apparition with such enthusiasm that, as Maritain put it, they seemed to regard it as a timetable of future events. This suggested a project to him.

He would take up the question of LaSalette in all its amplitude and, given the role of the "secret of Melanie," he would gather together everything bearing on the value of her testimony, driven only by a passion for the truth. The observations and memories of all who knew her must be collected while there was still time. He even linked the task to his grandfather, recalling Jules Favre's suit against those who accused his client of fraudulently tricking the young seers. Oddly, Maritain spoke of his own tendency, inherited from Jules Favre, to be a Don Quixote of lost causes. But in the case in point, Favre was a victor. (This is one of the rare references on Maritain's part to his antecedents.)

Maritain had been most impressed by Dom Delatte, the abbot of Solesmes, when he met the leader of the exiled Benedictine community on the Isle of Wight. Delatte had been sent there by Charles Péguy, as we shall see shortly. Jacques and Raïssa regarded the abbot as God's envoy to them during their early years in the Church. Consulted by Maritain about the LaSalette project, Delatte was completely opposed. In 1912, when Maritain had sent him a copy of Bloy's edition of the life of Melanie written by herself, he had been cautioned by the abbot against any mysticism not solidly grounded in the conceptual and doctrinal teaching of the Magisterium. Maritain replied with a long letter in which he sought to show the coincidence between what Melanie had written and Catholic teaching. Delatte, who was a burly virile fellow, replies with an expression of distaste for "the feminine path to the supernatural" (April 4, 1912). Say what you will, the Church has no need of such a supernatural which has done so much harm. Did Delatte perhaps think of the "little flock of three," with Jacques bracketed by two sisters?

Jacques said that he consulted his confessor, the Vicar General of Versailles, who approved and encouraged the project. And he again consulted Delatte. "In his reply, dated August 29 [1915], he condemned my project (which he said would ruin all the service Jacques would be able to give Truth and the Church and place him in discredit), but the condemnation was put in terms so violent that it had more the effect of annoying me than influencing my judgment."[7] Jacques says that, although Delatte occupied a pedestal for him, this disagreement did not change his plans. There were to be future storms that led to the estrangement between the two men. Another Benedictine, the abbot at Oosterhout, was favorable to Jacques's project when he was consulted.

The sketch of the project Jacques gives in the course of these memories is as follows: the apparition; the two witnesses; the public message; the secret of Melanie. Maritain consulted two priests who had known Melanie, one of whom had been her confessor. After praising the virtues of these priests, Maritain added that one had a passion for Nostradamus and the other had a tendency to want to "chronologize the Apocalypse." No matter, there were most fervent champions of Melanie in Italy "who were more interested in the depths of her soul than extraordinary supernatural things." Presumably there was no question in wartime of consulting the several Italian bishops mentioned, but Maritain felt that the two French priests cited gave him a solid sense of the character and virtues of the shepherdess of LaSalette, although he was relying on earlier visits to them.

Just when he was making good progress on his memoir, a group of LaSalette devotees launched an attack on the bishops of France that compromised the whole question of the apparition. On January 12, 1916, the Holy Office issued a decree forbidding any sort of treatment or discussion of the Secret of La Salette under any pretext or in any form, such as books, pamphlets, signed or anonymous articles. So here was Jacques Maritain, with his memoir well under way, more than ever convinced that he had been right to undertake it, but stymied now by an official prohibition. What to do? In these circumstances he felt that he must himself go to Rome with his memoir to see if an exception to the ban might be made for it.

Two years passed between the initial thought of the expedition and its execution. Many complicating factors arose. Europe was engulfed in war. Could Raïssa undertake so fatiguing a voyage? It never seemed to occur to Jacqes that he might go without her. He characterized himself as naive (and adds that he hopes to remain so all his life) but not unaware of what he might face. Here he was, a convert, a godson of Léon Bloy, one who had become a Thomist and received a doctorate from Rome, now squandering his prestige on the cause of a seer who was little loved by the French clergy and whose prophetic message was, to say the least, a cause of controversy. All the objections seemed to counsel prudence in the modern sense of the term, grounded in the way this trip might harm him.

While valuable, these reasons were not decisive for one who, if he had been moved by comparable reasons, would never have sought baptism. Hadn't he thought that he would have to renounce philosophy in order to become a Christian? That earlier experience of letting truth trump every other consideration influenced him now. And he cited the persuasiveness of Raïssa. One day she felt it was time to make the trip to Rome. Jacques had undertaken his memoir for the sake of the truth and in the hope of serving the wishes of the Blessed Virgin. If it came to that, he was ready to obey a negative decision in Rome if his memoir were judged to come under the interdiction of the Holy Office. Men might run the Church, but Jacques had confidence in it. His later experience as an ambassador confirmed his lifelong conviction that those who sought to proceed by intrigue and calculation invariably failed in their purpose, whereas those who gambled on candor and grace always in the end won through—though not always, he mordantly added, this side of the grave.[8]

So off to Rome on March 26, 1918, went Jacques Maritain and his frail wife. His plan was to consult immediately with his Dominican friend and mentor, Father Reginald Garrigou-Lagrange. The Maritains were met in Rome by the future Carmelite, Bruno of Jesus and Mary, who was studying at the Angelicum, the Dominican university in Rome. Bruno became their guide around the city, and they made pilgrimages to all the basilicas, to the catacombs, to the room in which Saint Benedict Labre died, and many other places as well. More apropos, Garrigou-Lagrange read and liked Jacques's memoir. "The Blessed Virgin indeed loves you," the saintly Dominican said. "You will suffer much." Jacques was advised to go see the pope. On the morning of April 2 the Maritains were received by Benedict XV who addressed Jacques as *Monsieur le docteur,* asked after the bishop of Versailles and went on to Big Bertha, the cannon with which Paris was being bombarded. And finally to the reason for the visit. The pope was quick to reveal his sentiments toward LaSalette. "The apparition itself is beyond doubt, but the words of the Blessed Virgin to Melanie, especially the severe judgment of the clergy, can they be certain?" It is not that there could not be a general complaint about the clergy, but the exaggerated claims attributed to her by Melanie were fantastic, no matter the girl's sincerity and good intentions. The papal judgment on the secret message: *"Quoad substantiam concedo, quoad singula verba nego:* As to the substance, I agree, but as to the particular words, no." The Holy Office wanted to avoid unnecessary scandal. The pope then asked Jacques whether he himself thought the Blessed Virgin had spoken thus.

"What to do? Contradict the pope? All I could see is that in any case I was going to displease someone, either the pope or the Blessed Virgin. So, without hesitation, it would be better to displease the pope. So I answered like a great nincompoop—but it is one of the rare moments in my life that I had the impression of performing an act with which I could be truly satisfied."

Jacques told the pope Melanie was a saint and that what she had reported was true. Soon Raïssa broke in to add her own arguments.

The upshot was that the pope referred Jacques to Cardinal Billot, suggesting that he first talk about philosophy with him, then bring up LaSalette. The pope went on to give detailed advice on how to approach the cardinal. Jacques refused, saying he had resolved to speak to the pope alone about his memoir and he did not want to compromise himself as a philosopher by bringing it up with Billot.

This is a remarkable account. And it is of fundamental importance for showing how profound was the influence of Léon Bloy on Maritain's spirituality. On the margin of the account, other important factors come to the fore. The reference to Jacques's confessor tells us that, apart from daily

Mass and communion, he frequently availed himself of the Sacrament of Penance. Moreover, he had a number of spiritual directors, not least Dom DeLatte, the abbot of Solesmes. Nor should we overlook his relative independence of his advisors. Dom Delatte strongly advised against the path he was on with respect to LaSalette, and Jacques contested him at length. Others give him the go-ahead, but we are not told on what their assurances were based. In Rome, Garrigou-Lagrange set up the meeting for him, doubtless desirous that a man he could rightly think of as his protegé in things Thomistic have an audience with the pope. (It was from the Angelicum, where Garrigou-Lagrange taught, that Maritain received his Roman doctorate in 1917.) The account, whether reconstructed at the time of the *Carnet de notes* or a contemporaneous account, shows us the young convert in his mid-thirties unintimidated by the pope, telling the Holy Father that he regards Melanie as a saint and her words true. But the two priests Maritain himself has met are scarcely disinterested parties—one is a Nostradamus enthusiast—and the Italian bishops Maritain had not consulted were presumably known to the Vatican.

All this is to be remembered when Maritain's swing to the right is considered. Some have sought to explain this by Maritain's susceptibility to the advice of his spiritual advisors. Everything points in the opposite direction.

But let us return to Heidelberg and those first days in the Church.

5

The three—Jacques, Raïssa, and Vera—had been baptized on June 11, 1906, in the church of St. John the Evangelist in Montmartre. Jacques and Raïssa arrived on August 27 in Heidelberg, where Jacques would study the current state of biology in Germany, thanks to a fellowship that had been granted him by the Michonis Fund. The original plan had been to visit all the chief German universities, but Raïssa's illness prevented this. In the summer of 1904, an abscess in her throat almost choked her, and in the country she submitted to an operation that saved her life but left her open to recurrences of the same problem. When they were married on November 26, 1904, Jacques perhaps already realized that he had taken a semi-invalid for his wife. Thus it was that their German plans had to be altered, and they settled in Heidelberg, where Jacques followed the work of Hans Dreisch.

But while ordinary academic pursuits continued, the young converts were trying to find a *modus vivendi* between those pursuits and the quest for holiness. Jacques records on October 28 that he had embarked on an *Introduction to the Life of Raïssa*, written only for the three of them, the introduction of which he had completed. He indicates that he was influenced by Léon Bloy's fascination with Raïssa's Jewish background as well as by the novelist's style. Although he sounds sheepish, he includes some pages of this project in the *Carnet de notes.*

> Goodness. Purity. Raïssa always goes to the end with a right intention and honest will. Her courage is incalculable and her pity defenseless. Where there is no beauty she is suffocated and cannot live. She has always lived for the truth and has never resisted it. She has never tricked her mind nor lied about her sorrow. She gives always, holding nothing back. For her heart as for her understanding it is the essential reality that matters; no accessory of it can cause her to hesitate. Her thought and genius bring her always to intuition. Being completely interior, she is completely free. Her mind can only be content with the real, her soul with the absolute.[9]

One wonders what need there was for such an introduction if it was indeed written for only the author and the subject. Raïssa's sister had not yet become a part of the household. But these pages tell us that early on, Jacques was convinced that his wife had already reached the goal for which they were striving. What effect did he imagine reading these pages would have on Raïssa? Even making allowances for the excesses of French expression, it is difficult to read these pages without some embarrassment. The writer is a man who, mere months before, had found the world he had entered by baptism uncongenial and foreign. His ambitions had been described politically and socially rather than in terms of the inner life. The famous episode in the *Jardin des Plantes* did not envisage a contemplative outcome, but rather a clearing away of obstacles to a life of action. Now, as it must seem abruptly, Jacques Maritain has adopted a quite different conception of the aim of life, the acquisition of holiness; and he seemed to think his wife had already attained it. He loads onto the portrait of her life every known virtue and heroic stance. Much of this is connected with Léon Bloy's singular interpretation of the relationship of Judaism to Christianity. It is as if Raïssa had inherited all the virtues of the great women of the Bible and, simply by dint of being Jewish, had entry to the higher reaches of holiness.

One might regard this as understandable excess, an enthusiastic young husband's devotion to his fragile wife; but the fact is that a note is struck that will be struck again and again, reaching its climax when Jacques published his wife's journal after her death—having edited it and prepared it for publication himself. He first circulated a private printing among a few friends, not all of whom seem to have shared his enthusiasm for the project, and then published it in a commercial edition. Jacques Maritain wanted the world to see his wife as a mystic on the order of Saint Thérèse of Lisieux.

The finished pages seem to have had an immediate therapeutic purpose. "Raïssa, when you are afflicted, remember my testimony."[10] Was this fulsome praise meant as a palliative to Raïssa when she was down with one of her numerous and somewhat mysterious illnesses, her reclusive moods that would increasingly be described as mystical episodes?

In November they received the news that Jacques's sister Jeanne intended to have her daughter Eveline baptized, and they would be the godparents. Eveline would be the first of a long line of godchildren of Jacques and Raïssa Maritain. Like their own godfather, they regarded Catholicism as a good to be shared, and they were to see Raïssa's parents relax their opposition to their daughter's conversion, which at first they had regarded as treachery, and eventually come into the Church themselves. Jacques's mother Geneviève remained adamantly outside the faith that had once been hers, and she persisted for some time in thinking that Raïssa had led her son astray. She appealed to Péguy, with whom she had become close friends. It was the case of Charles Péguy that acquainted Maritain with the perils and pitfalls of evangelizing.

6

Charles Péguy did not share Maritain's admiration for Léon Bloy. He claimed never to have read a page of Bloy's and seems never even to have met the man. When Bloy sent him an ingratiating letter, Péguy refused to answer. Did he perhaps see in Bloy a rival for the role of surrogate father that he had been playing for Jacques? In any case, Péguy's situation vis-à-vis the Church was complicated. His wife was violently anticlerical, and his children were not baptized. Yet when Jacques began to move toward Catholicism, Péguy intimated to him that he too considered himself a Catholic: so much so that he sent Jacques on a mission to a boyhood friend, now a Benedictine monk with the community of Solesmes, which was then exiled to the Isle of Wight. Péguy had a message for his old friend so confidential that he did not wish to entrust it to the mail. Raïssa attributed Péguy's caution to his concern lest the subscribers to his *Cahiers*, hearing of his return to Catholicism, should abandon him. The journal, along with a bookshop, constituted Péguy's livelihood. Apparently what he wanted Jacques Maritain to do was assure the monk that he had returned to the faith but that he intended to keep this secret.

Maritain set off for the Isle of Wight and arrived on August 24, 1907, carrying the good news to Father Baillet. It was on this occasion as well that Jacques met the abbot, Dom Delatte, a man who was to play an important role as spiritual advisor to the Maritains over the next decade and more. While Jacques was on this mission, Péguy told Geneviève Favre that he had sent her son off in order to remove him from the influence of Léon Bloy. Jacques returned with the message that Baillet thought Péguy must, above all, see to the baptism of his children. When Jacques returned from Heidelberg the following summer, he found that Péguy was still in a state of indecision. Moreover, he resented being pressed on the matter, and observed that he was senior in age to Jacques. He had devised a special status for himself, in the Church but not of it, returned to the faith but without scaring off his socialist and Dreyfusard subscribers with this alarming news. If Péguy was equivocal, Maritain was categorical.

Strange alliances were formed. Jacques's mother was the ally of Péguy against her son, and she also became close to Ernest Psichari when relations between him and Jacques threatened to break. Geneviève Favre seemed determined to prevent her son from influencing, in the direction of the faith, any of his friends. Did she know that the conversion of Psichari was a constant object of Jacques's prayers?

Maritain now functioned as a rebuke to Péguy, whose conscience was obviously speaking against his rationalized behavior. Things came to a climax when Jacques undertook to approach Madame Péguy and explain to her the need for the children to be baptized. Péguy's wife was obviously the stronger of the two in this matter and, unable to bring her with him into the faith, Péguy himself believed everything but remained nonpracticing, his children unbaptized. Jeanne Maritain accused Péguy of cowardice, and he told her to go tell it to his wife. In the end it was Jacques, not his sister, who undertook this delicate and doomed commission. Both the wife and the mother-in-law of Péguy took on the visitor and sent him packing.

Bitterness and estrangement between the two old friends followed, and harsh words were written by both. We are told by Raïssa that the two men reconciled in 1914, on the eve of the war. Like Ernest Psichari, who had converted, Péguy was a friend who was killed in action early in World War I. The second volume of Raïssa Maritain's memoirs indicates how tumultuous many of Jacques Maritain's friendships were.

The Péguy episode, however maladroit Maritain's behavior, introduces what would be a lifelong characteristic of the convert. His evangelizing impulse was strong, and, over his long life, he was the occasion for many gaining the grace of faith and comng into the Church. The number of his godchildren grew correspondingly. But the maladroitness and what he himself called naiveté never went away. The instances of Jean Cocteau and André Gide can be added to a list of the big fish that got away.

Versailles

I

As the academic year 1908 drew to a close, Raïssa was in bed for a month with a sore throat—Jacques himself had diptheria—and when they left Germany they lived for several months with Raïssa's parents. After that, there was a month on the Normandy coast where Raïssa was constantly ill. Their first home in Paris was on the Left Bank, not far from the Sorbonne and the shop of Charles Péguy. But in that same year, they moved to Versailles. They had a house there in which they lived until 1923, when they moved to a larger house at Meudon, their residence until the outbreak of World War II when they fled France.

In the Paris home, Jacques undertook to write for the publisher Hachette a *Lexique orthographique* with the help of Vera Oumansov, work obtained at the suggestion of Péguy. Jacques went on to more such hack work, a *Dictionnaire de la vie pratique.* Raïssa explained this, somewhat unconvincingly, as a deliberate decision to retain his philosophical independence. Her own illnesses continued, but with the resolution to avoid doctors, since she had never encountered any good ones. She went on a rice-and-water diet, with some vegetables included. In Paris they saw few people: Ernest Psichari, the Bloys, Péguy. And then one day they went to Versailles to meet Father Humbert Clérissac.

The trip to the Isle of Wight on Péguy's behalf had brought Jacques into contact with Benedictine spirituality. Jacques was in the first flush of his conversion, driven by the hunger for sanctity he had learned from Léon Bloy. The abbot, Dom Delatte, in response to a question, discussed with Jacques the advisability of a spiritual director. Reading the lives of the saints would have acquainted him with the advisability of such an advisor for one who sought holiness. Raïssa's account of the role of Delatte, in the second volume of her memoirs, written in 1944, could be called a species of revisionism.[11] It would be important to her treatment of Jacques's involvement in Action Française to attribute this to Jacques's alleged susceptibility to his spiritual directors. Thus, her initial description of the abbot is ambiguous. Having called him magnificent and genial, "a veritable high priest, impressive for his authority and prestige," she continues, "as also for his haughtiness and his intransigence. But it was only many years afterwards that we became aware of these defects which cast a shadow upon this great personality." It is unfortunate that we have only Raïssa's account of a conversation that took place on a channel isle while she herself was in Paris. She portrayed the abbot as trying to loosen Jacques up by telling him there were only three cases in which one needed spiritual direction: when one was uncertain over his vocation, if one were morbidly scrupulous, or if one had extraordinary experiences, visions, and revelations. He told Jacques to pray about it for a year and, if a director was indicated, he would send him to his good friend Clérissac.

Raïssa's ambiguous introduction of Dom Delatte in her memoirs is difficult to reconcile with the continued closeness of Jacques with the Benedictine abbot. In 1926, for example, he urges Julien Green to visit Delatte. As for Jacques's supposed malleability, we have already mentioned that he ignored Delatte's advice in 1918 on the matter of the trip to Rome to seek an exemption to the ban on writings about LaSalette.

When the year's wait that Delatte had advised was up, Jacques and Raïssa went to Versailles to see Father Clérissac. Now this would have put it in 1909. But the Maritains had moved to Versailles in 1908, so Raïssa's comparison of this first trip to their prospective spiritual director with the trip up the steps of Montmartre the first time they visited Léon Bloy must refer to the feelings they had. *Their* director: in Raïssa's account, we are given the impression that they were directed together. By contrast with her account of Delatte, Raïssa is lyrical in her praise of Clérissac. But in the case of the Dominican father, we have Jacques's own account of the man in a review he wrote for a posthumously published unfinished work of Clérissac's, *Le mystère de l'église*.[12]

Because religious orders could not maintain communities in France because of the hostility of the government to religious belief, Humbert Clérissac fulfilled his vocation as a member of the Order of Preachers by giving retreats in various countries—Italy, notably, but also England, where he was acquainted with Monsignor Robert Hugh Benson. Among the books Clérissac recommended for reading was Benson's *Lord of the World,* and Maritain commented intriguingly, "I have always thought that Benson, who knew him [Clérissac] well, thought of him in describing the personage of the Pope in *Lord of the World.*"[13] And Maritain reports Father Clérissac's enigmatic remark that he knew that Oscar Wilde had died in the faith because he was at his deathbed.[14] While somewhat hagiographic, Maritain's portrait of his first spiritual advisor is obviously an expression of filial gratitude. And it provides us with clues as to the spirituality to which the Dominican priest would have introduced Maritain.

A much repeated remark of Clérissac's was: "Christian life is based on the intelligence." He was devoted to Saint Thomas Aquinas, and it was on his urging that Thomas Aquinas entered the intellectual and spiritual life of Jacques Maritain. His ideal was to live the truth. "God is above all else the Truth, go to him, love him under this aspect."[15] This was, in effect, a gloss on Saint Augustine's *gaudium de veritate: rejoicing in the truth.* Clérissac loved the Church and his love for the religious life was an expression of that love. The three vows of religion—poverty, obedience, chastity—are publicly accepted by the Church, which officially consecrates the human person somewhat as it does a chalice or an altar. A religious person is one whose life is devoted to the acquisition of perfection, of holiness. The many religious orders play different roles in the Church, but Clérissac thought of his own, the Dominicans, as especially called to fidelity to the truth. They were a *race intellectuelle.*

The Mass and the Divine Office were at the center of Clérissac's spiritual life, but Maritain adds that Clérissac had a horror of "ostentatious poverty."[16] He was devoted to the writings of Saint Catherine of Siena and read and reread Dante. How does Maritain describe him as a spiritual advisor? That he was inspired by two masters after his own heart, Saint Paul and Saint Thomas, as well as by Christian antiquity. He warned against preoccupation with oneself and was on the watch for individualism, meaning by it a tendency to make either sentiment or external activity dominate. Attention should always be on God, on divine truth, and the rest should be left to God. He advised prayer and contemplation over ascetic practices, seeing in them a surer way to be united with the Church. The ladder of perfection had two rungs, doctrine and liturgy. The liturgy was the life of the Church and he rejected any opposition between liturgy and private prayer. For all that, the *opus Dei*, the liturgy, was prayer par excellence. His devotion to the Blessed Virgin was marked, and Maritain gave an intimation of how this came out in the last series of sermons he heard Clérissac preach at Notre Dame-de-Lorette in May 1914.

Speaking of Saint Teresa of Avila with great praise and of the concerted effort to acquire virtue, Clérissac added, "But don't forget that you are Merovingians, from a feudal society, what am I saying? Primitives. Never forget that you must let divine grace work in you and hold for nothing the products of your own activity. . . ."[17] Maritain recalled an evening walk with Father Clérissac in front of the cathedral at Versailles when the old priest gave him very specific advice. "Jacques, it is not enough that a work be certainly useful for the good of souls in order for us to make haste to accomplish it. It is necessary that God wills it at that time—and then, no delay. But God has time. . . . Do not go more quickly than God. He wants our thirst and emptiness, it is not our fullness that he wants."[18]

Raïssa tells us that for several months Jacques went every morning to see Father Clérissac on the Boulevard de la Reine where he served his Mass and afterward had long talks with him. Doubtless these provided the memories that enabled him to write the moving preface to Father Clérissac's posthumous volume. A recent biographer of Maritain, speaking of the six years when Father Clérissac was Jacques's spiritual director, notes that his influence was powerful and decisive and, "for good or ill," nothing in Maritain's long life would be unaffected by it. "Occult counselor as well as confessor, director of conscience as much as eminence grise?"[19]

2

Father Clérissac eventually received Ernest Psichari into the Church as well as into the Third Order of Saint Dominic. Third orders are means whereby people in the world can participate to some degree in the life and works of a religious order. Certain obligations are taken on—the daily recitation of the Little Office, other pious practices—with an eye to fulfilling more perfectly the demands of Christian life. The whole question of spiritual direction had arisen when Jacques spoke with Dom Delatte, the Benedictine, but it was Delatte who referred him eventually to Dominican Father Clérissac. Would the abbot have done this if he were not exiled on the Isle of

Wight while Clérissac was installed in Versailles? However that may be, Clérissac introduced Jacques to the spiritual life in a way that had a Dominican flavor to it. His devotion to Thomas Aquinas, which Maritain soon shared, would have been another link to the Order of Preachers. Nevertheless, Jacques and his wife and sister-in-law chose to become oblates of Saint Benedict, equivalent to a third order, and thus to pursue a Benedictine spirituality. The Rule of the Order of Preachers was a modification of the Rule of Saint Augustine. How did this come about?

There seems to be no answer to this question. The household at Versailles and later at Meudon—Jacques, Raïssa, and Vera—took on the appellation of the "little flock," and we know what the schedule of their day was. Raïssa wrote extensively on her own and Jacques's spiritual life and said that it was at Father Clérissac's suggestion that they became oblates. That he might have suggested they join the Third Order of Saint Dominic is clear from the fact that Clérissac installed Psichari as a member.

In the *Carnet de notes*, an entry of May 10, 1911, reads: "The Father Abbot Jean de Puniet just came to see us, saying that we are a little branch of Saint Paul's of Oosterhout, and that Saint Benedict loves everything small. 'You need wish to do nothing apart from your life, it is your life that is your work.' [Today begins the year of novitiate in preparation to be received as oblates of the Abbey of Oosterhout.]" Perhaps it was this minimalist description of their life as oblates by the abbot that explains the absence of reference to what would seem to have been, in the lives of these intense converts, a very important step.

Jacques tells us that his journal for 1911 after October 18 is missing. Writing in 1954, he recalled the year as an unhappy one: Raïssa always ill, money worries, hateful family discussions with his mother and his brother-in-law. But they had kept to their schedule, more or less, and their novitiate was completed and "we were in open country." Not a picture of domestic bliss. A few years before in Germany, Maritain had noted "*Das Hauskreuz*, c'est ainsi que les maris designent gentiment leur femme: My House Cross, that is how husbands refer gracefully to their wife."[20] Not *The Kreutzer Sonata*, of course, but an intimation that Jacques was human and found the constant illnesses and other domestic aggravations wearing. Then there is this later recollection (1954) of that year.

It was in 1911 or 1912 that I was suddenly assailed by violent temptations against the faith. Until then the graces of baptism had been such that it seemed to me *sight*, that it was evidence itself. Now I had to learn the night of the faith. No longer carried in the arms, I was put roughly on the ground. I remember long hours of interior torture on the Rue de l'Orangerie, alone in the room on the fourth floor I had turned into a kind of redoubt for work. I kept myself from speaking of it. I came through the test, by the grace of God, the stronger, but I had lost my childhood. I consoled myself with the thought that doubtless it had to be if I were to be of any service to others.[21]

The year 1911 was also when Jacques associated himself with Action Française, a decision he came to regret and that he and Raïssa and others have sought to attribute to his naive compliance with the direction of Father Clérissac.

3

In October of 1909, the Maritains had taken up residence in Versailles on the Rue de l'Orangerie in order to be closer to Father Clérissac. They lived at that address until 1913 when they moved to a larger apartment in which they could set aside a room for Father Clérissac when he visited Versailles from Angers, where he was then living. The move became possible after Raïssa had received some relief from homeopathic medicine for her chronic illness. Nineteen thirteen was the year in which Jacques's first book appeared, *La philosophie bergsonienne.* From October 1912, Jacques began teaching philosophy at the Collège Stanislas and in June 1914 became an adjunct professor at the Institut Catholique. The remarkable courses he gave during this first year at the Institut Catholique were in the history of modern philosophy. We will be examining Jacques's philosophical achievements later. For now, we must look more deeply into the roots of his spirituality.

Nineteen fourteen was a year of both horror and consolation. World War I had begun and the Maritains were soon to lose several dear friends. Péguy and Psichari, who had returned to the faith or been converted to it, were among the first to fall in the war. War was declared on August 2. Psichari was killed in action on August 22 and Péguy on September 5. And on November 16, Father Clérissac died. He was replaced in the role of spiritual director by Father Dehau.

Father Reginald Garrigou-Lagrange, who had first become aware of Jacques at the Sorbonne, where the bearded young student had gained the reputation of being a follower of Bergson, and who was himself to play a most important part in the intellectual and spiritual life of Maritain, recommended Father Dehau to Jacques. Dehau had a soothing effect on Raïssa, and Vera too benefited from his counsel. "As for me, I passed hours, priceless hours, reading John of Saint Thomas with Father Dehau, and listening to his comments. How many keys he gave me, what light I received from that gentle intelligence."[22] Father Pierre-Thomas Dehau continued in the role of Maritain's spiritual director for twenty-five years. Recalling these matters in 1954, writing in Princeton, the aging philosopher made a list of guides, companions, and protectors. Léon Bloy occupies pride of place, then Dom Delatte, Abbot of Solesmes ("during the first years of our Christian life, after our return from Heidelberg; subsequently our routes diverged and finally his attachment to Action Française caused him to break roughly with me at the time of *La primauté du spirituel*"), Dom Jean de Puniet, many others, then Father Garrigou-Lagrange, with a heartfelt tribute. Next Jacques adds those who had the deepest impact: Father Clérissac, Father Dehau, the eventual cardinal Journet. . . . He gives this portrait of Father Dehau. He was "not only wrapped in shawls and blankets but also in a secret. Half blind, he passed among souls as a friend of God charged with awakening them to the things of their Father. . . . I thought of him for the personage of Theonas in the book of that title, but using only surface and accessory traits which would not imperil his incognito."[23]

4

In September 1912, Jacques, Raïssa, and Vera went to the Abbey of Oosterhout in Holland and were received as oblates of Saint Benedict by the abbot, Dom Jean de Puniet. It was an occasion for the taking of religious names to seal the entry. Jacques took the name of Placidus, Raïssa became Agnes, and Vera, Gertrude. From that time on, the three formed the simulacrum of a religious community in their home. But there was more. On October 2, 1912, in the cathedral of Versailles, Jacques and Raïssa took a vow that profoundly altered their life together. They took a vow of chastity, renouncing sexual relations, in order the more surely to bind themselves to God. This extremely private decision was of course kept secret throughout their marriage, but as an old man, Jacques decided to reveal it in the privately circulated *Journal of Raïssa*. The reaction of friends prompted him to remove it from the public edition, but in his *Carnet de notes* he included a long chapter, written in 1962, on love and friendship.

Jacques was thirty years old at the time, Raïssa even younger, and they took this step only after long counsel with Father Clérissac. By common agreement, "they had decided to renounce that which in marriage not only satisfies a profound need of the human being, flesh as well as spirit, but is legitimate and a good in itself. . . ." Thus they also renounced the possibility of sons or daughters. The vow was not based on any contempt for nature, Jacques adds, but in their course toward the absolute and their desire to follow at any price, while remaining in the world, one of the counsels of the perfect life in order to clear the way for contemplation and union with God. A temporary vow of one year preceded the definitive vow. "Now she and I," he wrote in old age, "in one way or another, have finished with the earth, and I no longer feel bound by the silence we always maintained on these matters."

The Villard Bequest

Cette vie n'est pas nôtre oeuvre, mais celle de Dieu en nous.

I

On April 18, 1917, Jacques Maritain received a letter from a soldier who had once taken his course on German philosophy at the Institut Catholique, one Pierre Villard. It seems possible that Maritain had little if any memory of the man who, in a lengthy and heartfelt letter, poured out the current state of his soul. In following Maritain's lectures he had discerned, behind "the philosopher following with a clear eye the chain of causes and effects, the personality of a man for whom the difficult question of how to live well had been put in all its gravity, and who had solved it." It was this that prompted him to lay open to Maritain the emptiness of soul that oppressed him. Villard's letter was a cry for help addressed to a man he was confident could help him. But the letter seemed to shut the door on any obvious kind of response Maritain might have made. Villard, about to go on leave in Paris, asked if Maritain would see him. Maritain noted the visit in his journal.

21 April 1917.—Visit of Pierre Villard. One discerns in this poor soldier with the meditative countenance a soul thirsting for purity and the
absolute, for whom to *sense* the things of the spirit has become the great
need and the loss of faith (if indeed he has truly lost it) has left
in an irremediable vacillation: he is too perspicacious to be content with
a substitute. He is in a great trouble that resembles a spiritual test sent
by God.

It is noteworthy that Jacques Maritain, still in his thirties, had made
such an impression on a student that years later it encouraged the student to
bare his soul. The letter was not an invitation to a philosophical exchange.
It was a plea for help in finding the very meaning of life. Maritain answered,
and thus began a correspondence that would extend over the next fourteen
months. Despite himself, Maritain was playing the role of spiritual advisor.
It was a role he had played before and it was a role that he was to play for
many others as the result of this correspondence with Villard.

2

Maritain was to see Villard several times in the course of the latter's army
leaves, but it is the letters that preserve the tack he took with the young soldier. Villard had already been reading Pascal, Bergson, and Péguy. Maritain
gave him a life of Saint Catherine of Siena, which Villard found cloying, and
the saint's *Dialogue*, which pierced the defenses he had built up. While encouraging Villard's sense of inwardness, Maritain assured him that there is a
truth far more beautiful than any the soldier would find in that way.

There is a truth infinitely more beautiful than any you have guessed in
that way; or rather what was given you in an unstable intuition and that
doubtless you will later find troubling and all too much of the earth, is
the same Truth which is completely pure in the light of Revelation and
that teaches us about the all-good Father from whom we come. There
is only one stable, truly divine and deifying way in which to possess it.
And that is to receive it from God by the public, universal, catholic, intellectually defined teaching of the Church, Christ's mystical body, from
that mysterious Society, visible as a city built on a mountain although
secret in its profound life and in its spirit, which alone says: I have the

deposit of the infallible Word and I am myself infallible, I give birth to divine life, I can heal souls and forgive their sins, I give them the grace of my sacraments, I ceaselessly produce saints, I distribute the Blood of God, I offer uninterruptedly a sacrifice which is neither fictive nor symbolic, but true and real, in which every sacrifice has its exemplar and its power.

This was the heart of what Maritain told Villard: the Church is a mystery; do not confuse it with its all-too-human career through history, although that is indeed part of the mystery. But the visible Church on which to keep one's eye is the Teacher and dispenser of the sacraments, conduits whereby the grace won by Christ is made available through the centuries. But it is the interior life that must complement and make one's own the life of grace. Villard wanted to be a mystic. Maritain fostered and encouraged the desire but he sent him a *Catechism of the Council of Trent* and a copy of Robert Hugh Benson's *Christ in the Church* as well as Père Clérissac's *The Mystery of the Church*.

Some twenty-three letters from Villard were to reach Maritain over the course of the next year. Ten of his replies, usually much longer than those the soldier found time to write from the front, have survived. The final item in the dossier is from the chaplain informing Maritain of Villard's death in combat. Villard had spoken to the chaplain of his correspondence with Maritain. The chaplain had judged Villard to have returned to the Church when he came to him and asked for the Sacrament of Penance. The request was granted.

3

If this were an isolated event in the life of Maritain, it would be touching, perhaps edifying, but not defining of the man. But Villard was not alone in finding in Maritain a philosopher—that is, a professed seeker of wisdom—who really seemed to be engaged personally and wholeheartedly in that quest. But whatever wisdom can be gained from philosophy, it is as nothing compared to a life lived in union with Jesus Christ. Perhaps it was because Maritain had himself been rescued from a confusion every bit as profound as Villard's that he responded to the soldier's plea. Perhaps Villard sensed that his old professor had pursued a path he unconsciously wished to follow. How many philosophers are likely to be asked by their students, "What must I do to be saved?" Over the course of his long life, many men and women turned to Maritain for spiritual as well as intellectual advice. The number for whom he was an instrument of conversion is even greater than the number of his literal godchildren.

Maritain reprints the correspondence with Villard in his *Carnet de notes*. It makes up chapter 4 and runs from page 139 to page 182 of the French original. One might well ask why Maritain drew attention to such a matter, however frequently it was repeated in his life. Villard never won through to the serenity and certainty he saw in Maritain. Of all those in whose conversions Maritain had played a role, why should this somewhat equivocal one be given such pride of place? The reason is given in the *Carnet de notes*.

Maritain never says that he had remembered Villard when he was a student in his class. When the young man visited the philosopher, he came wearing the uniform of his country, and that doubtless conferred a kind of anonymity on him. During the year of correspondence, Villard's mother died; and he writes that, after the war, he hoped to transfer the remains of both his parents to Nancy. The soldier had become an orphan. Sometime after Villard's death at the front, Maritain received a letter from a lawyer, informing him that he had been named joint heir with Charles Maurras of the estate of Pierre Villard. To Maritain's astonishment, the young man had extensive worldly goods. He had left land to the city of Nancy's orphanage, but the rest was to go to Maritain and Maurras. "I was astounded that someone I took for a poor student was the heir to a considerable fortune." The following letter to Maritain, dated July 12, was included with the will.

What is the living principle that will save me from both intellectualism and sentimentalism? Where get the spirit of submission necessary for a clear view of sorrowful realities and the strength to surmount them?

I open Pascal. You know, Monsieur Maritain, what light appears to me there and delights me. But you also know what are still my hesitation and unease.

I have not yet found the happiness to live the life of positive faith. Still, it seems to me that the true Christian is only a higher expression of the conscientious and obscure laborer that, in my capacity as soldier, I train myself to become. Will loyalty to self, to the work to be done, to France, lead on to loyalty to a God I do not yet know?

I am convinced that happiness belongs to those hearts which are perpetually ready to pray, perpetually pure. I envy these limpid souls which are the living mirror of God. I hope that through them, the Church will arise from the profound abasement in which we now see her. I do not want to encourage mediocrity: I think that one single holy soul is more useful to humanity than a crowd of believers deprived of any mystical elan.

The words of this not quite unknown soldier, who gave his life for his country in a brutal war without precedent for pointless bloodshed, come to us across an interval of over eighty years. These words were written a year before his death, at the beginning of his correspondence with Maritain. But he had already determined that he wished to support what Jacques Maritain was and meant for his country.

4

The bequest caused some confusion in Maritain and his wife. Léon Bloy, who had been instrumental in their conversion, had lived a life of extreme poverty. Jacques and Raïssa had resolved to live their lives *"par des moyens pauvres,"* by slender means, modestly. Suddenly they were wealthy. After prayer and consulting his confessor, Maritain decided to accept the windfall. "I will use the means given me by Pierre Villard in the service of Christian thought and spirituality: 1. By my efforts in the philosophical and culture order; 2. By an action exercised on souls thanks to some center of spiritual influence."

Maritain was no longer dependent on the pittance then paid professors at the Institut Catholique. And he bought the house at Meudon, which was to be the center of spirituality, made possible by the generosity of a fallen hero; a house in whose chapel, by a special dispensation, the Blessed Sacrament was always reserved and where, we can be sure, prayers went up for the repose of the soul of Pierre Villard.

Action Française

I

Jacques Maritain's long involvement with Action Française, the movement run by Charles Maurras, gave him and his wife and many others great difficulty to explain. Indeed, the tendency, first present in Raïssa's memoirs, is to portray his association with this antidemocratic movement spawned by the Dreyfus Affair as the result of his docility to his spiritual directors. That a young man who had vowed to be a revolutionary socialist should become, after his conversion to Catholicism, a subscriber to Action Française may be explained in part by the fact that his spiritual advisors were enthusiastic supporters of Maurras and saw his movement as the hope of the Church in France—Delatte and his Benedictine community had, after all, been exiled to the English Isle of Wight by the Republic. This can scarcely be regarded as a sufficient explanation, any more than Maritain's allegiance to the tenets of Action Française can be described as half-hearted or tenuous. For all that, when the Church condemned the movement, Jacques was swift—many thought too swift—to embrace and defend the papal condemnation.

2

What was Action Française? First of all, it was a newspaper of that name and, derivatively, the movement the newspaper represented. Charles Maurras, whose paper and movement it was, although he became the darling of Catholics if not of the Church, was not himself a believer. His movement took its rise in the wake of the Dreyfus Affair, the condemnation of Captain Alfred Dreyfus, a Jewish officer convicted on trumped-up charges of treason followed by his almost immediate pardon. The "Affair" engaged every Frenchman one way or the other, pro or con; and to be anti-Dreyfusard was almost by definition to be anti-Semitic. This only serves to underscore the anomaly of Maritain's involvement with the movement. He was married to a Jewish woman; he had paid for the reissue of his godfather's *Salvation Through the Jews;* throughout his long life he would meditate on what he called the "mystery of Israel"; as a boy he had been passionately enlisted on the side of the Dreyfusards. The affair produced a host of intellectuals—on the Left, anticlericals, and on the Right, anti-anticlericals—who found Maurras's vitriolic condemnations of democracy attractive. The political struggle was one in which society was being progressively secularized and the Church marginalized. The struggle went on in the field of education, with leftist teachers siding with freemasons, whose numbers were steadily increasing, and among the teachers in the Catholic schools. The Left was united in the desire to somehow reverse the Dreyfus verdict. The affair had become symbolic, taking on a meaning far beyond its original and quite particular elements. Historians see French society as polarized around religious faith and secularism: it was almost as if there were two nations. The roots of this can doubtless be found in the nineteenth-century critique of the Enlightenment associated with Joseph de Maistre, according to which the supposed triumph of liberty would end in the enslavement of men. The rise of anti-Semitism in France reflected the tripling of the number of Jews there in the years prior to World War I.

Action Française was founded in 1898 in the wake of the Dreyfus Affair. Charles Maurras joined in 1899 and soon became the leader of the movement, with Jacques Bainville, historian, and Léon Daudet, editor of the paper, in the front ranks. Maurras distinguished between the "legal" country and the "real" country. The former was the republican regime with its centralized administration, political parties, and parliamentary charades that had been superimposed on the real France, made up of those who lived and worked. The remedy was to be found in the restoration of the monarchy. Maurras had been influenced by Auguste Comte, the positivist, and considered politics a science. He called what he advocated an integral nationalism. The Camelots du Roi was formed: a group of young men whose ostensible purpose was to sell the journal *Action Française,* a group with which Georges Bernanos was associated. (The Camelots du Roi was dissolved in 1936 because of incidents associated with the funeral of Jacques Bainville, when socialist Léon Blum, was roughed up.)[24]

3

Jacques Maritain was associated with Action Française for fifteen years, not breaking with the movement until it was condemned by Pope Pius XI in 1926. It seems doubtful that Maritain would have been a beneficiary of the will of Pierre Villard if he had not been associated with Action Française. The young man had followed Maritain's lectures at the Institut Catholique, but he bequeathed a million francs jointly to Charles Maurras and to Maritain. That Maritain asked Maurras not to mention his own sharing in this windfall has been interpreted as misgivings about Action Française, but surely there could have been other reasons. In any case, in 1920, at Maurras's suggestion, the two men contributed 50,000 francs each to found a review to promote the ideas of Action Française. This has been interpreted as an astute move to coopt the young philosopher—Maritain was nearly forty— a theory that collides with the founders' intention not to stress the connection of *La Revue Universelle* with Action Française. Doubtless they thought that it could reach beyond the already convinced, but it was recognized as being linked to Action Française. "In spite of his desire to remain politically detached, he was closely associated with the movement in the mind of the general public, so that at one time he was known as the official philosopher of Action Française. This impression was fostered, in particular, by his participation in the early 1920s in the founding and editing of *La Revue Universelle.*"[25] Jacques Bainville became director of the new journal and Henri Massis editor-in-chief. Maritain was philosophy editor, since along with the ideas of Action Française, Thomistic philosophy was to be promoted by the journal.[26]

4

Jacques Maritain himself gave the revisionists their lead. Writing to Henri Massis in 1932, he says that he began reading Maurras at the instigation of Père Clérissac, who urged him to join Action Française. "I accepted that, along with all the rest of it, with complete docility, out of obedience and submission to my director, convinced that this decision was one with all that I had accepted when I entered the Church."[27] He likens it to the way in which he had accepted the suggestion that he give a critical course on Bergsonism although he had been a student of Bergson. Maritain then suggests that the problem is not his actions but the motivation of his director. The famous trip to Rome, against the advice of some of his spiritual advisors, does not suggest someone who responded like a robot to the obiter dicta of Père Clérissac. Nonetheless, his analysis of Clérissac's motivation is important.

> But Père Clérissac's point of view was above all that of a theologian aware of the dangers then posed by Modernism to the dogmatic statement of the faith. The fact that Action Française fought these errors from outside, denouncing relentlessly the influence of Bergson, the anti-intellectualism of a Blondel or Laberthonniere, endeared it to him, and all the more because he was upset by the ravages these errors made among young priests and seminarians. . . .[28]

As for himself, Maritain says he was so wrapped up in metaphysics and theology, that this motivation of Clérissac convinced him that only Action Française provided the political means of correcting these dangers.

5

In order to accept this portrait of the political *naif* we have to imagine that Maritain did not read Maurras, did not read *Action Française*, did not really participate in *La Revue Universelle*, and did not make in his own name any number of antidemocratic political remarks. Maritain's allegiance to the movement was not a matter of parlor room asides or vagrant responses, but a sustained and public connection that, as Doering said, earned him the reputation of being the philosopher of Action Française. Doubtless this was the basis of Pierre Villard's decision to leave his million-franc fortune to Jacques Maritain and Charles Maurras.

Many Catholics, writers, intellectuals, priests, theologians, and philosophers were seduced by Action Française by concentrating only on certain aspects of its message and ignoring others. The movement had come to seem the most promising means whereby the Church could overcome the secularizing tendencies of the times.[29] On the other hand, many like François Mauriac associated themselves with liberal Catholic movements. It was scarcely Action Française or nothing. Whatever the explanation, there is something astonishing in Maritain's making an 180-degree turn from the fervent socialism of his youth and student days to alliance with a monarchist antiparliamentarian movement. And, when the condemnation came, he turned another 180 degrees, embracing with enthusiasm the condemnation.

Maritain imagined himself a man of action from the time of his boyish fantasizing about the revolution with the husband of his mother's cook. His fifteen-year association with the polar opposite of those early beliefs therefore surprises, just as his putting them aside in a trice suggests that naiveté was a constant of Maritain's practical political views rather than a lapse that was overcome in 1926. A practical opacity is also present in the liberal views he adopted in the 1930s and clear as well in the later *Reflections on America.* This is not merely another instance of the romanticism of the intellectual, as manifested in radical chic, for instance—although there was a good dose of that in Maritain. The deeper fact is that he was far more interested in atemporal things, and his excursions into the practical put one in mind of Plato's philosopher being dragged against his bent into the political realm, something that happened again and again over Maritain's long career. If his involvement with the movement is susceptible of benign interpretation, so is that of the spiritual directors to whom he attributed his connection with it. But it must be emphasized that, along with what he himself regarded as naiveté, there was often great lucidity on the level of practical theory. Nor is this surprising since, as we shall see, Maritain developed a very calibrated theory of degrees of practical knowledge.

6

The Villard legacy thus proved to be an ambiguous boon. On the one hand, it provided Maritain with a financial cushion that would enable him to develop as a philosopher and to pursue at leisure the quest for holiness. He came to regret his association with Action Française, but the movement's popularity with Catholics probably had much to do with accelerating his wider influence. However unconvincing are the efforts, by the Maritains and others, to make light of his association with Action Française, his publications make clear that he moved more surely when he sought to spell out the philosophical implications of Pius X's *Pascendi*. Maritain's early writings make clear that he had enlisted in the fight against Modernism.[30]

PRIME
(1918–1923)

Chronology

1919   July. Maritain signs Massis's manifesto *"Pour un parti de l'intelligence."*

1920   January 9. Jacques and Charles Maurras contribute fifty-thousand francs apiece of the Villard inheritance to the founding of *La Revue Universelle.*
        January 26. Lecture at Louvain: "Some Conditions of the Thomistic Revival."
        Publishes *Art and Scholasticism* and volume 1 of his *Elements of Philosophy,* the *Introduction to Philosophy.*
        Beginning of what would become the Thomistic Study Circles.

1921   Raïssa ill; convalescence in Switzerland.
        Consults Reginald Garrigou-Lagrange, O.P., about the study circles.
        Publishes *Theonas,* the first title in a projected French Library of Philosophy under Maritain's direction.

1922   March–April. Drawing up of the statutes of the Thomistic Circles. Garrigou-Lagrange becomes advisor of the circles.
        Prayer and Intelligence (De la vie d'oraison) by Jacques and Raïssa.
        July 1–September 20. Stay in Switzerland, where Jacques meets Charles Journet, lifelong friend and future cardinal.
        September 30–October 4. First retreat of the Thomistic Circles preached by Garrigou-Lagrange at Versailles.
        Antimoderne published.

LES CERCLES D'ÉTUDES THOMISTES

I

Of the two things Maritain said the Villard bequest would enable him to do—continue his philosophical work and conduct a center of spirituality—the second was begun at Meudon in a house the Maritains were able to buy with their new and unexpected fortune. But both objectives were pursued at the same address. It was at Meudon that Maritain began the Thomistic Study Circles.

An indication of the importance Maritain attached to the study circles and retreats that were held at his house in Meudon is the fact that he devotes nearly one quarter of his *Carnet de notes* to the subject. This project, which would continue until the beginning of World War II, when Jacques and his wife left France for the United States, and which represents one of the most sustained efforts on Maritain's part to influence the culture of his native land as a convert to Catholicism, must be understood in all its successes and failures.

The meetings at the Maritains' seem to have begun without any thought of regular recurrence. Jacques tells us that he found in a notebook this entry: "First reunion of Thomistic studies at the house, with Picher, Vaton, Barbot, Dastarac, Massis." The date of the entry was Sunday, February 8, 1914.

There was no immediate sequel to that meeting, not surprisingly: World War I broke out in 1914. It was five years later, in the fall of 1919, that regular meetings devoted to Thomistic studies began at the Maritain home in Versailles. Jacques had been on leave of absence from the Institut Catholique during the year 1917–1918 (the last year of the war), engaged in writing two introductory books in philosophy.[1] The names of those attending the first meeting were hardly household words, and Maritain describes the participants of the second meeting, which would indeed begin a series, as personal friends and students of his from the Institut Catholique. It was still an informal gathering, and it stayed that way until 1921 when the decision was made to formalize the meetings and to stabilize their point. The participants were those "for whom the spiritual life and the pursuit of wisdom (philosophical and theological) had major importance. . . ."[2]

From the time of their conversion, the Maritain household had been on a schedule that took its rationale from a dual purpose—the pursuit of study and the pursuit of sanctity. In Germany, there had been only an accidental connection between the two, with prayer merely surrounding studies more or less unrelated to the goal of the spiritual life. The discovery of Saint Thomas had opened up the possibility of a more integral connection between the life of the mind and the life of the spirit. This was a discovery that Edith Stein too would make.[3] When the Maritains became oblates of Saint Benedict under the motto *Ora et Labora: Work and Pray*, their regimen of prayer and study had taken on a particular stamp, but the Thomistic Study Circles acquired their own character. There was the continuation of the conviction that laymen too were called to sanctity, but the spirit of Versailles was more Dominican than Benedictine, a movement prefigured in a way in Thomas Aquinas's move from the Benedictine Abbey of Montecassino to the Order of Preachers.[4] Most of the participants were lay people—old and young, male and female, students and professors—but there were priests and religious as well. The lay people represented a wide range of vocations, not just professional philosophers, but doctors, poets, musicians, businessmen, scientists. Catholics were in the majority, but there were also unbelievers, Jews, Orthodox, and some Protestants. Some were already experts in Thomistic thought, others mere beginners. It was interest in the thought of Thomas Aquinas, albeit in different degrees, that brought them together.

What was the atmosphere? It wasn't a class or a seminar—the participants did not come as students in that sense; nor was it a soirée with drinks and cigarettes. Rather, people came to a home as guests. Jacques goes on about the need for feminine influence for the success of such a venture and characterizes the participants as guests of Raïssa. There were three women hostesses: Raïssa, her mother, and her sister Vera. The samovar was readied, and later there would be dinner. Writing as a lonely widower, Jacques insists that Raïssa was the "ardent flame" of the reunions, taking an active if discreet part in the discussions. And she prayed constantly for the success of the reunions. "It is clear that without her—or without her sister—there would have been no Thomistic Circles, anymore than there would have been a Meudon (or for that matter a Jacques Maritain)."[5]

The discussion would go on throughout the afternoon, through tea and on into dinner, though not all stayed for that. At midnight, they bade goodbye to the last guest and collapsed with fatigue.

2

It is significant that Jacques insists on the role of Raïssa in the reunions. Her motive was certainly and chiefly the dissemination of the thought of Thomas Aquinas, but of course there was also a wife promoting her husband's career and influence. As time went on, the reunions became the occasion for many conversions to Catholicism; and the relevance of Thomism for all aspects of culture gave the reunions the air of a salon that sought to exert influence in the artistic and literary life of Paris. The very public contretemps with Jean Cocteau and the effort to rival the literary influence of André Gide are facets of that, as we shall see. But these were far in the future when the effort began.

For the first ten or twelve years, the topics were the great problems of philosophy and theology, treated technically. Texts of Thomas would be read, the great commentators consulted—special mention is made of John of St. Thomas—and an effort made to "disengage from the intramural disputes of Second Scholasticism the truths whose appeal transcended the prison-like setting of the texts." What were the themes? Faith and reason, philosophy and theology, metaphysics, poetry, politics—all the issues raised by the culture around them.

Jacques was the leader, as we learn when he tells us that he prepared his expositions of the texts the night before or Sunday morning, "hastily, but carefully." Among his papers, he found notes for the meetings, and we are not surprised to hear that these took the form of synoptic tables and great schemata on large sheets that could be affixed to the wall. The subjects he

treated, by way of analysis of texts, included the following: angelic knowledge; how angels know future contingents; singulars and secrets of the
heart; intellectual knowledge; the agent intellect; knowledge of the singular;
the vision of God and the light of glory; the desire for that vision; theoretical and practical knowledge; is sociology a science? in what sense? medicine; politics; justice and friendship; the Trinity; subsistence, person, the
divine persons; Original Sin; the incarnation; the human nature of Christ;
free will. . . .

3

Maritain recalled these topics from the first decade of the reunions, which
should mean through 1929. As the chronology at the beginning of this section indicates, these were tumultuous years—the public flap with Cocteau;
the attempt to dissuade Gide from publishing *Corydon;* the establishment
of *Roseau d'Or*, the Golden Rose, a series of books meant to rival Gide's influence on French culture. And it was during this decade that Action Française, with which Jacques was associated, was condemned by Rome.

Before looking at the contretemps with Cocteau and with André Gide
over what might be called Jacques Maritain's apostolate to the homosexu-
als, which had very mixed results, let us examine the little book Jacques
and Raïssa wrote to express the vision of the intellectual life that lay behind the circles. But first we must consider the constitution that governed its
meetings.

4

The statutes governing the Thomistic Study Circles can be found in an appendix of Maritain's *Carnet de notes*, published many years afterward, in 1964.
Section I, which states the general principles of the circles, is of more interest than the section devoted to organization.

"In making Saint Thomas Aquinas the Common Doctor of the Church,
God has given him to us as our leader and guide in the knowledge of the
truth." Maritain's mind had been formed by the philosophy of the day—
negatively, for the most part, but more positively in the case of Bergson.

After his conversion, he did not immediately see the significance of Thomas Aquinas in the intellectual life of the Catholic. It was nearly four years after his conversion that he began to read the *Summa theologiae*. Doubtless motivated by docility at first, he soon became personally convinced of the wisdom of the Church's designation of Thomas as chief guide in philosophy and theology. Thomas has pride of place among the Doctors of the Church, and professors should present his thought to their students. The characterization of Thomas's doctrine in the statutes stresses its formality. "It addresses the mind as a chain of certitudes demonstratively linked and is more perfectly in accord with the faith than any other." It carries with it the pledge of a sanctity inseparable from the teaching mission of the Angelic Doctor who all but effaced his human personality in the divine light. However attractive the person of Thomas is and however much a model of the Christian life, Maritain quoted with enthusiasm the statement of Leo XIII in *Aeterni Patris: Majus aliquid in sancto Thoma quam sanctus Thomas suscipitur et defenditur: there is in Thomas something greater than Thomas that we receive and defend.* It is because of his sanctity as well as his intelligence that Thomas can be a vehicle of the truth and a model for the pursuit of it.

After providing a succinct indication of Leo XIII's reasons for designating Thomas Aquinas as guide in philosophy and theology, the statutes go on to observe that the human mind is so feeble by nature and weakened by the heritage of Original Sin that it needs supernatural help to grasp a doctrine so metaphysically and theologically exalted as that of Thomas. The saint is seen as a special assistant of the Holy Spirit in dispensing the graces necessary to achieve the aim of study. "Especially in the present time so replete with error and above all lacking the discipline and graces proper to the religious life, we believe it to be impossible for Thomism to be maintained in its integrity and purity without the special help of a life of prayer."

The spiritual life and the life of study are found to be united not only in Thomas but also in his major commentators; for example, in Bañez, who was the spiritual director of Teresa of Avila, and in Gonet, who dedicated his *Clypeus thomisticae theologiae* to her, and in the theologians of Salamanca (*Salmanticenses*), faithful Thomists who found in his theology the foundations of the spiritual teaching of both Teresa and Saint John of the Cross.

In modern times it is necessary for lay people as well as religious to pursue this union of study and prayer. How else can the modern mind be won over to the truth? It is also necessary to become knowledgeable in all that has been taught since Thomas, according to the circles' statutes: to accept what is true and reject what is false and, by combining old and new, to make progress toward an intellectual renaissance in all areas of culture, not only in theology and philosophy, but in art and letters as well. The statutes envisage writers and painters and poets moving off from a Thomistic base to creative work in their various fields.

But this cannot be regarded simply as the acquisition of knowledge. Indeed, knowledge is dangerous if one does not have the appropriate motive and spiritual preparation for it. "Experience shows that the danger of the 'materialization' of Thomism is not imaginary." It is to forestall that and to promote the opposite, the unity of study and prayer, that the study circles have been formed. The spiritual and supernatural is the most important aspect of this effort. As to what form this should take, members are left to follow their own best lights.

5

The circles were not a third order—would the Maritains have chosen the Benedictines rather than the Dominicans if that had been their intention?—but they were certainly modeled on such affiliates of religious orders. Those who took the aims of the statutes seriously would not only live lives different from those of other intellectuals, artists, and writers; they would be leading lives of reparation for the follies committed in the name of their art or science. While this will seem an unusual way to view one's intellectual or artistic life, Maritain would doubtless reply that what was at issue was simply taking one's Christian belief seriously. Prayer and study, living a life sustained by grace, are not mere options for the believer. What the circles did was to articulate what the demands of the faith are in the various activities that make up a society's culture. That the demands were racheted up a notch or two is undeniable; that a demanding pattern was proposed is equally undeniable. Lay people were advised to spend at least one hour each day in prayer, and this was to animate everything else done during the day.

The circles were put under the patronage of the Blessed Virgin Mary and were open to those living in the world who "wished to work for the spread of Thomism or to be inspired by it, resting faithful to the thought and teaching of St. Thomas which lives in his great disciples, such as Cajetan, John of St. Thomas and the [anonymous] Theologians of Salamanca." Members would take a private vow to devote themselves to the life of prayer to the degree that their state of life permits. A year's trial and the advice of a confessor is recommended before taking the vow for a year or even perpetually. But such a vow is not an absolute requirement for membership.

The director of studies would always be a religious of the Order of Saint Dominic. The first Director General of Studies, appointed by the provincial of the order in France, was Father Reginald Garrigou-Lagrange, professor of theology at the Angelicum in Rome. His guidance in forming the circles is acknowledged and among his continuing roles was to assure the purity and authenticity of the Thomism of the circles. There would be an annual meeting, as much a retreat as an opportunity to understand Thomas better. The statutes end with a prayer: *Doctor Angelice, ora pro nobis: Angelic Doctor, pray for us.*

6

Complementing the statutes of the circles was a little book written by the Maritains in 1922, the year the circles were formally organized. It was first circulated privately and not published and made available in bookstores until 1925. The authors disclaim that their work is meant to substitute for a treatise on spirituality or even serve as an introduction to the most elementary work in that area. What they have sought to do is lay out in the spirit of the Christian tradition and of Saint Thomas, in the simplest way, the grand lines of the spiritual life of persons living in the world who devote themselves to the life of the mind.

The book is prefaced by the testimony of Reginald of Piperno, the *socius* of Thomas in the Dominican Order who worked closely with him and could thus describe the saint with authority. "My brothers, while he lived, my master prevented me revealing the wonderful things of which I have been witness in his regard. One of them is that he did not acquire his knowledge by human industry but by the merit of prayer, for each time he intended to study, discuss, read, write or dictate, he would first withdraw for private prayer, and he prayed with tears that he might find the truth of the divine secrets, and thanks to this prayer, although before he had been in a state of uncertainty, he came away instructed. . . ."

The intellectual life is in any case a mysterious thing. Describing it after the fact is one thing—formalizing it into arguments and setting forth presuppositions, premises, relevant supports is another. How does it actually evolve? Where do ideas come from? What is the source of the insight that comes seemingly without prelude? The life of reason can seem to ride upon a sea of mystery. Of course, like self-made men, thinkers take credit for their thoughts as if they brought them forth with full lucidity and intention. But the image of the apple hitting Newton on the head suggests another possibility.

That being said, it will not seem that Thomas is taking unfair advantage in having recourse to prayer, asking divine light on the task before him. An argument for prayer in the schools is lurking here. No less an authority than Alfred E. Newman said it was the only way he could have graduated. More seriously, what we have here is what Saint Augustine, whose motto is taken from Matthew's Gospel, emphasizes in his *On the Teacher:* You have but one teacher, Christ. The capacity to learn is given: the human teacher can only address it, invoking a light that ultimately comes from the Word of God, the eternal logos.

Our tendency to think that prayer is a brief recess from acts over which we have full control and of which we are the sole causes is in conflict with Paul's injunction: *whatever* you do. . . . Once more, the animating principle of the circles is seen to be only a special case of the general condition of Christians.

7

De la vie de l'oraison has two parts: The Intellectual Life and Prayer, and The Spiritual Life. Anyone acquainted with the opusculum called *De modo studendi*, attributed to Thomas Aquinas, will be reminded of it when he opens this little book by Jacques and Raïssa Maritain. Each of the nine chapters (three in part 1, six in part 2) bears as its title a Latin citation on which the text is a commentary. But of course it is the conjunction of the intellectual and spiritual lives that gives the book its stamp, and one which, in the modern world, will surprise.

The progressive secularization of philosophy has had its effect on the sense of what the vocation of a philosopher is. Of Descartes's account of knowledge Maritain remarked that it bore a peculiar similarity to Thomas Aquinas's account of angelic knowledge. Methodic doubt led Descartes to the first certainty that, even if he were deceived about any and everything he might think, of one thing he could not be deceived, of the fact that he was thinking. From this starting point the Cartesian project of reconstruction began. Descartes regarded himself as a thinking something, a *res cogitans*, and his project was to see if he could get outside his mind, mind being all he is at this point. This is the origin of the so-called mind-body problem. It is not surprising that such an understanding of the philosophical task has influenced the philosopher's notion of his calling. It comes to be seen as an almost exclusively cerebral pursuit of knowledge unrelated to the wider life that, presumably, the philosopher leads. The madman, Chesterton said, has lost everything except his reason.

This impoverishment of the pursuit of truth is something to which Maritain responded in a variety of ways. The later discussions of Christian philosophy are obviously related to it. The distinction between the nature and the state of philosophy, between philosophy and philosophizing, obviously addressed this issue. But from the beginning, after their conversion and consequent pursuit of a spiritual life under the guidance of a director, any philosophizing would necessarily be seen in the context of the spiritual life. The book on the life of prayer—in English it would be called *Prayer and Intelligence*—was first published anonymously in 1922, reprinted under the names of the authors in 1925, then with changes in 1933, and with more changes still in 1947. The basic text of the book remained the same, with the variations occurring in the notes and addenda. This history of the book may be taken to underscore that its subject represents a profoundly abiding concern of the authors.

"O Wisdom, which proceeds from the mouth of the Most High, reaching from end to end mightily and sweetly disposing all things, come and teach us the way of prudence." The technique of the book is to provide brief reflections on a series of Latin tags coming from various sources. The first part meditates in order on the following:

1. *Verbum spirans amorem:* The Word breathing forth love.
2. *Et pax Dei, quae exsuperat omnem sensum, custodiat intelligentias vestras:* May the peace of God which surpasses all the senses take over your understanding.
3. *Sint lucernae ardentes in manibus vestris:* Let there be burning lamps in your hands.

Verbum spirans amorem: the Word breathing forth love. It is necessary that in us too love proceed from the Word, that is, from the spiritual possession of the truth in Faith. And just as whatever is in the Word is found in the Holy Spirit, so too what is in our knowledge must pass into the affections by way of love, and come to rest only in it. Let love proceed from truth, and knowledge be made fruitful in love. Our prayer is not what it should be if either of these two conditions be lacking. By prayer we mean above all that which takes place in the secret of the heart and is ordered to contemplation of and union with God.

Union with God is the ultimate end of human existence, the common goal of all. Once again, we are reminded that the reflections before us are only a special instance of the common human vocation. That end will be reached by action aided by grace or sometimes simply by an act of God with the soul in the passive condition described by the mystics. Saint Gertrude is cited but also the *Summa theologiae*'s discussion of the gifts of the Holy Spirit. Thomas makes clear that God moves man in a way appropriate to his nature: man is not a mere instrument or tool of the divine action. "But man is not an instrument of that kind, for he is moved by the Holy Spirit in such a way that he himself also acts as a creature endowed with free will" (*Summa theologiae*, IaIIae, q. 68, a. 3, ad 2). Deliberate effort on our part, moved by grace of course, can prepare the way for God's special action in us. Our intellect can only develop to the full its highest capacities if it is strengthened by a life of prayer. "There is a quite special connection between the intellectual life and the life of prayer, in this sense that prayer seeks to remove the soul from the realm of sensible images so that it might rise to the intelligible and beyond, but, reciprocally, the activity of intellect is the more perfect as it is freed from these same sensible images." Again this echoes Saint Thomas (IIaIIae, q. 15, a. 3; *In Boethii de trinitate*, q. 6, a. 2.). Prayer alone can unite us with absolute fidelity to the truth and fill us with charity toward our neighbor, "in particular, a great intellectual charity." Prayer alone will enable us to move from truth to practice.

In those whose lives are dedicated to intellectual work, prayer must be sustained and nourished by theology. Theology makes surer and shorter the spiritual path and can spare us a host of errors along the way: in the Purgative Way, the first and ascetic step mentioned by the saints whereby we wean ourselves from base desires and self-love; in the Illuminative Way, theology has a purifying power that turns the human self toward God alone; and finally, in the Unitive Way, it roots the soul in faith and divine truth, a disposition essential to the life of union.

Charity takes pride of place, not least because in this life we can love God more perfectly than we can know him. God lifts up the most simple to the sublimest contemplation, but knowledge can become an obstacle because of our perversity and vanity. However, it would be presumptuous to expect an infusion of doctrinal lights that are in our power to attain. The normal way, for those given the grace, is to pursue both paths: to unite the life of intelligence to that of charity and let the one be of aid to the other, remembering that the second is far more valuable than the first.

8

The Maritains make passing mention of the character of the intellectual life in modern times; and no reader will fail to see how fundamentally different from the modern is the vision of the life of the mind set forth in this little work, a vision that underlies the Thomistic Study Circles. Jacques Maritain did not see the faith he had been given as a mere garnish, something added to his workaday life in a more or less incidental manner, something that might lead perhaps to saying a prayer before sitting down to study. The Christian faith initiates a life, and grace is to pervade all aspects of it. This required Maritain to embed the intellectual life into the common Christian vocation, thereby transforming it.

9

The second part of this little work meditates on the following Latin phrases:

4. *Estote perfecti:* Be thou perfect.
5. *Caritas vinculum perfectionis:* Charity the bond of perfection.
6. *Mihi autem adhaerere Deo bonum est:* It is good for me to cling to God.
7. *Qui spiritu Dei aguntur, ii sunt filli Dei:* They who are moved by the spirit of God are the sons of God.
8. *Averte oculos meos ne videant vanitatem:* Turn away my eyes lest they look on vanity.
9. *In omnibus requiem quaesivi et in hereditate Domini morabor:* In all things I have sought rest and I will dwell in the inheritance of the Lord.
10. *Qui volens turrim aedificare, non prius sedens computat sumptus:* He who wishes to build a tower without first counting the cost. . . .

11. *Praebe mihi cor tuum:* Show me thy heart.

12. *Si qui vult post me venire, abneget semitipsum, et tollat crucem suam, et se-quatur me:* He who wishes to come with me must first deny himself, take up his cross and follow me.

The second part begins with an appeal to the Rule of Saint Benedict; cites Père Lallemant, author of a work called *Spiritual Doctrine,* and Saint Bernard of Clairvaux; Thomas Aquinas; his commentator Cajetan; Saint Albert the Great; John of St. Thomas; Pseudo-Denis the Areopagite; and, explicitly and implicitly, of course, Sacred Scripture. Saint Francis de Sales, Saint Teresa of Avila, Père Humbert Clérissac, and Cassian are invoked as well. Despite their disavowal, the Maritains have in these few pages provided a florilegium of texts from the Christian tradition of reflection on the spiritual life, arranging the texts and invoking the authorities with the special purpose of laying out for others, as doubtless they first did for themselves, the only way in which, as Christians, they could continue to pursue the life of study. It is imperative that this be seen as the bedrock of Maritain's long and industrious life. The spirit in which he thought and taught and wrote makes him a congenial figure even if one is initially less than persuaded by what he says. The voice that one hears is not that of a careerist, an academic, a man jealous of his reputation.

10

A personal remembrance: When I was a very junior member of the faculty at Notre Dame, Jacques Maritain visited. He would speak that evening in the auditorium of what was then the new Moreau Seminary on the far side of St. Joseph's Lake on campus. We walked along the road that leads north from the Grotto under autumnal trees still aglitter with golden leaves, scuffling through those that had already fallen. Before reaching the community cemetery where, under identical crosses, the dead members of the Congregation of Holy Cross lie in a kind of clerical Arlington, we turned to the right and continued on to Moreau. Much of the audience was made up of seminarians, and we all took our seats and waited until an old man was led down the aisle, stooped, his hair white but still full. Around his neck he wore a scarf in the way a priest wears a stole, but this was a layman, one of the most beloved and respected figures of the Thomistic revival. I cannot say that I remember much of what he said—he spoke on the philosophy of history—and this not only because his English was difficult. It was the man one heard first of all, the person speaking; what he had to say was filtered through a self that had spent a long life trying to avoid the one tragedy of which he had read in Léon Bloy so many years before. This was not just another lecture, because he was not just another lecturer. The ideal of the intellectual life he embodied inspired generations of laypeople who decided to devote their lives to philosophy or theology or to see whatever they did *sub specie aeternitatis.* That was a long time ago, over forty years ago, and since then the faculties of Catholic colleges and universities have taken more secular models for what they do. There have been many changes. Changes, not improvements.

VAE MIHI SI NON THOMISTIZAVERO

I

The foregoing chapter should make clear that when Maritain amends the cry of Saint Paul, "Woe is me if I do not preach the gospel," into the slogan that provides the title of this section, he is not putting Scripture to secular use. The study of Thomas, the intellectual life, was not something separate from the spiritual life for Maritain. What grounded his conviction that in taking on the Catholic faith he was effectively taking Thomas Aquinas as his main mentor in things intellectual? We have seen that this did not come home to him immediately. Some years passed after his conversion before he began to read Thomas Aquinas. But once he began, nothing was ever the same again.

In 1879, a quarter of a century before Maritain's conversion and three years before his birth, Leo XIII issued an encyclical known from its *incipit* or opening words as *Aeterni Patris.* As its title made clear, the pope wanted Christian philosophy in the manner of the Angelic Doctor, Saint Thomas Aquinas, to be established in Catholic schools. Thomas Aquinas had been recommended time and again by the papal Magisterium; he held pride of place in the intellectual training of members of his own order, the

Dominicans, as well as others. Editions of his works continued to appear, but by the time of Leo XIII, Thomas no longer played a significant role in the intellectual life of the Church. How this came about has much to do with the extraordinary character of Leo's encyclical.

The *Summa theologiae* and the Bible were displayed on the altar during the sessions of the Council of Trent as the principal works of reference for the bishops gathered to consider what was to be done about the issues raised by the Reformation. The renewal in the Church occasioned by the defection of Luther and others was characterized by the reform of seminary education. The prominence given Thomas Aquinas at the Council's sessions would seem to promise that he would function as mentor in philosophy and theology. But the Tridentine Church does not seem to have enjoyed anything like a Thomistic revival. Rather, historians provide us with an increasingly bleak and fragmented picture. When John Henry Newman, recently converted to Catholicism, came to Rome in 1846 expecting to find a bastion of Thomism, he found anything but. "I have read Aristotle and St. Thomas," a Jesuit told him, "and owe a great deal to them, but they are out of favor here and throughout Italy. St. Thomas was a great saint—people don't dare to speak against him, but put him aside."[6] We may wonder what had happened since the time of Descartes at the Jesuit College of La Fleche, where he was introduced to at least the tail end of the Thomistic tradition, i.e., the commentator on the *Summa*, Toletus.

2

One thing that happened was Descartes himself, who, putting away what he had learned as mere opinion and verbiage, set out to put philosophy on so firm a foundation that the endless quarrels that had characterized its previous history would come to an end. Descartes was a Catholic; when he died in Stockholm, where he had gone as a guest of Queen Christina, it was feared that he was trying to convert her to Rome—a conversion that did indeed eventually take place after Descartes's death: Christina's life ended in the eternal city. The Cartesian method was not aimed at undermining religion, but with Descartes we see the beginnings of a philosophy self-consciously separating itself from Christian faith. In time, philosophy would come to see itself as completely secular, an alternative to Christianity; but this was far from the immediate result. Well into the nineteenth century, philosophers saw themselves as providing the only defense of Christianity possible in modern times. In the eighteenth century, Kant would recommend a religion that kept within the limits of reason alone; while in the nineteenth, Hegel saw his philosophy as the apotheosis of Christianity: philosophy as the truth of religion. The modern philosophy that dominates the history of the discipline can seem merely an extension of the Protestant Reformation—and this despite the role that Descartes, Malebranche, and Pascal, Catholics all, played in its first generation.

Catholic thinkers seemed to take as their first task the assessment of Descartes's rejection of scholasticism. With the success of what may be called the epistemological turn, with the endless variations on it that were to come, confronting the claims of the moderns, as such, pretty well filled one's plate. It is an old story that one who spends his life refuting another will end by being more like than unlike his foe. The case of Claude Buffier, S.J. (1661–1737), is interesting in this regard. His writings exhibit a fascination with Descartes as well as the intention to save from the possibility of doubt certain truths of common sense.[7] Buffier thus anticipates the Scottish School; indeed Thomas Reid has been unfairly accused of plagiarizing the Parisian Jesuit. Buffier may be taken to represent a kind of philosophical minimalism, the defense of those common truths that guide men's lives because the suggestion that they may all turn out to be false is socially and morally disruptive. Buffier recognized the difference between beliefs that recommended themselves only because they were familiar and the prejudice of the times and did not of course defend as true whatever was commonly said. Defenses of common sense notoriously become quite sophisticated, and Buffier leads the way in that, as in much else.

Taking Buffier as a bellwether, we might see Catholic thought as more and more defined by positions it was disposed to contest, defensive, giving up territory by inches, fighting a losing battle. Hence the hodgepodge Newman encountered in the schools of Rome where ecclesiastics were trained, many of them destined to become bishops and have seminaries of their own.

Here and there during the nineteenth century, circles were formed dedicated to rediscovering Saint Thomas. Presumably the Dominicans had never lost him, but they do not seem to have been vigorously engaged in making him felt in the wider world. Of course, in France, with the Revolution, the religious orders were suppressed; indeed, the political and social upheavals of Europe are the background against which the development to which we refer must be seen. Italy was in tumult; the pope was chased from Rome in

1848 and then brought back from Gaeta to become the prisoner of the Vatican. The fruits of modern thought were becoming visible all around, and they were not favorable to the faith.

3

Perhaps these irresponsibly sweeping remarks are enough to ground an understanding of the twofold aim of *Aeterni Patris*. It reposed on a negative assessment of modern culture and of the philosophy that had produced it. The effects of modernity were to be seen within the Church as well, so what Leo wanted was a revival of Christian philosophy *ad mentem Sancti Thomae* in the Catholic schools, in order that modern errors could be effectively countered and their danger to the faith neutralized—but only after the truth had been grasped.

It was Jacques Maritain's dissatisfaction with the philosophy he had encountered at the Sorbonne that disposed him for the grace of faith. Modern thought reduced man to matter, made life pointless, and led to despair. If it was true, death would be preferable to life. First Bergson and then Bloy showed Maritain that there was an alternative. With the grace of faith came the certainty that life had a meaning, a meaning that was pursued along a path very different from that traversed by modern philosophy. In the first years of his life as a Catholic, Maritain continued his biological studies and then engaged in humdrum editorial work as an alternative to taking a post teaching philosophy in a lycée where the curriculum was set by the thinkers he had rejected. Raïssa was given Thomas as spiritual reading; she passed on her enthusiasm to Jacques and the rest, so to say, is history.

Maritain's own way of coming to Thomas colors his career as a Thomist. First and primarily, there is the enthusiasm and delight that the reading of Thomas gave him, the conviction that at last he was coming into possession of the truth. But this brought the secondary conviction that Thomas was the remedy and refutation of the errors that had infested the Sorbonne. The fundamental truth was that the human mind is designed to know reality. This apparent truism had been called into question in a variety of progressively more inventive ways by modern philosophy. And it all began with Descartes.

The Dream of Descartes was published in 1932, but the first three chapters of the book were written contemporaneously with *Prayer and Intelligence*. Maritain did not come to the reading of Thomas with his mind a philosophical *tabula rasa*, and it is inevitable that he should compare what he was learning from Thomas with what he had been taught in school. (Notice the surface symmetry of the trajectories of Descartes and Maritain: each departing from what he had been taught toward what was certain and true, but Maritain seeking to recapture what Descartes had flung away, albeit in a doubtless disposable form.)

4

Jacques and Raïssa Maritain were on the Isle of Wight, and thus effectively in Great Britain, when World War I broke out in August 1914. They had left for the Isle of Wight, where the Solesmes community was in exile, in June, despite the impending danger to France. Jacques was in his thirty-second year; but Charles Péguy, his senior, and Ernest Psichari, his coeval, fell in combat during the first month of hostilities. Jacques's mother, Geneviève Favre, was appalled at her son's absence from the country and suggested, perhaps sarcastically, that he take up permanent residence in England, as France would be an uncomfortable place for those who had not risen to her defense. In response, Jacques claimed that he was being held prisoner on the isle. Moreover, his monarchist beliefs came into play. Democracy, he told his mother, had exiled the monks whose only crime was that they prayed. As for himself, he would remain where God had put him. As it happens, Jacques had an exemption, although later, in the spring of 1917, he would be temporarily mobilized. But he would have a different kind of war from his fallen friends.

Jacques had been teaching at the Collège Stanislas since 1912, but in June 1914, just before he left for the Isle of Wight, he was appointed an adjunct professor at the Institut Catholique. It was there that he gave, in the academic year 1914–1915, a series of lectures in which he probed the underlying causes of the enmity between France and Germany. These lectures were published in the journal *La Croix*, the first in its entirety, while the remaining twenty-one lectures were summarized.[8] While many of the ideas contained in this series of lectures were adumbrated earlier and would be extended and developed in later writings of Maritain, here we have them hot off the press, as it were. In them, Maritain speaks not of the material combat but of the underlying moral and intellectual conflict.

There is a false image of the war that must first be confronted. France is seen as the champion of world democracy and of the Revolution, whereas Germany is the champion of reaction. There may be some Frenchmen who imagine they are fighting for the revolutionary ideals of 1789, but the vast majority, Maritain says, are fighting simply for France, and a subclass of these see France, as the eldest daughter of the Church. As for the ideas of the French Revolution, they have prospered in Germany more than in France. Germany has the kind of despotism that results from the ideals of the Revolution and is the antithesis of the principles of order and tradition. Germany has developed technological marvels, but they are "at the service of an ego immersed in nature alone, at the service of a humanity freed from every spiritual and supernatural principle."[9] In short, Germany enshrines the individualism and naturalism of the Reformation.

Maritain had spent two years studying biology in Germany, but there is nothing anecdotal about his analysis. We might say that the tone of these lectures is reflective of the rhetoric of wartime, and there is something to that, but these were not fugitive notions in Maritain's development. His "true image" of the war is as severe against his own country as it is against Germany.[10]

If the French Revolution set in play political ideals that changed the face of Europe, it was the Cartesian revolution that was the source of the modern philosophy on which Maritain passed a negative judgment throughout his career. His instinctive dissatisfaction with modernity is present from his student days. As his thought developed, the theory in terms of which he underwrote that distaste varied. What Descartes set in motion in the world of thought, Luther a short time before had set in motion in religion: the solitary individual standing in judgment on tradition, having to verify for himself each and every claim on penalty of being less than human, or less of a Christian. But Maritain's philosophical appraisal of modernity proved to be far more durable than the undoubted Action Française mentality that animated Maritain. As a boy he had been a socialist. Now he was a monarchist for whom democracy and its ideals were anathema. Eventually Maritain would claim that democracy is the best political expression of Christianity, but he is a long way from that in 1914, and will have to go through a number of political convolutions in the intervening years to get there.

5

But if Maritain's political theories were to vacillate back and forth between Left and Right, there is a solid continuity in his moral and intellectual appraisal of modernity. With his conversion, Jacques began to see the world through the lens of his faith and he could scarcely overlook the atheistic tendencies of the Left. The view of man and his destiny that was predominant in the modern world—at least in culturally influential circles—was at odds with the Christian view. When Maritain turned to Thomas, he found not only a theologian who articulated revealed truth, but one whose conception of theology presupposed a philosophy that could arrive at truths about man and the world and God independently of Revelation. Throughout his long career, Maritain steeped himself in the thought of Thomas and sought to do in his own times something analogous to what Thomas had done in his.

And this meant that the culture had to be redeemed. It would not do to abandon art and literature and philosophy to forces hostile to religion and to withdraw into a sectarian redoubt waiting for the end times.

TIERCE
(1923–1926)

Chronology

1923   June 5. The Maritains move to 10 rue du Parc at Meudon, where they will live until war breaks out in 1940.
September 26–30. Second retreat of the Thomistic Circles at Meudon. These will continue annually until 1940, save for 1936.
October 13. Jacques and Henri Massis interviewed by Frédéric Lefèvre.
Lecture at Avignon, "Saint Thomas, the Apostle of Modern Times."
Volume 2 of *Elements of Philosophy*, the *Introduction to Logic*.
December 14. Attempts to persuade André Gide not to publish *Corydon*.

1924   July. Jean Cocteau at Meudon.
Reflections on Intelligence (*Réflexions sur l'intelligence*) published.

1925   March. *Roseau d'Or* founded. First title, Jacques's *Three Reformers*, dedicated to his mother.
Meets Nicholas Berdiaev.
Jean Cocteau meets Père Henrion at Meudon and three days later makes his confession.
August 2. Raïssa's mother baptized.
August 29. Maurice Sachs baptized.
September. Paul Claudel visits.

1926   January. Cocteau's *Letter to Jacques Maritain* published and, at the same time, Maritain's *Reply to Jean Cocteau.* The exchange was published in English as *Art and Faith.*

Georges Bernanos, *Under the Sun of Satan (Sous le soleil de Satan)* published by *Roseau d'Or.*

Meets Julien Green.

August. Cardinal Andrieu makes a declaration about Action Française and Pius XI responds.

September 25. Meeting at Meudon of Maritain, Maurras, Massis, and Garrigou-Lagrange.

October. "An Opinion about Charles Maurras and the Duty of Catholics."

December 20. Pius XI condemns Action Française.

MARITAIN'S KULTURKAMPF

I

Jacques's most active involvement in Action Française was from 1920 through 1926, thanks to his connection with *La Revue Universelle*. Jointly financed by Maurras and Maritain from money they had each received from the fallen Villard, it was meant to convey the ideas of Action Française to readers beyond those who subscribed to the official publications of the organization. Maurras had begun his career as a literary critic, and Maritain was now disposed to turn his attention to the world around him.

During the year following the end of the war, Jacques was granted a leave of absence from the Institut Catholique, and the Maritains—meaning the little flock of three: Raïssa, Vera, and Jacques—retreated to Vernie, near Solesmes, where they lived in a rectory. The ostensible purpose of Jacques's leave was to enable him to write the first volumes in a manual of philosophy he had agreed to do, but it was to be a year when a fundamental change in Maritain's understanding of his vocation occurred.

The three members of the little community sought to live a life in communion with the Benedictine ideal; all three were oblates of Saint Benedict. An intense spiritual life governed the household and provided the background for Jacques's intellectual work. Jacques compared the two sisters to

Martha and Mary, Vera being a solid practical presence while Raïssa was ethereal and withdrawn, given to closely monitoring her spiritual life and recording it in her journal. She was clearly influenced by what she read about the saints and mystics, though it is doubtful that any of *them* kept so obsessive a record of the ups and downs of their inner life. It is clear that Raïssa longed for mystical experiences. She withdrew into her room to devote herself to hours and hours of prayer and then noted in her journal how things had gone. But accounts of her health vie with accounts of her spiritual experiences. We will return to this when we discuss the posthumous publication of her journal and Jacques's interpretation of it and of his wife's spirituality. For now, this contemplative penchant of Raïssa's, plus the removal of any financial concerns thanks to the Villard legacy, made plausible the idea that the three would simply withdraw from the world and develop contemplative spiritual lives. A recurrent question in Raïssa's journal is wondering what God wants her to do.¹ If the withdrawal did not happen, the reason was Raïssa.

When Raïssa emerged from prayer, she sometimes brought with her a decision as to what was to be done. Thus it was Raïssa who broke the log-jam of conflicting advice about the proposed journey to Rome to see the pope while war was raging. So too, during the year of seclusion at Vernie, it was Raïssa who decided that they must seek to have a direct impact on the world in which they lived.² It seems clear that one of the things bothering Raïssa was how her life was to fit into Jacques's. His lectures attracted attention, his book on Bergson had been a sensation, he was invited here and there to talk. Raïssa notes that her health mysteriously deteriorates as soon as he leaves. The vow that they had taken clearly required a prolonged effort if their celibate life and their intimate cohabitation were to be reconciled. Raïssa sometimes sees Jacques as a rival with God for her love. When young, they had fallen madly in love with one another and now, as a convert seeking ever closer union with God, Raïssa had fallen madly in love with her creator. *Amour fou* is the phrase Jacques uses. She vows (May 22) to detach herself from "everything to which she is particularly drawn," such as to follow Jacques in his work and to help him. One thing she did help him with was a book he was writing that would be called *Art and Scholasticism*. This little book, which was destined to have a tremendous impact throughout the century on working artists, suggested an outlet that was denied Raïssa so far as philosophy was concerned. Culture was not exhausted by abstract thought, and the path of the poet seemed analogous to that of the mystic. Thus was born Raïssa's decision that they must return to the world and seek to influence their time through its artists and poets. The 1919 entries in her journal that reflect this new direction reveal an original and interesting mind.[3] "It is a mistake to isolate oneself from men because one has a clearer view of truth. If God does not call one to solitude, it is necessary to live with God in the multitude, and make him known and loved there."[4] By May 12, 1919, she is speaking of the different ways to God: a mystical way, the way of truth, the way of beauty, and so forth.

2

So it was that the Maritains returned from Jacques's leave of absence with a richer sense of their common vocation. The life of solitude was not to be theirs, but their involvement was not to be limited to Jacques's teaching and his philosophical writing. The *Cercles d'études thomistes* took on new scope and the range of intellect was seen to be appreciably broader.

As a signatory of the 1919 *Pour un parti de l'intelligence*, Jacques aligned himself with those who saw France as the chief guardian of civilization, a vocation that could be fulfilled, however, only insofar as a true understanding of the nation was had. The key role of Catholicism in France and western culture generally was emphasized.

ART AND SCHOLASTICISM

I

Although Maritain had been given leave to write two introductory manuals of philosophy[5]—a task that might have recalled his hack work of 1908—it was the little book in which he sought to expand the scholastic conception of art and apply it to fine art that represented an important new direction in his thought. Originally destined for appearance in a review, the study, fortified (and more than doubled in size) by appendices and notes, became a veritable treatise on aesthetics. It was also Thomistic, but only in the sense that Maritain had found in Aquinas the elements of the theory. However, it was far from being a reconstruction of a possible medieval aesthetics. Maritain was seeking in Thomas principles that could be applied to contemporary art and thus link the effort of the artist to his effort as a Thomist. Despite its small size, this first essay of Maritain into aesthetics is full of wonderful things. Here we shall concentrate on the way in which Maritain develops the analogy between the moral and/or mystical life and the work of the artist.

Aristotle distinguished between two virtues that perfect the practical use of our mind, prudence and art. Prudence or practical wisdom is aimed at directing the agent's acts to his true good with the result that the agent becomes good. The aim of prudence is the good of the agent. When the mind puts itself to the task of making something, on the other hand, the virtue of art insures that the thing will be well made. In his discussions of art, Aristotle has in mind building, shoemaking, medicine, and the like: the acts, as we might say, of the artisan. Although the *Poetics* deals with tragedy and speaks of imitation, we find in Aristotle no effort to bring sculpture and poetry and drama under the same umbrella as medicine, architecture, and shipbuilding. No more do we find in Thomas, who followed Aristotle in this regard, any discussion of aesthetics in a later sense. Maritain begins his discussion by underscoring this. Before he can show the relevance of a scholastic aesthetics to contemporary art, he must first show that there is such an aesthetics.

There is perhaps no more accessible example of the nature of Maritain's Thomism than *Art and Scholasticism*. Elements are brought together from various works of Thomas. Often an aside in an answer to an objection in the *Summa theologiae* will loom large. Extending the workaday discussions of "making" in Aristotle and Thomas to artistic creation is no easy task, and Maritain relies on the analogous sense that can be given to terms whose native habitat is the discussion of how to build a boat or how to bind up a wound. But it is the transcendental concept of beauty that is at the heart of Maritain's argument.[6]

2

Students of Thomas's teaching on the transcendental properties of being often have trouble with beauty as a transcendental. In the early discussions of being and its transcendental properties, beauty is not mentioned. And indeed Thomas's teaching on this subject has to be pieced together from discussions having quite different ends. The beautiful, Thomas quotably remarked—James Joyce embraced this account—is *that which, when seen, pleases: id quod visum placet.*[7] Maritain takes this to mean that there is an intuitive knowledge of beauty that gives joy.

The beautiful is what distinguishes the fine arts from the products of the artisan. The latter is chiefly concerned to make something useful— shoes for walking, a house to live in—whereas the fine artist. . . . Well, how does he differ from the mere artisan? Like the artisan, the artist makes something, and there may well be, as in the case of the sculptor, a good deal that is quite sweaty and servile in that making. Maritain suggests that the making component arises from man's sensible nature, whereas the beautiful component answers to that which is spiritual in him. He then suggests the analogy between contemplation and art. The fine arts should turn our minds to the transcendent, should sublimate the material so that it signifies the immaterial.

As he develops a theory of fine art from hints and asides in Thomas, Maritain is at the same time applying it to contemporary artists. This entails a critique of modern art that echoes his critique of modern philosophy. "From this point of view, it seems that modern art, having broken with the metiers, tends in its own way to the same claim to absolute independence, *aseity*, as modern philosophy" (note 44). It is clear that Maritain is not fashioning a Thomistic aesthetic that will serve merely as descriptive of what is going on in the arts; it is meant to provide both a criticism and a guide.

The definition of beauty as that which, when seen, pleases, might seem, in the case of the fine arts, to apply to the viewer rather than the maker. One of the most distinctive contributions of Maritain to the Thomistic aesthetics that he fashioned is the concept of poetic knowledge. This is antecedent to the making or, in any case, not simply the technical knowledge required to write a poem or paint a picture. This knowledge was dubbed connatural by Maritain and thus required that he spell out the similarities and dissimilarities of the artist's knowledge and action from those of anyone acting morally. This is so because Thomas's most noteworthy employment of the term "connatural" is in the context of moral knowledge. This is not to say that it figures prominently even in those texts. But its few occurrences catch the eye and, when pondered, open up what he is saying about moral knowledge.

3

Thomas contrasts the general or universal knowledge that one might have about how to behave—general rules, reflections on action, anticipations of moral difficulties—and the knowledge that is embedded in particular actions. It is a melancholy commonplace of human life that we can know what we ought to do yet not do it. Moral philosophers and theologians can give good general advice about how we ought to act even when they themselves do not act in accord with the knowledge they are passing on to us. To such a figure, Thomas opposes one whose moral advice is rooted in the life he lives and is not expressed in terms of universal rules and principles. Thomas imagines us asking these two kinds of advisors for advice in a matter of chastity. The moralist will base his advice on a general understanding of human nature, what is fulfilling and what is thwarting of it, and in this learned way advise us against taking such and such a course. The advisor whose wisdom has been wrung from the life he has led would perhaps reply, "Well, what I would do. . . ."

The chaste man makes judgments, and may give advice, based on his kinship with the ideal of chastity, on the fact that his will and desire are fixed on the ideal of bringing his sense desires under the sway of his mind and thereby humanizing them. Thomas calls this judgment one that is *per modum connaturalitatis* or *per modum inclinationis*. Acting chastely is second nature to the chaste man because he is inclined to, has affinity with, the good of chastity.

Of course one could go on about this distinction in its moral import, and elsewhere Maritain does. Here he is interested in suggesting that the poet's knowledge, that out of which his creation comes, is like that connatural knowledge of the virtuous person. This creates a problem for Maritain, needless to say, since he has begun with and has not abandoned the notion that prudence or moral wisdom is one virtue, having as its aim the perfection of the agent, and art another, whose aim is the perfection of the thing made. But in the case of the fine arts, Maritain wants not so much to erase this distinction as to develop a close analogy between the procedures and assumptions of the fine arts and moral wisdom, the discursive activity of the virtuous person.

A feature of the analysis of effective moral judgments, particular judgments, is that moral virtue is a necessary presupposition of them. That is, unless and until the true good is my good, I am unlikely to direct my particular acts to that good or in the event even see my circumstances in its light. The reason is that my bent tends to take me elsewhere. If I have a long history of unchaste actions, that very history inclines me to act in a similar way in the future. I may know at some level of generality that such acts thwart me and distance me from the end that alone can fulfill me, but in the crunch I act as I have so often before. This is the reverse of the inclination and connaturality of the virtuous person. It is the wrong kind of behavior that is second nature to me: hence the recurring question as to the relation between knowledge and virtue. Knowledge at a level of generality is compatible with a life lived in conflict with that knowledge. Moral change thus requires more than information. It requires a change of disposition, acting against what has become one's inclination, a long and choppy effort to bring one's life into conformity with moral truth. The knowledge of the good that follows on the good having become *my* good is efficacious in a way mere general knowledge can never be.

It is that kind of affinity with its object that Maritain ascribes to poetic knowledge. What is more, he even suggests that there are analogues of the moral virtues that insure that the judgment of the artist does not go awry.[8]

When we connect the aesthetic theory developed in *Art and Scholasticism* with the decision made at Vernie to eschew the life of seclusion for a more active involvement in society, we have the means for understanding one of the motivations behind the formation of the *Cercles d'études thomistes*, the apostolate to contemporary intellectuals and artists.

Contesting the Hegemony of Gide

I

It was in 1920 that Maritain became the cofinancier as well as collaborator in *La Revue Universelle*. While *Action Française* origins of the review are incontestable, equally incontestable is the fact that increasingly Maritain saw his social role as a Thomist in more commodious terms. Two books, which followed on the publication of *Art and Scholasticism* and the at-first privately circulated *De la vie d'oraison*, were gleaned from Maritain's contributions to the review, namely *Theonas* and *Antimoderne*. But it was Jean Cocteau's association with the discussions at Meudon and with Maritain personally that suggested the possibility of another effort.

André Gide had become the undisputed leader of the literary and artistic circle gathered around the *Nouvelle Revue Française*. A gifted writer who had been raised a Protestant, Gide was a perverse and fascinating figure for those who saw the return to Catholicism as the best hope of French culture. Gide had a way of suggesting an openness to Catholicism that first drew the efforts of Paul Claudel. Claudel, a ferocious Catholic, was tireless in his proselytizing efforts, and he saw in Gide someone ripe for conversion. That Gide took delight in encouraging an effort for which he felt little true sympathy is clear from the voluminous correspondence of the two men that was eventually published.[9] Now it became Maritain's turn to address Gide.

Maritain regarded Gide as a sinister figure, and he threw down the gauntlet in 1923 when, with Henri Massis, he granted a lengthy interview to Frédéric Lefèvre that appeared in *Les Nouvelles Littéraires*. Maritain described Gide as suffering from a spiritual sickness and accepted his self-description as a heretic among heretics. "But nothing is more monotonous than heresy. Heresy is incapable of development, it can assimilate nothing to itself. Only dogma progresses, only truth is capable of enrichment and novelty."[10]

Gide was a homosexual at a time when this mode of life was receiving notable literary attention, as in Proust's *A la recherche du temps perdu*. Gide had written a book, *Corydon*, the publication of which would be his emergence from the closet. The book celebrated homosexuality, and Maritain took upon himself the task of dissuading Gide from publishing the book. He wrote to Gide and asked to see him. Gide agreed. The meeting, which took place on December 10, 1923, failed of its purpose; Maritain was revealed as naive, *Corydon* was published. It is Gide's account of the meeting that we have.[11] Out of this ill-considered effort, an idea formed. Gide must be countered by forming a rival group. In part, this was the role of the *Cercles d'études*, but it was to be supplemented by books to be published under the heading of *Le Roseau d'Or*, the title suggested by the Apocalypse and signifying that "the things of the spirit have a measure which is not of this world." The series was launched in 1925 and had the support of Paul Claudel, Paul Reverdy, Jean Cocteau, and others. But this series soon revealed the risk of seeking to wed authentic values with new directions in the arts. Perhaps no more surprising conjunction could be imagined than that of Jacques Maritain and Jean Cocteau.

2

Cocteau, an *enfant terrible* of artistic innovation, a man whose lifestyle was even more flamboyant than that of Gide—a homosexual drug addict, but a poet and dramatist of undoubted flair—sought Maritain out at Meudon. What drew him there? He came into an atmosphere that stood in stark contrast to his own mode of life, and Maritain discerned a spiritual hunger in the young man. Soon he was urging Cocteau to return to the faith, make his confession, and end his evil ways. At the same time, Maritain became an en-

thusiastic supporter of Cocteau's poetry and drama. This unusual friendship between Jacques and Raïssa Maritain and Cocteau flouirshed.

Before pursuing that, it should be noted that the *Roseau d'Or* occasioned
the first breach between Maritain and his fellow Catholics. In his effort to
evangelize culture, Maritain was giving support to some rather equivocal
works. He treated gently an iconoclastic work on Joan of Arc by Joseph
Delteil. Many were shocked. Maritain's response to this criticism took the
part of the artist against pious Catholics. "It is important not to be silent
about the truth, but it is also important not to turn over to the side of the
devil, out of incomprehension and misunderstanding, a whole movement of
art and poetry which nowadays, amid a thousand follies and some anguish,
seeks the true light. It is on the side of intelligence that the Catholic renaissance now has its best chance."[12] The risk involved in going an extra mile in
order to win the seemingly hostile poet to the cause is nowhere more clear
than in the case of Cocteau.

When the young Cocteau came to Maritain in 1924, the philosopher
assured him that he had come in search of God. God would give him no
rest. He must watch and pray. Cocteau had recently lost his companion
Raymond Radiguet and had plunged into opium, thus threatening his
health. He felt suicidal impulses and was unable to write. Finally, in 1925,
Maritain convinced him to undertake a cure. Maritain continued to see the
young man's problem as a spiritual one. When he emerged from the clinic,
Cocteau took part in a meeting of the directors of *Roseau d'Or*, to which
he promised to contribute a book. The car that was to take Cocteau back
to Paris was late in coming to Meudon and thus it was by chance that he was
still in the house when Father Charles Henrion strode in.

Henrion had converted under the influence of Paul Claudel, become
a priest, and was a missionary in the Sahara associated with Father de Fou-
cauld. He was a dramatic figure in a white habit, and his entrance stunned
Cocteau. The poet's reaction seems undeniably one of infatuation, and he
thought that Maritain had arranged the dramatic entry in order to over-
whelm him. Maritain seized upon this reaction to further Cocteau's return to the practice of the faith. Not many others shared Maritain's interpretation of Cocteau's sudden interest in the faith. In any case, Maritain set
up an interview with Henrion, brought Cocteau to Meudon for the occasion, and the poet and priest retired. Then Raïssa heard their footsteps as
they went to the chapel in the Maritain home. Cocteau made his confession.
The following morning at Mass, along with the Maritains he received the
Eucharist from the hand of Charles Henrion. The news of Cocteau's conversion did not long remain secret.

3

The names of those Maritain was instrumental in bringing back to or into the Church would make a very long list indeed. For many men and women over his long lifetime, he proved to be the occasion for a profound spiritual regeneration. He had a knack for knowing what might prove the catalyst of conversion. He gave a young poet, André Grange, John of the Cross to read. Pierre Reverdy, after his conversion, burned all his manuscripts and retired to a little house near Solesmes in 1926, where he remained in seclusion for thirty years. And there were others, such as Max Jacob and Erik Satie and Maurice Sachs.

The reversals of these conversions were often dramatic and made Maritain look naive and hasty. Sachs was another homosexual, an habitué of *Le Boeuf sur le toit*, where jazz and booze diverted such men as Picasso, Aragon, and Erik Satie. As an adolescent, Sachs fell in love with Cocteau who made him his secretary and cast him in minor roles in his plays. Cocteau's mention of Maritain sent the young man to Meudon. Sachs was eighteen in July 1925. Two months later he received the sacraments in the chapel at Meudon. But first fervor died, and soon Sachs felt the pull of the life he had thought to leave behind. Nonetheless, he decided to enter the seminary and was encouraged by Raïssa. Claudel, in one of his visits to Meudon, was introduced to Sachs and remarked upon the unlikely convert in his journal.[13]

Maritain's influence should not of course be assessed in terms of backsliders, and Sachs and Cocteau were certainly that. What impresses about these efforts is Maritain's refusal to exclude anyone from the call to pursue holiness. The more troubled the person, the more obvious the need. The published exchange of letters between Maritain and Cocteau doubtless had a radiating effect on many. As for Maritain, even in his last years, living with the Little Brothers, he wrote of Cocteau to one of the young persons who continued to seek his advice and counsel. "Cocteau came to see us because he felt, by his poetic intuition, that the very evil that shocks and scandalizes us makes us cry out to the innocence of God and that if we have to suffer the intolerable and inadmissible, it is because on the other side of the tapestry, hidden from our view, there is a love infinitely more true than all the misery through which we must drag ourselves."[14] Claudel put it in a way that seems initially harsh, but in the end makes a similar point. "Evidently Maurice Sachs and the characters of Proust are similar to vermin. But doesn't Job say to the worms: you are my brothers and sisters?"[15]

SEXT

(1927–1940)

Chronology

1927   July. *Primacy of the Spiritual.*
Conversion of Charles de Bos. Meets Yves Simon and Olivier Lacombe.
October. *A Few Pages on Léon Bloy (Quelques pages sur Léon Bloy).*
December. *Why Rome Has Spoken,* by many authors, among them Maritain. Jacques had been summoned to Rome by Pius XI and asked to plan such a book.

1928   Peter Wust visits Meudon. Emmanuel Mounier frequents Meudon.
October. First number of *Vie Intellectuelle,* in which publication Maritain played a decisive role.
Maritain leaves chair of modern philosophy and assumes that of logic and cosmology.

1929   March 23. Gabriel Marcel baptized.
Ecumenical meetings at Meudon and at Berdiaev's home.
July. *The Angelic Doctor* published.
October. *The Clairvoyance of Rome.*
Jacques takes leave of absence to write major work.

1930   *Religion and Culture* kicks off new series of books called *Questions Disputées,* edited by Charles Journet and Jacques.

1931   Friendship with Etienne Gilson begins.
        First visit, in company of Nicholas Nabokov, to Kolbsheim, chateau
        of Antoinette and Lexi Grunelius, eventual resting place of Raïssa
        and Jacques.

1932   *The Dream of Descartes* and *The Degrees of Knowledge* published.
        June 1. *Roseau d'Or* is replaced by *Les Iles*, edited by Jacques with the
        assistance of Stanislas Fumet.
        September. *Journée d'études* of the Thomist Society at Juvisy on the
        topic of phenomenology. Edith Stein visits the Maritains.

1933   First trip to Toronto's Pontifical Institute of Mediaeval Studies (di-
        rected by Gilson). Visits University of Chicago.
        May. *On Christian Philosophy.*
        "Christian Philosophy" is the theme of the French Philosophical
        Society: contributions by Jacques, Gilson, and Emile Bréhier.
        December. *Du régime temporel et de la liberté (Freedom in the Modern World).*

1934   *Pour le bien commun*, statement by Maritain and others about repres-
        sion of riots in Vienna.
        Lectures in Rome at the Angelicum, at Nimegen, and at Santander
        in Spain on "Spiritual and Temporal Problems of a New Christi-
        anity." Second visit to Canada and United States.
        Sept leçons sur l'être (A Preface to Metaphysics).

1935   *Frontiers of Poetry* and *Philosophy of Nature.*
        Manifesto on war in Ethiopia.
        Letter on Independence.
        Science and Wisdom.

1936   July 26. *Integral Humanism.* Accused of being a Christian Marxist.
        Visits Argentina and Brazil.

1937   Writes *Manifesto of Protest by Catholic Writers against the Bombing of Guer-
        nica.* Maritain declared Public Enemy Number 1 in Spain.
        Sept suppressed by ecclesiastical authorities. Foundation of *Temps
        Present*, in the first issue of which Jacques publishes "*Profession of Faith.*"

1938   Stormy lecture, subsequently published: *Les juifs parmi les nations (A Christian Looks at the Jewish Question)*. Signs many manifestos—against the Anschluss, against aerial bombing in Spain. Defended by Mauriac.
Questions de conscience.
October–November. United States, first visit to the University of Notre Dame.

1939   Lecture, subsequently published: *Le crépuscule de la civilisation (The Twilight of Civilization)*.
Quatre essais sur l'esprit dans sa condition charnelle (Scholasticism and Politics).
Attacked by Marcel De Corte and Paul Claudel.
September 3. Declaration of War.

1940   January 4. With Raïssa and Vera, leaves France for America.

Primacy of the Spiritual

I

The 1930s represent a golden period of Jacques Maritain's life as a Christian philosopher. During this decade he produced his masterpiece *The Degrees of Knowledge* and a host of other works of greater or lesser importance, but all testifying to the magisterial role he now played for so many. His guidance was not confined to the intellectual or spiritual lives. Maritain's liberation from Action Française, which had been accompanied by estrangement from and even enmity with former comrades, permitted his original political and social predilections to come to the fore. The young boy who had discussed socialism with the husband of the family cook in the kitchen of his mother's home, the young student who had agitated for various causes, had been supplanted by the young husband and philosopher whose chief aim was to acquire holiness. The attraction of Action Française for many French Catholics was that it represented an alternative to the secular drift of the French Republic. It is impossible to dismiss as simple dupes the large numbers who rallied to the banner of Action Française. That their allegiance required a willfull blindness seems clear in retrospect. When the movement was condemned by Rome, the scales fell from Jacques's eyes. This change took place at a time of unprecedented turmoil in the West.

The Great Depression cast a pall over the western democracies. The Wall Street crash prompted a new and critical look at capitalism. The John Dos Passos trilogy of novels *U.S.A.* provides a vivid sense of the political and social upheaval in the United States, where the Depression had begun. Leaving Action Française might have stirred up the political enthusiasms of his youth, but Jacques Maritain did not find a ready-made solution to the economic and political crisis in which the whole world seemed to be embroiled. To switch one's fealty from the Right to the Left involved difficulties of an intellectual and spiritual kind that Maritain was unlikely to overlook. He began a series of meditations on the political order, the nature of democracy, and the principles of political philosophy. And in *Integral Humanism* he proposed a project of breathtaking scope that would address the secular present, not by a nostalgic attempt to replicate medieval theocracy, but by finding a new path between authentic secular values and those of Christianity.

The thirties of the last century were not simply an occasion for leisurely and academic debate. The Left represented by Communist Russia seemed to be making inroads in the European democracies brought low by the ravages of the Depression. French Catholics seemed to have distanced themselves from the aspirations of the working classes, where the politics of the Left became *de rigueur*. And in Germany, Adolph Hitler battened on the economic chaos as well as German resentment of the terms of the Versailles peace treaty and rose, improbably as it must have seemed, to power. On the level of power politics, a militant communism seemed pitted against a rising fascism. In this chaotic time it was not easy to find one's way. Maritain, on the level of discussion and theory, made signal contributions. In the practically practical order, as he might have put it, his actions were somewhat ambiguous. The flashpoint for him was the war in Spain.

2

Even apart from that, Maritain had misgivings about the emphasis on attracting writers to the meetings at Meudon. As the preceding decade wound down, he expressed doubts on this score to Julien Green in a letter of May 1929. Doubtless such second thoughts were powerfully aided by Georges Bernanos's attack on Maritain, accusing him of presumption in seeking to lead a literary movement. "I lend my poor voice to those for whom you are an intolerable scandal," Bernanos wrote on May 2, 1928. "You say you are there on the part of Our Lord Jesus Christ. You have no authority from the hierarchy, your only authority comes from your books, your talent, your deeds. The role of voluntary judge, benevolent executioner is less yours than perhaps you think. I love you with all my heart because no one has done me more harm than you."[1] Bernanos was always a crusty character, and became more so with age. He attacked Paul Claudel with something approaching venom for reasons not obvious to others. Maritain had, it appears, suggested revisions in Bernanos's first novel, and of course no writer accepts advice easily or soon forgives a favor. For all that, Maritain came to see that the *Cercles d'études* must emphasize the spiritual and the intellectual, philosophy and theology.

The *Primauté du spirituel* marks the change, as does the formation of new friendships, among them with Yves Simon and Gabriel Marcel. But another note was introduced by Maritain's friendship with Emmanuel Mounier, whose journal *Esprit* would be the controversial vehicle of personalism. In the *Primauté*, Maritain rejected the notion of a theocratic utopia, and he began to explore political notions with Nicholas Berdiaev as well. Indeed, Maritain's mother, Geneviève Favre, began to frequent Meudon. Pondering the example of Mahatma Ghandi and influenced by Massignon, Maritain sought to put together the inner purification brought about by the spiritual life, on the one hand, and political action on another.

Bernanos's accusation draws attention to a feature of Maritain's career that is so obvious it can easily be overlooked, perhaps by seeing it anachronistically through post–Vatican II eyes. Jacques Maritain was a layman. As a Christian he had the missionary impulse to share the good news: to be a believer was to be an evangelist.

CONTROVERSY OVER CHRISTIAN PHILOSOPHY

I

Questions as to the relationship between the mind's quest for understanding, on the one hand, and religious faith, on the other, are as old as Christianity. Has faith overcome the need for philosophy? Is there a necessary enmity between faith and reason? In what sense can one who is a believer be a philosopher? Maritain had confronted such questions in a personal way almost from the outset of his Catholic life. And eventually he addressed them abstractly as well.

When the *Société Thomiste* convened in September 1933 to discuss the topic of Christian philosophy, Jacques Maritain had already published a little book with that title. And, indeed, his views on the matter were closely discussed, praised, and criticized throughout the meeting whose participants were the leading Catholic philosophers of France. Maritain himself was unable to attend, which is a shame. Etienne Gilson, whose Gifford lectures *The Spirit of Medieval Philosophy* had also appeared prior to the meeting, became an increasingly active participant, and the exchanges between him and Father Mandonnet are among the most illuminating of the session, since they express views that are diametrically opposed.

The president of the society was Marie-Dominique Chenu, O.P., and the day was organized around two papers: in the morning, that of Aimé Forest, then of the Université de Poitiers; in the afternoon, that of Father Motte, professor at the Saulchoir. Each paper was followed by a lively discussion, both of which are valuable for seeing how the question of Christian philosophy polarized the participants. Indeed, the proceedings may be said to cover the essential pros and cons of the topic.[2] Chenu, in opening the meeting, said that Gilson had shown that history provides a sense of what Christian philosophy is and that the conjunction of Christianity and philosophy, unlike that of, say, German and philosophy, involves more than a factual connection. There is an intrinsic influence of the faith on philosophizing. It is that intrinsic link that he hopes will be the focus of the meeting.

2

Father Motte, in his paper, gave support to the view that there is an intrinsic link between faith and philosophy. The world Thomas Aquinas lived in is one in which man had been called to the supernatural order. The distinction between reason and faith, between the natural and supernatural, does not disturb this whole. "For Saint Thomas there are not two compartments of being, two creations, the second of which by improvisation comes to the help of the first; there are not two final ends, one for natural man, the other for man raised to the supernatural level, no more than there are two gods, a natural God and a triune supernatural God, but one and the same God, whose nature is precisely to transcend all nature and to burst into a trinity."[3] Man is made for grace and the beatific vision.[4] Although grace is a complement to nature added from without, it is nonetheless an essential element in the concrete plan of predestination. Without grace, man cannot enjoy the privileges of his own nature.[5] In short, the supernatural organization of the world is a fact; and for Saint Thomas, the enclosing of nature within a higher order acquires a *de iure* value.

The supernatural thus answers to a kind of structural necessity, as is clear, Motte says, from Thomas's description of the final end of our rational nature. "Insofar as rational nature knows the universal nature of good and being it has an immediate order to the universal principle of being; the perfection of the rational creature, therefore, does not consist only in that which belongs to it given its nature, but also in that which is attributed to it by a supernatural participation in divine goodness."[6] Motte's main point is that wisdom is one: integral reality answers to a wisdom that can only be one. "Saint Thomas saw this better than anyone. But in explaining for us the law according to which nature and grace unite without being confused with one another in the total order of providence, he has also perhaps at the same time furnished us a precious key to resolve the problem of the Christian influence on philosophy without touching the just aspirations of philosophy."[7]

Reason as such is insufficient to gain the vision of integral reality Motte has put before us. Philosophy is essentially inadequate because it cannot grasp things beyond its range, and there is more in heaven and earth than is dreamt of in any philosophy. How then can philosophical wisdom fail to distort reality? If it takes for everything what is *not* everything, it is a snare and delusion. "The autonomy of philosophy must therefore be legitimated. From the unity of being, we must come to a distinction of points of view. At least, knowing that on the side of the real the bridges are not blown, let us understand that revelation and philosophy, as distinct as they are, can encounter one another."[8]

How does all this agree with Thomas's teaching of a twofold truth, that of reason and that of revelation?[9] Our mind is such that its activity depends on what is first grasped by the senses; what we think about is either the nature of sensible reality or that which can be known with reference to sensible reality. The sensible world, as the effect of God, leads to knowledge of him; but the richness of the cause is infinitely impoverished in the being of its effect, and the world cannot enable us to gain access to God's proper being. It is this defect that deprives philosophy of its claim to be the sovereign wisdom.

Is unbaptized reason then incapable of truth? Saint Thomas doesn't think so, and that is the point of his *duplex veritatis modus*. There are limits to what unaided reason can do, but within those limits it is capable of astonishing accomplishments. "The human intellect has a form, namely, the intelligible light itself, which is in itself sufficient for knowing some intelligible things, namely, those to knowledge of which we can arrive through sensible things."[10] So it is not a matter of everything or nothing. Knowledge need not be exhaustive in order to be true. To abstract is not to lie.

In a discussion that might be called the *grandeur et la misère* of philosophy, Motte draws attention to the aspirations and the limitations of natural reason. "From the mystery of the divine being the limits of philosphical knowledge flow: creation, obediential potency, the angelic world, ultimate finality and eschatology and the interpretation of history mark the points where reason sees its object escaping it."[11] Motte concludes a philosophical pluralism from this. "In short, although the sciences have a true existence and represent bodies of universal truths that impose themselves on all (and are moreover susceptible of growth), philosophy does not exist, there are only philosophies and philosophers who reflect on the same problems but do not arrive at solutions on the basis of evidence that conquers all minds. The contradictions and groping of the history of philosophy show more than the history of any science that these are not accidental facts: they respond to a fundamental difficulty, which comes from the very object of philosophy."[12]

In any case, philosophy and revelation do not meet as equals, and philosophy confronts a choice. It might simply surrender its autonomy or, remaining free, receive from revelation what it can be given without losing its nature. The first choice is, in effect, to become theology; the second, if it results in a true philsophy, it will be one that can be called Christian. Motte enters into an extended discussion of theology, in which philosophy is put to the service of the faith. The question then becomes: if philosophy in the old sense can still go on, will the Christian engage in it? "Supposing a Christian who philosophizes, who means to do pure and authentic philosophy, can he and his speculation not be affected with a quite specific sign? That is the problem."[13]

Taking philosophy in the sense of metaphysics, Motte reminds us of how difficult it is to lay hold of its subject, being as being, even for Aristotle. "Judeo-Christian revelation in naming God 'He who is' and in making the world depend on him to the depths of its being, imposed this point of view right off and by that fact truly gave metaphysics to itself."[14]

3

It is at moments like this that one wishes Maritain had been there. Motte's defense of Saint Thomas is radically confused because he has a different view of Aristotle's achievement than does Thomas himself. What Motte has said makes sense only if we think that Aristotle failed to assign a first cause of the being of things. But this is precisely his achievement, according to Thomas Aquinas. If Thomas is right, Motte's plea for a constitutive influence of Christianity with respect to metaphysics has to be rejected. Of course this lapse is not peculiar to Motte; it comes to characterize the Thomism that develops in the wake of the Christian philosophy controversy.

When Motte goes on to see analogy and its application to metaphysics as a Christian deliverance, it becomes even clearer that the niceties of historical accuracy have been left behind. That Christian revelation tells us massively more about God than philosophy could discover, that the angelic universe receives a detailed characterization on the basis of Revelation quite beyond anything philosophical—all this is of course true. But what is not made clear by Motte is whether this additional knowledge is intrinsically dependent on revelation or not.

Maritain, for his part, had insisted on the difference between the speculative and practical orders in their dependence on theology. There is no suggestion from him that the *praeambula fidei* presuppose for their acceptance the faith they are a preamble to. But Maritain has surprises in store when he turns to the moral order. Motte himself rejects Maritain's notion of a "moral philosophy adequately considered."[15]

4

Already in *The Degrees of Knowledge*, Maritain had made suggestions about the grades and levels of moral knowledge that had attracted a great deal of attention. Moral discourse is grounded in the principles of synderesis—natural law—and moves toward the judgment of prudence as its term. If the action is the conclusion and natural law provides first principles, attention soon turns to the middle distance between these two, the knowledge through which one passes from generalities to this here-and-now act. It is in that middle distance that Maritain proposed a distinction between what he calls "speculatively practical" and "practically practical" knowledge. Maritain was trying to make room for the moral relevance of such writers as Saint John of the Cross. Important as this distinction is, and controversial as some found it, it paled in significance to Maritain's description of what a morally adequate moral philosophy must be.

The governing principle of what Maritain has to say is the fact that man has been called to a supernatural end: that is the ultimate end of human endeavor with reference to which actions must be assessed as good or bad. Any discussion of human action that ignores the fact that we are called to a supernatural end and that there is no other ultimate end for human agents must be inadequate to its subject. An adequate moral philosophy, accordingly, must be governed by a truth it borrows from theology, namely, our supernatural vocation.

That, roughly, is what led Maritain to say that, in order to be considered adequate, moral philosophy must be subalternated to theology. One of the basic underpinnings of this view is Saint Thomas's position that the virtues discussed by Aristotle in the *Nicomachean Ethics* are virtues only in a sense, *secundum quid*, not perfect virtues. In order to be the latter, they must be informed by the theological virtue of charity. Maritain took this doctrine to be warrant in Thomas for the view that moral philosophy can only be adequate when subalternated to theology, just as acquired virtues can only be truly virtues insofar as they are animated by charity.[16]

Can there be no purely philosophical moral philosophy? As a practical science, morals aims at the regulation of the concrete singular act. As a science it is in that middle distance between the most common principles and the judgment of prudence. The question we are considering concerns what Maritain called speculatively practical science. Maritain contested the claim that a purely philosophical morality could be a true practical science. It would be possible in the state of pure nature, before the Fall; "But in the state of fallen and redeemed nature in which we actually live, a purely philosophical moral science would *prescribe good acts*, because it would be based on natural right—such as not to lie, not to commit injustice, to practise filial piety, etc. But the prescription of certain good acts is not enough to form a practical science, a true science of the use of freedom, a science which prescribes not only good acts, but which also determined how the *acting subject* can live a life of consistent goodness and organize rightly his whole universe of action."[17] Before examining what it could not do, we must note what Maritain allowed a purely philosophical moral science could do: it can provide us with a system of ends, of rules, and of acquired virtues. But it is because it would not be seeing these as directed to our de facto ultimate end that it falls short of true practicality. How could it direct us to an end it knows not of? That was the nub of Maritain's view of a purely philosophical ethics. In order to be adequate, ethics must be governed by our true ultimate end. But the supernatural end is not something that is knowable in pure philosophy. Therefore moral philosophy adequately considered has to depend on a higher light—faith, theology—if it is to be organized in terms of man's true ultimate end.

Of course Maritain did not want to deny that natural ethics exists. But it would have to be a false morality unless, as with Aristotle, this is avoided thanks to the "unsystematic character of his ethics."[18]

At the Juvisy meeting, Father Sertillanges advocated an across-the-board dependence of philosophy on theology, and he was surprised that Maritain, who rejected this at the outset, embraced it when it was a matter of moral philosophy. He found that illogical.[19] Either the whole of philosophy is dependent on theology, or none of it. But the real dynamism of action and the deep exigencies of willing suffice to establish the deficiency of a purely natural moral theory.

The abiding tension between believers and philosophers is the tendency of philosophy to regard itself as self-sufficient and as wisdom while the believer knows philosophical wisdom is only partial. The philosopher is likely to regard faith as a priori unacceptable, as too much to ask—or at least as something that can be ignored: believers can operate with the faith, but we philosophers must be content with philosophy. "Combatting this position within philosophy, by showing its insufficiency and lures to the faith it offers of itself, is a far more fundamental effort of Christian philosophy if not more profound than that which deals with the partial objective benefits and subjective reinforcement that comes to philosophy in a Christian setting.[20]

But he was not done. He went on to agree with Mandonnet that, strictly speaking, there cannot be a Christian philosophy! The influence of Christianity on philosophy can be assigned to the order of discovery; but in the order of demonstration, either the argument is good or it isn't. For example, Thomas believed in creation. When he went on to demonstrate it, he then held it on that basis. So Christianity might inspire the philosopher, but so can poetry. But he was willing to call that philosophy Christian which was in fact stimulated by the faith, whether objectively or subjectively. Such a philosophy might live in a Christian setting, but there was nothing Christian in its very notion.

5

By the end of the day at Juvisy, repetition had set in, unsurprisingly. What has been the upshot of the discussion? While some of the participants come close to saying that in Christian philosophy there are some truths held because they have been revealed or on the basis of their having been revealed, there was no formal assertion of this. Indeed, whenever Maritain's notion of moral philosophy adequately considered was mentioned, it was regarded as pure theology.

Gilson, the liveliest voice at the meeting, had persuaded everyone of the historical fact of the influence of the faith on philosophy. But to admit this was a far cry from holding that there is a continuing formal, objective dependence of philosophy on the faith.

What was and was not confronted was the idea that philosophy in the standard modern sense is taken to be an activity that proceeds without any analogue of the Christian influence that occupies the participants. Philosophy that seeks to be autonomous was said to conceal its own inadequacy from the philosopher. But whence comes this antecedent desire for autonomy? What are the existential conditions for philosophizing *tout court*, however they might differ between believers and nonbelievers?

In his work devoted to the subject of Christian philosophy, Maritain made the important distinction between the essence of philosophy and its state. Maritain's little book arose out of a lecture he gave at the University of Louvain in December 1931 that expanded the communication he had made to the Juvisy conference devoted to the subject, a conference he himself did not intend. "The fact that a theologian of the stature of Father Garrigou-Lagrange and philosophers such as Etienne Gilson and Gabriel Marcel saw fit to express their accord with the view I upheld on those occasions provided the necessary encouragement to have them published in their present form."

The position Maritain intended to avoid was that which denied any autonomous character to philosophy but which makes it intrinsically dependent on divine faith. "The rationalists—and even some neo-Thomists—infer that because philosophy is distinct from faith it can have nothing in common with faith, save in an entirely extrinsic manner."[21] Emile Bréhier represents the rationalist position. Maurice Blondel functions in a very complicated way in Maritain's little book. Blondel inveighed against a *separated* philosophy, which is the spirit of the times and which sets philosophy against the faith, looking "upon the philosopher himself as dwelling in a condition of pure nature."[22] But Blondel's effort, one that would be shared by Henri de Lubac, to introduce apologetics into the heart of philosophy, was one that Maritain rejected. "To achieve its purpose, apologetics, by its own nature and essence presupposes the solicitations of grace and the operations of the heart and will on the part of the one who hears, and the light of faith already possessed on the part of the one who speaks; whereas philosophy by its nature and essence exacts neither faith as in the one nor the movements of grace as in the other, but only reason in the one who searches."[23]

The distinction required to maneuver between such extremes is that which is between the order of specification and the order of exercise, "or again, in the terminology which I shall adopt, between 'nature' and 'state.'" That is, he proposed that we distinguish between what philosophy is in itself and the historical conditions in which it may exist from time to time in the human subject. Natures subsist in subjects: the nature of philosophy is specified by its object, but it is a flesh-and-blood individual who philosophizes here and now. From the first point of view, there is a whole range of truths attainable by the human mind relying on its natural powers. Philosophical wisdom is captured, Maritain suggests, by the Thomistic phrase, *perfectum opus rationis: perfected rational activity.* This means that calling a philosophy Christian does not refer to the essence of philosophy; as philosophy, it is independent of Christian faith. What then is the Christian state or exercise of philosophy?

"To philosophize man must put his whole soul into play, in much the same manner that to run he must use his heart and lungs."[24] That human nature is weak is something both Christians and non-Christians have realized; both recognize as well that many errors can be made on the way to the acquisition of wisdom. When that wisdom is pursued by a human subject who has the faith, the pursuit is assisted in objectively observable ways. Gilson's *The Spirit of Medieval Philosophy* laid out the objective case for the way in which Christianity has prompted philosophical gains. Maritain mentioned clarity about creation, about nature, about the person. In the moral sphere, there is the concept of sin. Gilson spoke of "revelation begetting reason," and Maritain observed that, strictly taken, this would apply to theology, not philosophy. Revelation is relevant to philosophy because it contains truths knowable by reason, preambles as well as mysteries of faith. There is also the presupposition of revelation that faith is a reasonable act; this has acted as a stimulus in resisting skepticism, as is clear from Augustine's *Contra academicos.*[25]

6

Maritain's reflections on Christian philosophy are central to his understanding of what he had undertaken from the outset of his study of Thomas Aquinas. It was not merely a question of winning an argument against such critics as Bréhier or of correcting what he took to be a mistake in Maurice

Blondel. Behind the discussion we can sense the response to the materialist flatland that Jacques and Raïssa had encountered as young students at the Sorbonne. He had been saved from that, first by Bergson and Bloy, then by Thomas Aquinas, and he had found a way of understanding his philoso-phizing as integral to the pursuit of holiness, which is the one thing need-ful. The distinction between the nature and state of philosophy enabled Maritain to recognize the autonomy of philosophical arguments without losing sight of the fact that it is concrete human subjects who philosophize. The condition in which philosophy finds itself can be either beneficial or the opposite to the attainment of philosophical truth. The philosophy of the Sorbonne came out of human subjects whose prejudices ended by thwarting the philosophical impulse, cutting the mind off from the spiritual, clearing the philosophical landscape of truths fully within the reach of reason. The great benefit of the faith is that it creates a subjective condition which may—there is no necessity about this—enable the subject to attain truths fully philosophical but hitherto undreamt of by philosophers of the kind that Hamlet chides.

Degrees of Knowledge

I

In 1928, Jacques switched from the chair in modern philosophy to that in logic and cosmology at the Institut Catholique. Toward the end of the following year, in October, he went on leave of absence to write the book that is his acknowledged masterpiece. *Distinguer pour unir: Les degrés du Savoir,* as it was originally called (Distinguish in Order to Unite), was soon known by its subtitle alone, *The Degrees of Knowledge.* The book is the fruit of his philosophical reflections over the many decades since he had turned to the guidance of Saint Thomas Aquinas. Many books have been written on the Thomistic "synthesis," mostly efforts to summarize the summaries that largely make up the work of Aquinas. Not all such books are pedestrian, almost none inspired. In *The Degrees of Knowledge,* Maritain both exemplified and amplified what he had learned from Saint Thomas. The main lesson he had learned provides the structure of the book. Things hang together. Beneath diversity there is a profound connection between things, and this is also true of the human efforts to address reality. No one has better expressed the fusion of the intellectual and the spiritual, the natural and the supernatural, the conceptual and the mystical, than Maritain did in *The Degrees.*

The book is, in an obvious sense, an account of the degrees of knowledge: the ascent through degrees of rational knowledge, science, philosophy of nature, metaphysics; and then the ascent through degrees of suprarational knowledge. But more essentially it is an account of degrees of wisdom. Wisdom is taken to be a supreme knowledge, universal, which judges things in the light of first principles. There are, Maritain says, three wisdoms.

First, there is the wisdom that defines philosophy. The love of wisdom passes through a number of disciplines and inquiries of interest in themselves, but, as philosophical disciplines, they are teleologically ordered to the acquisition of wisdom. Aristotle's development of the nature of wisdom occurs at the outset of his *Metaphysics*. It soon emerges that it is a divine science—both the kind of knowledge we would attribute to God and a human knowledge that aspires to such knowledge of God as is possible for human reason. This is so because wisdom is knowledge of all things in the light of their very first and ultimate causes. Unsurprisingly, Maritain's three wisdoms are three ways of knowing God.

Aristotle called the ultimate goal of philosophy theology, knowledge of God. The theology of the philosophers consists in establishing that He exists and what can meaningfully be said of him on the basis of what is known of the things of this world. Saint Paul's remark in the Epistle to the Romans that, from the things that are made, we can come to knowledge of the invisible things of God has long been taken as a scriptural account of the kind of knowledge of God that unbelievers and pagans and, of course, Christians too can have on the basis of their knowledge of the world.

Natural theology is the name given this philosophical effort, and obviously from a perspective beyond philosophy. The implicit contrast is with supernatural theology, that inquiry that applies the method of human science and argument to the truths God has revealed. The connatural object of the human mind is the essence of sensible reality, but this does not mean that the mind cannot know suprasensible things. Invoking a principle of Neoplatonist provenance that Thomas often uses, that in a hierarchical order, there is some participation in the higher by the lower, Maritain observes that in the human mind, *intellectus, nous*, is an opening to being as such. That is why the human intellect is not restricted to sensible things. "If our intellect is directly ordered, as human, to being as it is concretized in sensible things, it remains ordered, as intelligence, to being in all its amplitude, and the being grasped in sensible things is already an object of thought which surpasses the sensible[,] and spirit draws itself to conceive an area of being freed from the limits of the sensible and to seek in this area the high-est explanations of all the rest."²⁶

Above the theology of the philosophers is the discursive reflection on the Christian mysteries called sacred theology. "It develops in a rational manner and according to the discursive mode that is natural to us truths virtually contained in the deposit of revelation."²⁷ The principles of this sci-ence are the believed truths of revelation, truths about God that we cannot understand in this life and which are, accordingly, mysteries. Because of the certainty of faith and the source of the truths reflected on, the theology based on Sacred Scripture is higher than that of the philosophers. "Thus, it knows the very same thing that God and the blessed see in God in a very imperfect way, but the only way in which the revealed treasure can be com-municated to the human race."²⁸ In Scripture, God speaks to us in human language, proportioning truths about himself to our ability to understand. But the discrepancy between our mode of knowing and the truth that is God can be bridged only by analogy. Among God's effects, we come upon perfections that need not be limited as they are in creatures—justice, un-derstanding, being, goodness. And words like "just" and "intelligent" and "being" and "good" are analogically common to creatures, extended from their creaturely use to express something of what God is.

It is clear that what sustains theology in this sense is the grace of faith, thanks to which we accept as true what God has revealed. It is at this point that Maritain enters into a discussion of sanctifying grace and the state of grace as the Holy Trinity dwelling within the soul. The gifts of the Holy Spirit, enumerated in Scripture, developed in the *Summa theologiae* and in the great commentary on the latter by John of St. Thomas, provide the bridge from theology as discursive scientific meditation on the truths of faith—and intrinsically dependent on faith, so that only the believer can be a theo-logian in this sense—to the mystical life, the sustained effort to draw ever closer to God and to experience him as he dwells within the soul.

In the very first question of the first part of the *Summa theologiae*, Thomas Aquinas asks whether the sacred doctrine he is embarked upon can be called wisdom. Since the wise man is one who judges well, it is possible to dis-tinguish kinds of wisdom based on different kinds of judgment. Thomas illustrates what he means first of all in the moral order. If you ask for moral advice, you could get it from a moral philosopher or moral theologian, and they would give you an argument as to why a certain kind of conduct is right or wrong. Their judgment, Thomas says, is a cognitive one (*per modum cognitionis*), as good as the premises on which it is based. But you might ask advice from someone whose behavior exemplifies goodness. A young person goes to an older person who is not learned but manifestly good and asks moral advice. The reply would come in the mode of "Well, what I would do is such-and-such." This judgment arises out of the orientation of that person's life, what they are and not just what they know; Thomas says it is an affective judgment, a connatural judgment (*per modum inclinationis*). It is this distinction that enables Thomas to compare the wisdom of sacred theology and the wisdom that is the gift of the Holy Spirit. The former manifests itself in judgments that are *per modum cognitionis;* the latter in judgments that are experiential, dependent on a connaturality with the object, *per modum inclinationis.*

This explication of the third kind of wisdom, that of the holy person animated by a gift of the Holy Spirit, is the culmination of Maritain's masterpiece. He approaches it by a lengthy reflection on Saint Augustine and a comparison of Augustine and Thomas, but then turns to the great Spanish mystic Saint John of the Cross. The chapters of the second part of *The Degrees* are not unprecedented as such. It is clear that Maritain has learned much from his mentor in the *Cercles d'études*, Father Garrigou-Lagrange. Indeed, he dedicates the discussion to Garrigou-Lagrange. What is new, what is truly original, is seeing the links between and the hierarchy among the various kinds of knowledge and the kinds of wisdom discussed. No mere scholar could have written this book.

2

The Degrees of Knowledge is in many ways the roadmap of Maritain's life, a map on which all roads lead to mystical experience. Good Thomist that he is, Maritain does not think we can bypass the knowledge of this world gained by the sciences and philosophy. As a Christian, he knows we cannot be content with the theology that is an achievement of philosophy. Thomas Aquinas is author of landmarks of sacred theology, but it is clear that, in his own life, what he was seeking as the ultimate goal is union with God. Indeed, in the last year of his life he had a vision that caused him to stop writing and to leave the *Summa theologiae* unfinished, saying that everything he had written seemed to him now mere straw.

Thomas had spent hours poring over the texts of Aristotle and of the Fathers and such medievals as Peter Lombard, but he was above all a *magister sacrae paginae*, a professor of Scripture. What attracted Maritain to Thomas was that all these things were part of a single personal effort to become what one is meant to be. No one can understand the kind of philosopher Jacques Maritain was without assimilating the profound implications of *The Degrees of Knowledge*.

3

The Degrees appeared toward the end of 1932. As if accompanying it, *The Dream of Descartes* also appeared. This little book, a remarkable tour de force, in many ways more profound than the section devoted to Descartes in *Three Reformers*, recalls the mystical origins of the Cartesian method, the dreams in which Descartes, not unlike the ancient poet Parmenides, is granted an insight that will enable him to change the course of human thought. One is reminded of Pascal's "Memorial," the account of his conversion that Pascal had always with him, sewn into the lining of his coat, when one reads of Descartes's account of his fateful dream and his analysis and decoding of it. We are told that Descartes had this in written form when he died in Stockholm, but it has come down to us only indirectly and in the accounts of others. It had become the practice for historians to ignore all this, doubtless embarrassed by the fact that the father of modern philosophy, so grateful for the revelation he had received in a dream, vowed to make a pilgrimage to Loreto to which the house of the Holy Family had been miraculously transported. Descartes kept that vow.

But Maritain's little book is important for far more than paying attention to this important event in the life of Descartes and in the history of modern philosophy. It occurs to Maritain, the student of the Angelic Doctor, that the account Descartes gave of human knowledge bore a strong resemblance to what Thomas had said of angelic knowledge. The knowledge of the angels is not gained from experience but it is an infused gift; further, the essence of the angel is a means for it to know other things. Descartes, having applied the method of doubt to all candidates for knowledge, ended with thoughts and ideas and no way of establishing that they were thoughts or ideas of anything outside the mind. Only a proof of the existence of God, based on the claim that the idea of God in my mind is not one I could myself be cause of, so it must have an extramental cause: God—only this proof enables Descartes to get out of his mind. But this is to put the most difficult philosophical task, proving the existence of God, at the very threshold of philosophy.

Earlier, in *Three Reformers*, Maritain accused Descartes, along with Luther and Rousseau, of bringing about the rise of subjectivism that would prove to be the death knell of philosophy.

GILSON AND MARITAIN

I

Almost before Maritain and Etienne Gilson met, the two men were linked together as if they were two barrels of the shotgun that would scatter the confusions of the contemporary world with Thomistic pellets. One is reminded of the twinning of Hilaire Belloc and Gilbert Chesterton in England, productive of the armored vehicle George Bernard Shaw called the Chesterbelloc. But the relations between Maritain and Gilson were by and large at a distance, *à longe*. They exchanged compliments in print, not least on the issue of Christian philosophy, in which each man saw his views as complemented by the other's. Gilson was instrumental in Maritain's invitation to Toronto and tried unsuccessfully to sign his countryman to a permanent presence at the Pontifical Institute of Mediaeval Studies. But Maritain proved elusive. Published praise of the other continued to appear from the pen of each man. For the Thomistic revival, Maritain and Gilson were of supreme and all but equal importance.

2

When Jacques Maritain began to study Thomas Aquinas, he did not regard himself as an isolated individual confronting a text that had survived from the thirteenth century. He learned from such mentors as Reginald Garrigou-Lagrange that there was a tradition of interpretation, a Thomistic school, and that among the giants of that school were the commentators Cardinal Cajetan, John of St. Thomas, the anonymous Carmelites of Salamanca, and others. The commentary of Cajetan was included by the editors of the Leonine edition of the *Summa theologiae*. As Father Labourdette remarked, although many sought to confine themselves to simple Thomism, defined by the text of Thomas itself, looking askance at the commentators of the intervening centuries, "Jacques Maritain judged that the thought of St. Thomas was powerful enough to have opened a veritable tradition, a tradition that remained alive by confronting new problems and old."[29] In *Theonas*, Maritain had said that a living thought never ceases to grow and that in the hands of the great Thomists his [Thomas's] thought, far from petrifying, became more alive as it evolved. This disposition to benefit from the great commentators characterizes the Thomism of Maritain throughout his life.

As the citations suggest, there is another kind of Thomist. It came as a surprise to many, when the letters of Jacques Maritain and Etienne Gilson were published[30] to come upon a veritable campaign by Gilson to get Maritain's agreement to the Gilsonian vendetta against Cardinal Cajetan and even Aristotle. That this was indeed a campaign, and that the enlistment of Maritain in it was regarded as of tremendous importance, is testified to by Gilson's premature claim of victory in a letter to Anton Pegis. Gilson wrote that Maritain "does not believe in John of St. Thomas any longer but does not want the rumor to spread. He vaguely suspects that Cajetan is no better."[31] Gilson clearly mistook Maritain's diffident reaction to his intimidation for agreement.

Even more remarkable is the letter to Father Armand Maurer, included by Géry Prouvost in his edition of the Gilson-Maritain correspondence, in which Gilson essays a general comparison of Maritain's approach to Saint Thomas and his own. The letter was written in 1974, after the death of Maritain, and was occasioned by the posthumously published *Untrammeled Approaches*.[32] Prouvost provides the original English of the letter in his volume.[33] He finds the letter *bouleversante*, and one can only agree. How does the aged Gilson compare his own work with that of Jacques Maritain?

He begins by declaring that reading the posthumous Maritain had made him realize that he "had never understood his true position."

I was naively maintaining that one cannot consider oneself a Thomist without first ascertaining the authentic meaning of St. Thomas [*sic*] doctrine, which only history can do; during all that time, he was con-sidering himself a true disciple of St. Thomas because he was *continuing* his thought. To strive to rediscover the meaning of the doctrine such as it has been in the mind of Thomas Aquinas was straight historicism. We have been talking at cross purposes all the time. (P. 275)

At first blush, this seems to be an instance of a familiar opposition. Exe-getical and historical work on a text is often opposed to efforts to read it in the light of other and later discussions. This would appear to be a division of labor rather than a division of viewpoint on the text: not everyone can do everything, and there are editors and historians whose work provides an in-dispensable basis for replicating and extending the sort of thinking the text records. Where would Thomists be without the largely anonymous mass of scribes and editors to whom they owe the very presence of the text? Where would Thomists be without the careful historical recovery of the setting in which particular works were written, their occasion, and so forth? Doubt-less those who engage in the one kind of work regard their opposite num-bers warily; but for all that, their work would seem to be complementary rather than contradictory, as if one had to do either one or the other.

In part, this could be what Gilson is saying. Insofar as it is, it would be wrong to see him on one side of a line and Maritain on another, as if all Gilson's enormous corpus was historical in the sense of the above quotation. But it is clear that Gilson was stung by what he read in *Untrammeled Approaches,* not least a passage in which Maritain, writing about philosophy in relation to Vatican II, distanced himself from Gilson on the issue of the great com-mentators.[34] Maritain was still firmly a member of the Thomistic school that Gilson had come to loathe. Perhaps it was the realization that his long effort to persuade Maritain had failed that led him to continue the com-parison in an unfortunate direction. He ends with a blanket condemnation of all Maritain's efforts to assimilate and develop the thought of Thomas Aquinas.[35]

Magnanimity was not the besetting virtue of Gilson's last years, and this is an unfortunate valedictory. But it can be taken to underscore the nature of Maritain's interest in the thought of Thomas Aquinas. In an appendix to *Bergsonian Philosophy,* Maritain gives us a remarkable analysis of recent work on Aristotle and of the nature of the commentaries Thomas wrote on treatises of Aristotle. In the book in which he reflects on the meaning of the Church's proposing of Thomas Aquinas as major mentor in theology and philosophy, Maritain reveals the mandate for his own lifelong effort. The Thomistic revival is not an invitation to become a medievalist, an historian:

it is an effort to assimilate the thought of Thomas and bring it to bear on questions and problems of our own times.

3

From this point of view, one can marvel at the range and depth of the works of Maritain. It would be difficult to cite any of his works as historical in the Gilsonian sense, but this does not mean that he did not pore over the text. His copy of Thomas's *Quaestio disputata de veritate* is in the Jacques Maritain Center at Notre Dame, and the text is full of marginalia and there are slips of paper inserted in the volumes attesting to Maritain's close and analytical reading of the text. But when he wrote, his interest was to express what he had learned and to show its surprising relevance centuries after Thomas wrote. Moreover, the Thomism of Maritain goes into areas Thomas had not gone. His political philosophy, his aesthetics, amount to genuine innovations that have their source in Maritain's study of Thomas but cannot be parsed back into texts of the master. Maritain is never more Thomistic than when all the elements of what he presents are well known, but his putting them together provides a breathtaking synthesis hitherto unknown. I think, of course, of *The Degrees of Knowledge*.

SECOND THOUGHTS ON A FIRST BOOK

I

"Read Bergson. I have criticized him a lot, but read Bergson!" Thus Jacques Maritain spoke to Yves Floucat in 1960. Misgivings about the severity of his criticisms of Henri Bergson in his first published book, *The Bergsonian Philosophy*, were already expressed in the second edition. However profound Jacques Maritain's disagreements with Bergson might be, he could never forget the decisive role the philosopher had played in saving himself and his fiancée Raïssa from the despair induced by the philosophy taught in the Sorbonne at the turn of the century.

In her memoirs, written during their wartime exile in New York, Raïssa recounted in the unforgettable pages that bear the heading "In the Jardin des Plantes" the crisis the young couple had reached. Their cultural milieu, the ambience of the Sorbonne, was materialist and could not provide any answer to the most fundamental question of all: What is the meaning of life? Raïssa and Jacques did not see any reason to go on living if indeed there were no reason for living at all. This despairing gloom first began to lift when they were taken to the Collège de France by Charles Péguy to follow the Friday afternoon lectures of Henri Bergson. Here, the possibility of metaphysics, of something transcending the material, was opened up to them in a way that, years later, both Jacques and Raïssa were still effusive in describing.

No doubt it was precisely the profound impact that Bergson had on him that was the basis for Jacques's personal need to attack him when Jacques saw that a thinker who had once been so great a boon became an obstacle to the truth he had found in Saint Thomas Aquinas. But at those lectures in the Collège de France, Péguy, Ernest Psichari, Raïssa, and Jacques sat spellbound. The Bergson book, in its first version, was perhaps necessary to exorcize the defects of Bergson's philosophy as they were revealed to the eye of one schooled in Thomism. But it was only right that, this being done, Jacques should return to Bergson and moderate his criticism in the long preface to the second edition.

The vagaries of reputation in philosophy are a story unto themselves. There was a time when the writings of Henri Bergson were a constant point of reference. This is no longer so. It would be ironic if he became known to present-day readers only through such a massive criticism as that which Maritain leveled in his first book. When he wrote it, Maritain was taking on a superstar of the times, whose reputation seemed assured and could not have been mortally damaged even by so thorough a critique as that found in *The Bergsonian Philosophy*. Maritain would be the first to urge the reader to go to Bergson's own writings in order to appraise what is said of them in his book. Of course, not all Bergson's major works had appeared when Maritain wrote this book. But Maritain could assume a thorough knowledge of his opponent on the part of the reader. As he said to Floucat, *"Lisez Bergson!"*

Maritain's own reputation has known its ups and downs. When the Jacques Maritain Center was founded at the University of Notre Dame in 1957 under the triumvirate of Rev. Leo R. Ward, C.S.C., Frank Keegan, and Joseph Evans, it was envisaged as the eventual repository of Maritain's papers. Raïssa died in 1960 in France, to which they had returned for treatment; and from that point on, the center of gravity of Jacques Maritain's life returned to his native land. The more than dozen years of life left him came to be divided between Toulouse and the Little Brothers of Jesus, an order in which Jacques himself would take the three vows of religion in 1971, and the chateau at Kolbsheim where he was the honored guest of the Gruneliuses. It was there that Raïssa lay buried and where Jacques would lie beside her after his death in 1973. He was no longer a household word in his native land, perhaps, but Kolbsheim fittingly became the repository of his papers; there, under the capable administration of René Mougel, the groundwork was laid for the renaissance in which the sixteen volumes of his work edited by Mougel and others have played the major role.

2

Since his death, the reputation of Jacques Maritain has been recovering from the dip it took with the appearance of *The Peasant of the Garonne*, his mordant look at what some were making of Vatican II. The prescience of those misgivings has long been clear. Meanwhile, new societies devoted to the thought of Maritain have sprung up: in Kolbsheim, of course, but also in Rome, in Latin America, in Canada, and in the United States. John Paul II cited Jacques Maritain by name in his 1998 encyclical *Fides et Ratio* as a model of the continuing effort to effect a *modus vivendi* between faith and reason. Young Catholic intellectuals are finding inspiration in the motto Jacques Maritain took from John of St. Thomas, *Philosophandum in fide:* One should philosophize in the ambience of the faith.

On the occasion of the twenty-fifth anniversary of his first book, *Bergsonian Philosophy,* Maritain wrote a lengthy preface in which he expressed regret at the tone he had taken in criticizing Henri Bergson. It was not that he thought that the criticisms he had made were invalid, but that the book did not convey the tremendous role that Bergson had played in the thought of Raïssa and Jacques as well as of countless others. We have vivid word pictures of the lecture hall in the Collège de France in the late afternoon, the green shaded lamps on the professorial table lit, the seats filled with as heterogeneous a group as has ever attended philosophical lectures—but then Bergson was opening anew the path to the spiritual, for which there was a hunger on all levels of French culture. And there was another thing that would have influenced Maritain's mellower mood: Bergson too had come into the Church, if only on his deathbed.

Return to the Left

By accepting immediately the condemnation of Action Française and undertaking to explain and defend the Church's action, Maritain was effectively declaring independence of a political outlook that, while it was anti-capitalist and antibourgeoisie, also rejected democracy and parliamentarianism. Moreover, Maritain alienated many fellow Catholics who accepted only with difficulty, if at all, the papal condemnation.

After the dust settled, Maritain began work on *The Degrees of Knowledge* and for a year his life took on an almost monastic regime. The meetings of the Circle of Studies loom even larger in his life, and he continued to make new friends because of them. In September of 1931, the tenth annual retreat was held with Garrigou-Lagrange as director. In December of that year, Jacques visited Kolbsheim and the chateau of the Gruneliuses. Did he have any premonition that it was in the little graveyard there that he would bury Raïssa and later still be buried with her? The chateau is now the locus of the *Cercle d'Etudes Jacques et Raïssa Maritain*, and it is there that René Mougel and his associates edit the *Cahiers Jacques Maritain*. From Kolbsheim came the magnificent sixteen-volume edition of the writings of Jacques and Raïssa already mentioned. Work on the *The Degrees* continued through 1932, punctuated by meetings of the circle; and in September the annual retreat was held. Also in September occurred the visit of Edith Stein described at the beginning of this book. The following year, Jacques made his first trip to Toronto and visited the University of Chicago as well. *Freedom in the Modern World (Du régime temporel et de la liberté)* was published in 1933 and then, in 1934,

Pour le bien commun, a joint statement by Maritain and others on the repression of riots in Vienna. His lectures that year in Rome, in Nimegen, and in Spain, concentrate on the spiritual and temporal problems of Christianity. There is no diminution of more theoretical works; the interest in aesthetics continues, but one notices the increased involvement in practical questions and in direct action. In 1935, Maritain took part in a manifesto on the war in Ethiopia. When *Integral Humanism* appeared in 1936, some accused Maritain of being a Christian Marxist. In that year, Maritain visited Argentina and Brazil. In 1937 appeared the Manifesto of Protest against the bombing of Guernica. Maritain was named Public Enemy Number 1 in Spain. He spoke out against anti-Semitism, and a stormy lecture on that subject was later published as *A Christian Looks at the Jewish Question (Les juifs parmi les nations).*[36] Maritain's name appeared on many manifestos against the Anschluss and against aerial bombing in Spain. He had come a long way from Action Française, and François Mauriac felt compelled to come to his defense against Catholic criticism. In 1938, Maritain again went to North America and, for the first time, visited the University of Notre Dame.

By the end of the thirties, Maritain was manifestly a man of the Left. He found himself at odds, in political matters, with his spiritual and intellectual mentor Garrigou-Lagrange, something painful to both men. And there were others as well who lamented the change in Maritain.

DISPUTE WITH CLAUDEL

I

Among the old friends and admirers who were put off by Maritain's political activities during the thirties was Paul Claudel, poet, diplomat, dramatist. In a moving account, *Ma conversion*,[37] Claudel describes the cultural scene in Paris when he was a student and trying to find his path as a poet. The depressing materialism that the Maritains would sense a decade or so later lay like a heavy hand on the human spirit. The influence of Ernest Renan, the great apostate, was everywhere. Renan distributed the diplomas and prizes when Claudel graduated from the Lycée, and he was the grandfather of Jacques's boyhood friend, Ernest Psichari. On Christmas Eve, 1886, at Notre Dame in Paris, looking in on the liturgy out of aesthetic motives, Claudel felt his lost faith come surging back into his soul. Some years would pass before he brought his life into line with his recovered faith but that event in Notre Dame became an event in French cultural history as well as in the poet's biography. The visitor to Notre Dame will find Claudel's conversion memorialized on a plaque in the sanctuary.

Claudel's spiritual advisor had told him to read Thomas Aquinas, both of the summas, the *Summa contra gentiles* as well as the *Summa theologiae*, and to read them neat, without commentary. As a young consul in China, Claudel did this, and it was formative of him as a poet.[38] How could there not be a friendship between such a man and the Maritains? Of course, Claudel's life was spent largely outside France on diplomatic assignments in China, Brazil, Japan, the United States, etc. But surely, if belatedly, his genius was recognized in France. The Maritains recognized it from the outset, reading Claudel's *Art poétique*. In early 1921 Claudel mentions Maritain in his journal and in August records that Maritain had sent him a wonderful comment by Saint John of the Cross on Psalm 45, verse 5. (Claudel's immersion in Scripture was lifelong, ending in the volumes of commentary that make up a signifcant part of his collected works.) In December came the Christmas visit to Meudon when he met Maurice Sachs. In July 1930, he made another visit to Meudon and some weeks later wrote this: "Maritain says that the power of the system of Saint Thomas lies in the fact that he grounds it on the great truths of common sense that the human heart obstinately retains even when one verbally denies them: the existence of the world, finality, freedom, providence, the existence of God, responsibility, the existence and immortality of the soul."[39] Clearly here was a thinker Claudel admired. That it was mutual is clear from Maritain's participation in the issue of *Vie Intellectuelle* dedicated to Claudel in 1935.

In 1937, Maritain signed a manifesto on behalf of those Claudel characterized as the "Basque traitors." For his part, Claudel had written a long poem "To the Martyrs of Spain."[40] "I wrote to that imbecile telling him what I think of him." Strong words. On the same page Claudel quotes a Latin adage: *Plus potest objicere asinus quam solvere philosophus:* An ass can raise more difficulties than a philosopher can resolve.

Perhaps it was his professional absences from France that enabled Claudel to make friends among groups at odds with one another. He was uncontaminated by any connection with Action Française. As a servant of the Republic, he could scarcely embrace a movement that was fundamentally antidemocratic. And he was as repelled by facism as he was by communism. Consequently, one of Maritain's manifestos brought a severe reaction from the older man. Maritain had written, "So long as modern societies secrete misery as the normal production of their functioning, there can be no rest for a Christian." "Mr. Jacques Maritain is a great philosopher," Claudel responded. "Under that title, he would not be unaware of what the Scholastics call the *per se* and the *per accidens*, or in other words the normal and accidental result or effect. But he tells us that misery is the normal result of the functioning of current society, in other words the end for the sake of which it exists. This is to go further than Jean-Jacques Rousseau himself in whose steps our Thomist follows. It is excessive to pretend that the end of any society, as degraded as it might be imagined, is the misery of each or of some of its members."[41] Not only does Claudel seize upon the claim that the intended aim of modern society is the misery of its people, he also comments on Maritain's statement that "There is no rest for a Christian: *il n'y a pas de repos pour un chrétien.*" It is a Christian obligation in justice or charity actively to seek a remedy for the general imperfections of society. "This is to be beyond the founder of our religion," Claudel comments. Christ advises the apostles to wait for the harvest season before determining what is wheat and what is weed. Our competence and our power to distinguish evil is limited, Claudel observes. He ends by doubting that there is anything like the social question. There are particular problems to be addressed, of course, and he lists alcoholism, prostitution, pornography, the family, housing, and unemployment, not to mention education. For Claudel, the real cause of social ills is ideology and an unchecked sentimentality coupled with a blind confidence in one's own abilities and lights, the bane of the bookish and intellectuals. Maritain, in short, is naive.

2

In response, Maritain pointed to the social encyclicals of the popes. He denies that he meant that misery is per se the end of modern societies. "As for philosophers who treat the problems of social philosophy, it would seem to be precisely their duty as philosophers to bring about what they teach. If they are mistaken, attack their errors. But to blame them for undertaking a task that is part of their profession would be an obvious absurdity."[42]

Claudel replies that it is one thing to recognize social ills, ills he has never denied, and quite another to say that such ills are the normal product of the functioning of a society. "Mr. Maritain repudiates this and says that he did not mean what he said. I congratulate him. Nonetheless he said it. In so grave a matter it is usual for a philosopher to express himself with precision."

Well, one can see here a fundamental difference of the kind Gilbert and Sullivan immortalized. Maritain is a born liberal, Claudel is a born conservative. What is important here is that both are Catholic and both think and argue in a common context. To pounce upon the exaggeration of Maritain is a debater's trick, but then Maritain, in the heat of political zeal, opened himself to such critiques. No doubt, for Claudel it was their very different reactions to the war in Spain that underlay this later exchange. Claudel can stand for the large number of devout and intelligent Catholics who were offended by Maritain's apparent alliance with those who were persecuting the Church in Spain. There is no apologia for Franco in Claudel. Perhaps like the Bernanos of *The Moonlit Cemeteries*, Claudel would say that, on the political level, there was no good side in the Spanish Civil War. His critique of Maritain was not a defense of fascism anymore than Maritain's agitation against the atrocities committed by Franco was a justification of the martyred priests and nuns.

Nones
(1940–1948)

Chronology

1940   January 4. Leaves Marseilles for North America with Raïssa and Vera.
March 1. Having spent January and February in Toronto, leaves for New York.
De la justice politique published.
With the occupation of France and setting up of Vichy government, takes up residence at 30 Fifth Avenue.
October. *Scholasticism and Politics* published.

1941   January 4. Death of Henri Bergson.
March 6. First radio broadcast to France.
A travers le désastre published.
July. Raïssa finishes *We Have Been Friends Together.*
La pensée de saint Paul.
Confession de foi.
Ransoming the Time.

1942   January. "The End of Machiavellianism."
February. Ecole Libre des Hautes Études established in New York by Belgian and French exiles, with Maritain as vice president.
The Rights of Man and Natural Law published.

1943   January 9. The Maritain volume of *The Thomist* celebrates his sixtieth birthday.

April. *Christianisme et démocratie.*
June 26. Death of Maritain's mother, Geneviève Favre, in Paris.
August. *Education at the Crossroads.*
September 2. Begins weekly addresses on Voice of America.

1944   *Principes d'une politique humaniste.*
De Bergson à saint Thomas d'Aquin.
June 6. Normandy invasion.
July 10. On visit to New York, General de Gaulle proposes ambassadorship to Vatican.
Trip to Paris. Appointed French ambassador to Vatican.
Raïssa's *Adventures in Grace* published.

1945   April 1. Leaves for Rome, where on May 10 he presents his credentials.
Raïssa and Vera come to Rome via Naples.
Maritain becomes close to Monsignor Montini, the future Paul VI.

1946   Maritain under attack by Julio de Meinvielle of Buenos Aires.
November 15. "Message aux amis argentins."

1947   January 12. Concert of music of Sati, Lourié, Ibert, and Vlad presented by Maritains at Palais Taverna.
The Person and the Common Good.
Existence and the Existent.
UNESCO conference in Mexico; Maritain president of French delegation and president of the conference. His opening address, *La Voie de la paix.*

Exile in New York

I

"I left France in January 1940 to give the courses which for several years I had been offering at the Pontifical Institute of Mediaeval Studies in Toronto and for a series of lectures in the United States. I planned to return to Paris at the end of June, but the tragic events of the month of June and the German stranglehold on my country, prevented me from doing so."[1]

On January 4, 1940, Jacques, Raïssa, and Vera—the "little flock"—boarded ship at Marseilles and sailed away from war and into a decade that would begin and end in the United States, first as exile, eventually as professor of philosophy at Princeton. One can only imagine the despondency with which they left behind their defeated country and the anxiety with which they looked ahead. Such financial assets as Jacques had were abandoned to the vagaries of the occupation. The Gestapo sought him in vain at the Institut Catholique, proof of the wisdom of his departure. In southern France an allegedly independent French government was set up under the venerable Marshal Pétain and some, like Mounier and Fumet, moved into the Vichy territory in order to carry on the publication of their respective journals, *Esprit* and *Temps Present*. From London, Charles de Gaulle broadcast a defiant rejection of the armistice the Germans had offered, and in Paris the Resistance began.

After a few months in Toronto, they moved to New York, soon taking possession of a furnished apartment at 30 Park Avenue. Jacques was incapable of being anywhere for any length of time without exercising a magnetic attraction. Soon he was being looked to for advice and help from other emigrés. In New York, the emigrés founded a press that published their works in French. The Ecole Libre des Hautes Etudes was founded under the presidency of Henri Focillon, and Jacques, who would succeed Focillon as president of the school, began teaching there. He also lectured at Columbia and Princeton. And after Pearl Harbor, he began to broadcast to France, courtesy of the American government. These talks were collected, published, and translated into English.

2

The war forced on Jacques Maritain, Christian philosopher, the opportunity to develop in acute form the ideas that had begun to take shape after the condemnation of Action Française. Maritain's immediate need was to rethink, in the light of the Catholic tradition, the relationship between the temporal and the spiritual. In *The Primacy of the Spiritual*, he had, in an amazing tour de force, brought to bear on the twentieth century the Church's thinking on its relation to the temporal realm, the realm of politics. Arguing for the primacy of the spiritual and the Church's indirect power over the temporal order, something the condemnation of Action Française had made imperative, Maritain advanced an eloquent defense of the papal action. No Catholic can read the pages he devoted to the crucial role of the pope without being deeply moved and without seeing how distant the modern mind had become to the doctrine he defended. He invoked Joseph de Maistre and Bossuet, he touched on the Galileo affair, he cited Father Faber on the reverence in which a Catholic must hold the pope and the obedience he owes him. Action Française rejected the condemnation by claiming an autonomy for the temporal that Maritain saw as heretical. It was not that the Church denied anyone the right to be a monarchist or to be against democracy and parliamentary government. He recalled the time-honored truth that no single form of government was entailed by Christian belief. But when a political movement took positions that made it, in effect, a rival of the Church in the Church's proper domain, the Church had no choice but to condemn it.

This was a great turning point in Maritain's thought, as has been mentioned; and he worked his way gradually toward the proposal of *Integral Humanism*, in which he saw that a nostalgia for the medieval, the wish to return to some earlier state of affairs, was simply not an option. But the first requirement was to become a critic of humanism.

One can trace in Maritain's writings of the 1930s the emergence of the crucial distinction he drew between anthropomorphic humanism, the humanism of the Renaissance, and a theocentric humanism. Along the way to this clarity, Maritain aligned himself with questionable allies, as in the signing of various manifestos—allies who espoused the very humanism he theoretically rejected. He even congratulated André Gide when he openly espoused communism. He condemned the aerial bombing in Spain but seemed to many to accept uncritically the liberal version of the bombing of Guernica. In his own mind, Maritain believed he was not joining any side or any political party, and no one can doubt the sincerity of his denial. But we must not look to manifestos for Maritain's analysis of what had brought Europe to a flashpoint that would lead, inevitably it seemed, to World War II.

3

Perhaps it would be better to focus on the continuity of Maritain's thinking rather than a major change in the 1930s. His first courses at the Institut Catholique had been devoted to the history of modern philosophy. Of course, no French philosopher could escape the pervasive presence of Cartesianism. The work that inaugurated the series *Roseau d'Or*, a series meant to provide an outlet for an alternative literature to that of the *Nouvelle Revue Française* and André Gide, was Maritain's own *Three Reformers*. His cultural efforts were to be defined by an openness and receptivity to the modern; that and his association with Cocteau can be seen as efforts to assimilate and redirect surrealism. But in the inaugural volume, Maritain subjected Descartes, Luther, and Rousseau to a devastating critique, one in which he drew a relationship between the ideas and the persons who held them. This was not extending an olive branch to modernity but taking an axe to the roots of modern culture.

What these three "reformers" had done was to sever the relationship between man and the transcendent. In their emphasis on the individual man and their exaltation of humanity, Maritain saw a humanism that began perhaps only by bracketing man's relation to God, but ended by denying it. Culture, philosophy, became separated from Christianity. Maritain recalled that classical thought pursued the life of reason in order to rejoin "something better than reason and its source."[2] But the reason that emerged with Descartes cut itself off both from what was above it, the suprarational, and from what was below it, the infrarational. Such a humanism required that man be his own savior and that he produce by his own efforts a terrestrial paradise. No wonder that someone like Kierkegaard attacked the reason that presumed to encompass Christianity and to reduce it to its own categories: religion within the limits of reason alone!

Even today it is almost shocking to read Maritain's critique of humanism, so countercultural does it remain: a humanism based on man as autonomous, man equated with reason alone. Nietzsche attacked the culture that had been elevated on this exiguous view of man, but without offering a clear alternative. Insofar as he had one, it seemed a cure worse than the disease—a superman who would exercise power over the mindless masses of modernity. But Nietzsche gave way to Rosenberg, the theoretician of Nazi racism.

4

In 1939 Maritain had published a little book called *The Twilight of Civilization*, which summarized the social and political position he had been formulating. It is a resumé, as impressionistic as the preceding paragraph, but the power of the analysis is inescapable. The rejection of humanism is the rejection of a false view of man, and Maritain's proposal was that a true humanism must be based on what man truly is, a being called to union with God. The earlier discussions of Christian philosophy seem abstract when compared to the actual thinking of the Christian philosopher. Thanks to his faith, Maritain had accepted a truth that went beyond the truths the unaided human mind is capable of. What he accepted was not an opinion or a theory but a revelation. Only through faith can a man fully understand what he is. The man of faith inevitably observes philosophy even while he engages in it. For him, its truths are not the sum total of truths, and he will commence philosophizing from out of his faith (*philosophandum in fide*), will be guided by it as he reasons, and will relate the achievements of reason to truths beyond its reach.

In *The Twilight of Civilization*, after discussing the crisis of modern humanism, Maritain goes on to consider the great forces aligned against Christianity and the relation of the gospel to the pagan empire. Man is now threatened by totalitarianism, both the fascist kind and the Marxist kind. Marxism is seen as a grotesque caricature of Christianity, seeking a universal hegemony over mankind.[3] The atheism of Marx and the racism of Hitler seek to replace Christianity with a false and terrestrial faith. Maritain's grasp of what modernity had become did not lead, despite the melancholy title of the little work, to despair. He rejected a shallow optimism as well as pessimism and turned to the great alternative of a new humanism, an integral humanism: one based on a true view of man and of his potential, both natural and supernatural. The new paganism generated a view of politics expressed by Carl Schmitt, which required the community to be based not simply on friendship among its members but on hatred of an opponent. For Schmitt, the state requires a hated enemy in order to thrive. Maritain rejected this with eloquent vigor, recalling the simple truth of Christianity.

The solidarity of the race, grounded in the fact that man is created in the image of God and is called to a universal love that has no natural enemies, is the only possible basis for a genuine politics. Sin is to be hated but not the sinner. And then he turns to democracy.

The discussion of Christianity and democracy in this little book begins with an explicit reference to America. If the modern world requires a new humanism to supplant the anthropocentric humanism of the Renaissance, it calls for a new democracy as well. Democracy has many senses, as he had already argued in *An Opinion on Charles Maurras* and *The Primacy of the Spiritual*. A democracy based on an anthropomorphic humanism is only another form of the same problem. "It remains that if it is true that there are always temperaments of the right and temperaments of the left, political philosophy itself is of neither the left nor the right, it must be simply *true*."[4] So too Maritain envisages a democracy that transcends what are currently called democratic governments. "It is defined by the fact that it recognizes the inalienable rights of the human person and the vocation of the person as such to the political life, and which sees in those who have authority the vicars of the multitude, as Saint Thomas Aquinas put it" (p. 44). Individualistic liberalism stemming from Rousseau must be rejected, but—and here is a note, derived from DeMaistre, which will characterize Maritain's thought from now on—one must seek in a false humanism and the democracy to which it gives rise the authentically human aspirations from which it springs.

5

The way out of the debacle is not simply to provide the pathology of anthropocentric humanism; one must see that it is the perversion of an aspiration that has a defensible development. Jacques Maritain, who began as a self-described antimodern, has become a critic of modernity who sees it as a failure to recognize its own deep aspirations. One must plunge into anthropomorphic humanism in search of these aspirations if one would provide an alternative to it, a new humanism that is an authentic development of these aspirations. "An integral humanism and an organic democracy, democracy inspired by Christianity of which the American episcopate speaks, proceeds from a theocentric inspiration. They really respect human dignity, not in an abstract individual, atemporal and non-existent, which ignores the historical conditions and historical diversity and which pitilessly devours the human substance, but in each concrete and existent person in the historical context of his life" (p. 45).

What are those inalienable rights? Maritain finds them in Pius XI's encyclical *Divini Redemptoris:* the right to life, to the integrity of the body, to the means necessary for existence, the right to tend to one's final end along the path traced by God, the right of association, the right to possess and use property. . . . In *Human Rights and Natural Law,* Maritain addressed the vexed question as to the relationship between the traditional teaching on natural law—that there are moral guidelines anchored in our very nature—on the one hand, and the doctrine of natural rights, which had a quite different theoretical basis, on the other. In his postwar Walgreen lectures that became *Man and the State,* Maritain would present his matured thinking on this matter.

The Heart of the Matter

I

The increased tempo of Maritain's life as he settled into wartime exile in New York—the writing, lecturing, teaching, consultation with representatives of General de Gaulle, radio broadcasts—did not distract Jacques and his little flock from the one thing needful. His reflections on politics place squarely in the center of the picture the human person called to holiness. About this time in Oxford, C. S. Lewis was writing the remarkable essay, "Learning in War Time." How can we justify the pursuit of learning at a time of great danger when issues of life and death confront us? Lewis's answer could have been Maritain's as well: "The war creates no absolutely new situation: it simply aggravates the permanent human situation so that we can no longer ignore it. Human life has always been lived on the edge of a precipice. Human culture has always had to exist under the shadow of something infinitely more important than itself. . . . We are mistaken when we compare war with 'normal life.' Life has never been normal."[5]

2

Among the books Maritain wrote in New York is the remarkable *The Thought of St. Paul,* in which he reflects on the epistles with especial reference to the question of the "mystery of Israel."[6] In Paris, Jacques had been the object of some vituperation for addressing publicly the question of anti-Semitism. Raïssa was Jewish—doubtless one motive for Jacques's lifelong interest in the issue, largely from a theological point of view. "Salvation comes from the Jews." Maritain begins with this quotation from John 4:22. All the apostles were Jewish, of course, not least the Apostle to the Gentiles, Paul, originally Saul. "It is from Israel that the Savior of the World came; it is in the womb of a young Jewish girl—the only absolutely pure creature among all human creatures—that the Word by whom all was made took on human flesh, soon to be spared in the first pogrom of the Christian era, the massacre of the innocent Jewish babes by which Herod sought fumblingly to strike their king. . . ." It is with Moses that Maritain compares Paul. Moses transmitted to Israel the tablets of the Law; Paul taught the universal church by the sword of the word that had been entrusted to him, a "church composed of Jews and gentiles," the spiritual Israel that was "by the Law, dead to the Law, in order to live for God."

That is the Pauline mission and the source of Saint Paul's importance for human history. It was thanks to him that Christianity was freed from Judaism to become universal, catholic. It had to be understood that the Son of Man had not come only for the Jew, but for Man, for the human race taken in its unity. The great intuition of Paul that flooded his spirit, Maritain writes, was the universality of the Kingdom of God and that salvation comes through faith, not through the law. And there is another pillar of Paul's teaching: the liberty of the sons of God. "Saint Paul is the great teacher of liberty; the sense of liberty is rooted in the very marrow of the bones of the man who was Saul, the most fervent of the Pharisees, all the barriers of whose heart melted at the vision of the glorified Christ. From that point on, he knows no frontiers, but is at the mercy of Him whom he loves and who delivered him."

In this book on Paul the reader comes into contact with the scriptural bases of the spirituality of Maritain. The book has the deceptive look of being merely a florilegium of texts, and Maritain does indeed put many texts before the reader; but they are chosen to illustrate large themes and in their cumulative effect give a profound sense of the mission of Saint

Paul. In such a book, it is the role of the author to be self-effacing, to let his subject speak. But if it were simply a matter of listening to Paul, we need only read the epistles and the Acts of the Apostles. This is a book by one who has long immersed himself in those texts and has discerned the major themes illustrated far and wide in the epistles. And the art of the book is to make us unaware of the very knowledgeable guide we are following. Under the headings of the mission of Paul, law and grace, the greatest of these is charity, Christ the redeemer, the economy of salvation, and the new man, Maritain enables us to assimilate the message of Paul. But there is another theme as well, that of the mystery of Israel.

The Mosaic law prepared the chosen people for the messiah, as the natural law does others; and when the messiah comes, he is rejected. Paul bears witness for his own people, underscoring the enormous advantage of being Jewish: it is to the Jews that God has confided his oracles (Rom. 3:3). The Scriptures were put into the hands of the Jewish people. Paul's love of his fellow Jews—he would accept exclusion himself if it were the price of their accepting Christ—is the measure of his anguish at their rejection of Christ (Rom. 9:1–5). God has not rejected his people, but Israel's false step makes possible the salvation of the nations (Rom. 11). The reward of the Jews will be a greater spiritual abundance when at last they turn to Christ. The conversion of the Jews was looked forward to in the Middle Ages as to the third period of the Church and of Christianity. The gentiles have been grafted on to the olive branch of Israel (Eph. 2:11–18) and God will not withdraw the promises he has made to his chosen people (Rom. 11). They will eventually convert. Maritain closes this discussion with a quotation from Thomas Aquinas's commentary on John.

> The two peoples, the Jewish people and the gentile people are symbolized at the tomb of Christ by the two apostles. They run together toward Christ across the ages, the gentiles by the natural law, the Jews by the written law. The gentiles, like Peter, who arrives second at the sepulcher, come later to the knowledge of Jesus Christ, but like Peter they enter first. The Jewish people, the first to know the mystery of the redemption, will be the last converted to faith in Christ. . . . *Then*, the evangelist writes, *John will enter.* Israel ought not remain eternally at the entrance to the sepulcher. After Peter has gone inside, they too will enter, for in the end the Jews, they too, will be received in the faith.[7]

Adventures in Grace

I

And Raïssa? How could she possibly adjust to being transplanted to the New World, a stranger among strangers, after having established a *modus vivendi* at Meudon that enabled her to pursue in relative solitude the life of prayer? "Raïssa had lost the one place—Meudon, with the presence of the Blessed Sacrament in our home—where she felt some shelter on the earth and where, running the risk of dying of pain, she found conditions exceptionally favorable in spite of everything for recollection." Thus wrote Jacques, introducing that portion of her journal that runs from 1940 until 1960. But isn't it normal, he asks, that anyone who sets out on the road to God must one day be deprived of all the facilities for prayer that for so long a time had been granted her? Here is a description of Raïssa by their friend Julie Kernan. "At this time as Jacques was submerged in work, Raïssa was particularly unhappy. Distressed by the news that seeped through to her from France, missing the peace and quiet of Meudon, she shrank from the bustle and noise of the big city around her and spent much time at her desk, leaving the apartment as rarely as possible. Even so, she graciously received visitors, and coped as best she could with the domestic problems that arose."[8] By contrast, Vera is described as wading into the shops and markets, babbling away in the best English she could muster, the practical one of the trio who kept their ménage going, as she always had. Julie Kernan thought Raïssa had more knowledge of English, but she spoke it reluctantly, dreading to make mistakes—a fear familiar to many a monoglot. And yet she accompanied Jacques on his trips, for example, to Chicago in March where they stayed with John and Eleanor Nef and Jacques lectured at the university. As if contrasting his experience with her own, she wrote in her journal on March 25, "Jacques's lectures at the university. For me this exile is a terrible trial." On April 25, she vowed to die but then took it back when she considered how lonely that would leave Jacques and Vera. On January 5, 1941, she wrote, "Bergson died yesterday (January 4). Great pain for us. I think of all that we owe him, and that many others do as well. We heard in a letter from France that he had been baptized and did not want to declare it publicly out of consideration for the Jews subject to persecution in recent years. Our master, lost and found."

Judith Suther writes of this time. "It would nonetheless be inaccurate, as well as insensitive, to say that Raïssa ceased to contribute to the balance of love and mutual support that bound the 'small flock of three' together, or that she wailed in private while Jacques and Vera dealt with the world. What took place, to a greater degree than had occurred before, was a shifting of the balance and a sharpening of everyone's roles. Raïssa became more withdrawn, Jacques more politically and intellectually engaged, Vera more serviceable and nurturing. Under the pressure of war and expatriation, their natural tendencies became more clearly defined."[9]

2

However badly Raïssa took life in America, at least at first, nonetheless she solidered on. And what was she doing at her desk, as Julie Kernan describes her? She was writing her masterpiece in two installments, the first called in English *We Have Been Friends Together*, and its sequel, *Adventures in Grace*. Memoirs. Somehow the term seemed inadequate to what Raïssa put down on these pages. She evoked her childhood, meeting Jacques, the encounter with Léon Bloy, conversion, and then the quest for holiness. For generations of American Catholics, she made the French Catholic world vibrant with life. One felt that he had known Ernest Psichari and Charles Péguy; Bloy seemed a presence in the room as one read Raïssa. The artists and writers, the philosophers and theologians, a whole world, peopled it seemed by converts or reverts to the faith, for whom Catholicism was the central fact of their lives and the key to making sense of the world and oneself. And she is the keeper of the flame. She launched the explanation of Jacques's long connection with Action Française—he was too responsive to the urging of his spiritual directors, unquestioningly altering what he considered his natural leftism for the monarchical and antidemocratic movement of Charles Maurras. He was never a member, of course, and he says he did not subscribe to the movement's daily paper.

Raïssa's benign view of Jacques's involvement with Action Française is symptomatic. Jacques is the hero of every encounter, and she portrays herself in a thoroughly subordinate role. Her sensitivity to the mildest criticism of Jacques is palpable. All that may be true, but it does not detract from the accomplishment of these two memoirs, which ultimately were fused into one volume. Nothing Jacques himself ever wrote conveys as powerfully the persons they were: Raïssa, Vera, himself. But Raïssa makes them and their friends lift from the page and invade the mind and imagination of the reader. Nor has her memoir lost its power to evoke people who hungered for God, for the life of the spirit, for holiness. The motto of them all might have been taken from Bloy: There is only one tragedy, not to be a saint.

Ambassador to the Vatican

I

Jacques and his wife and sister-in-law spent some summer weeks of 1944 at East Hampton. Raïssa responded with uncharacteristic exuberance. "This landscape is delicious, the light extraordinary; trees, bushes, everything seems marvelous to me. It is the first time since we came to America that I have felt myself 'received,' sheltered, firm on the earth, on reality." But the best was yet to be. On August 25, Paris was liberated. In November, Jacques was flown to Paris in an American military plane. There he was persuaded by General de Gaulle and Georges Bidault, Minister of Foreign Affairs, to serve as French ambassador to the Vatican. Here was an opportunity to serve his country in a public way, a country that was still at war.

He was flown to Rome by military plane to take up his post and to await the arrival of Raïssa and Vera more than three months later. August 10, 1945, was their first day together in Rome. By then, the war was over in Europe and soon to be over in the Pacific. The great unknown of the postwar world loomed ahead.

In the nineteenth century, it was not unusual for American literary people to serve as American consuls in foreign lands—Hawthorne for instance, in England, William Dean Howells in Italy—but the practice had long since fallen out of favor. The French, on the other hand, seem to have been favored by diplomats who developed their literary reputations while serving: Paul Claudel and St.-John Perse, to name but two of the most distinguished. For all that, there is something unexpected and delightful in the naming of Jacques Maritain as his country's ambassador to the Vatican. During the years in New York, the ever-sensitive Raïssa had recorded her fears that critics of Jacques in Rome might have the ear of those in authority. There is no doubt that Jacques, the mildest of men, was regularly attacked by those who might more justly have seen in him an ally than an enemy. It would be possible to tell the story of his philosophical career in terms of the criticisms, even attacks, he was subject to.[10] But Maritain had always had powerful friends in Rome, and his arrival in 1945 could be described as triumphant.

Julie Kernan records Jacques's estimate of the France he visited in late 1944, when he agreed to the post at the Vatican. Certainly the somewhat furtive and unfriendly Parisians would have been emerging from a very dark period, and life was difficult with food and heat at a premium. But the larger question concerned the divisions that the occupation and the Vichy regime had created among the French people. Some bishops had been supportive of the Vichy regime, and of course the Free French of de Gaulle would have regarded them as near traitors. De Gaulle demanded the removal from Paris of all diplomats who had recognized the Vichy government, and this included the papal nuncio! He was soon replaced by Angelo Roncalli, who had served during the war in Turkey and had been a key figure in the Vatican's successful efforts to save some 860,000 Jews from certain destruction at the hands of the Nazis. Eventually he would become the beloved Pope John XXIII.

2

Installed in the Palazzo Madama, the Maritains acquitted themselves of their diplomatic duties with aplomb. Jacques was no stranger to the Vatican, of course. Here was a layman who had been granted special audiences with several popes, not least with Pius XI when Action Française was condemned. He held an honorary doctorate from the Angelicum and had many admirers in the Roman universities. Of course, as is ever the case with a philosopher, he had his critics as well; and, in Rome, intellectual criticism often sought to express itself in disciplinary moves. Charles Journet had alerted

Jacques to the animosity against him in some Roman circles on the eve of the war, but the German invasion blew all such intramural quarrels away. If France was divided, both in the temporal and spiritual realms, by accusations of collaboration with the Nazi occupiers, Italy was still reeling from its near fatal flirtation with Benito Mussolini. The devastation and poverty in Rome were dramatically worse than in Paris.

But still Rome was Rome. St. Peter's and the other great basilicas were all around them, and just off the Piazza Navona was the church of St. Louis of France. There and elsewhere, Jacques performed the tasks of a cultural attaché, encouraging discussion groups and lectures. Nor did his own philosophical work cease. The postwar phenomenon of existentialism in Paris provided an occasion for Jacques to address what he saw to be a most unfortunate turn in French philosophy.

3

Existence and the Existent was published in 1947, but Jacques had made use of the work in progress for a talk he gave to the Pontifical Academy of St. Thomas Aquinas as well as for an article in the *Revue Thomiste*. It is clear that the work was prompted by Jean-Paul Sartre. Sartre had made a name for himself in the Resistance and, in the postwar period, made the philosophical view that came to be called existentialism a popular phenomenon. Sartre himself joked that a staid lady who uttered a vulgarity when provoked worried aloud that she was becoming an existentialist. Sartrean existentialism draws the ultimate implications of atheism.

One who believes in God understands himself and the natural world as God's creation, and God is seen on the analogy of a human artist who has an idea and sets out to realize it. The artifact is a good one if it fulfills the expectations of the artist. Thus, for the theist, man embodies God's intention; he has a nature or essence that is the measure of his acting well or badly. An automobile that functions well as an automobile is a good one. Its functioning well is determined by what an automobile is for, its end or purpose. For the theist, human nature provides the clue to human flourishing and its opposite.

This sketch of theism is reasonably accurate, but Sartre provides it as a foil to his own view. What happens when you take God out of the picture? Man is no longer a creature; he has no nature or essence that provides a standard for his conduct. If the theistic view can be captured in the phrase "essence precedes existence," atheistic existentialism is summed up as "existence precedes essence."

In what had been his approach for more than a decade, Maritain sought to show that this despairing view of the human situation masked something important and true. Thus, he proposed not simply to question or refute existentialism but to argue that Thomism is the true existentialism. This was to view the movement as the tag end of a philosophical culture that still carried some echoes of its past, and there is truth to this. Thus it is that Maritain's book begins with a metaphysical discussion. But where Thomism engages existentialism is in the practical order, and it was Maritain's great insight to show this.

> Precisely because in ethics or practical philosophy Thomist existentialism is ordered, not to the existence exercised by things, but to the act which the liberty of the subject will bring into existence, the differences in metaphysical point of view, profound though they be, will nevertheless not preclude certain contacts between this existentialism and contemporary existentialism. As a matter of fact, it is in the domain of moral philosophy that the views which modern existentialism contributes seem to me most worthy of interest."

The tags Sartre offered for theism and existentialism make it clear that the existence involved is human action. If the theist holds that essence precedes existence, this means that what he does must be in conformity with his nature. For the existentialist, human action has no such guide. Metaphysical assumptions abound on both sides, but the focus is on action, and that is what Maritain stressed. It also tells us much of his motivation for addressing a philosophical movement that had, so to speak, spilled over into the streets and become a matter of popular culture. It was not simply a matter of some professional thinkers making mistakes about which one can argue; existentialism was providing an atmosphere of antinomian despair, and this involved souls. Maritain had long observed the paradox that philosophical movements that focused on the human subject quickly led to conclusions destructive of the human person. Existentialism, at first blush, seemed a kicking aside of all constraints on action, a call to insouciant pursuit of whatever you liked. But Sartre himself saw this as merely a middle-distance view. At bottom, the freedom of existentialism is a condemnation, a state of total responsibility with any effort to diminish it identified as *mauvais foi*, self-deception.

4

If Maritain's recognition that existentialism was far more an ethics than a metaphysics is true, this little book also relates to what came to be called Thomistic Existentialism. Of course, Maritain's point was that Thomism is the true existentialism, but it is when this is explicitly a metaphysical claim that critics stir. The existence that interested Kierkegaard was not the *esse* that Thomas distinguishes from *essentia*, however much the Satrean tags might mistakenly suggest that. Of course, Maritain was not maintaining that *esse substantiale* is identical with the incidental being manifested in this action or that. But attempts to express Thomas's thought in the jargon of the day can be risky. The prominence in the book of what Maritain called the "intuition of being" also puzzled his fellow Thomists and led to the kind of intramural disputes that dogged Maritain.

All the more reason for us to stress what seems to have prompted Maritain to take on existentialism. All we need do is recall the sense of despair that Jacques and Raïssa had as students of the Sorbonne to see why Jacques would have wanted to arm a new generation of youth against the fashionable despair of existentialism. One of the sections in the final chapter of the little book is called "Philosophy and Spiritual Experience." Here Maritain speaks in terms of the age-old issue of knowledge and virtue. He lauds the thought of Thomas Aquinas that recognizes various distinct intellectual enterprises but unifies them in a way that does not destroy the distinctions. Are we to be content with such cerebral unification? "The mortal danger run by those whose doctrine mounts towards the heights of unity and peace is that they may think they have reached their goal when they have only started on the path, and they may forget that for man and his thought, peace is always a victory over discord, and unity the reward of wrenchings suffered and conquered."[12]

Earlier he had pointed out the sterility of mere introspection, the morbidity involved in minute analysis of one's psychic innards. Such self-indulgence makes the self terminal, it is no longer an opening to the something more than self, as in Saint Augustine. The self is a creature and, as a creature, points to its creator. "What I should like to stress is that the spiritual experience of the philosopher is the nourishing soil of philosophy; that without it there is no philosophy; and that, even so, spiritual experience does not, or must not, enter into the intelligible structure of philosophy."[13]

The spread of a kind of matter-of-fact atheism in the postwar world drew many responses from Jacques Maritain. In contemporary parlance,

Sartre could be described as Nietzsche Lite, but a popular atheism is all the more pernicious. The exclusion of God from consciousness, the refusal to acknowledge the terms of one's own existence, is a tragedy—the only one, since the alternative to Bloy's sanctity is the loss of one's soul. Maritain devoted much thought to this after writing about existentialism, and lectures he gave at the Institut Catholique appeared in 1948 under the title *The Meaning of Contemporary Atheism.*[14] Anyone looking for Maritain's influence on the ecumenical council Pope John XXIII called, and which began meeting in 1962, need only look at this little work.[15] Maritain said that he wanted to "discover the spiritual sense hidden in the present agony of the world." While he is talking of a cultural phenomenon, Maritain seeks the roots of popular atheism in philosophical doctrines.

5

He begins with a discussion of the various kinds of atheism, pointing out that sometimes the "god" that is rejected is a false one, having nothing to do with the true God, and thus producing a pseudo-atheism. There are of course "absolute Atheists" who have a clear idea of the God they are denying, the one in whom believers believe. But even here, Maritain distinguishes a negative from a positive atheism in modern philosophies. The negative atheist is one who, rejecting God, does not replace Him with anything else, only a void. This can vary from the superficial atheism of the seventeenth century libertines—an absence—or it can take the form depicted by Dostoyevsky's Kiriloff, who asserts an absolute independence of the human self. What Maritain calls positive atheism might better be called an antitheism, a desperate, even heroic effort to reconstruct the universe in accord with the rejection of God. The tragic atheism of Nietzsche illustrates what he means, as does that of contemporary existentialism of the kind he confronted in *Existence and the Existent.* This is the character of contemporary atheism, and that is what Maritain discusses.

In seeking the source of such contemporary atheism, Maritain observes that one does not become a positive atheist by way of an inquiry conducted by speculative reason into the problem of God. Negative philosophical conclusions may be taken into account, and comfort is taken in the platitude that science has simply rendered the question of God meaningless. But all that is of secondary importance, not the primary motive. The contemporary atheist simply accepts those claims; he believes them; he chooses them. "The point of departure of absolute atheism in my view is a fundamental act of moral choice, a free and crucial determination."[16] As one rejects the subordination of childhood, one rejects all subordination as the requirement of moral maturity. Away with any moral law or ultimate end for man in a personal and free and deliberate act of choice. How could Maritain fail to notice that there is here a kind of degraded form of the act of faith? It is no longer a simple rejection of God, but a refusal and defiance. Any thought that conflicts with this fundamental choice is rejected as if it were a temptation to faith. But this calls for a constant and prolonged battle. Here is the first contradiction in atheism: proclaiming the disappearance of all religion, it becomes itself a religious phenomenon.

There is another contradiction in contemporary atheism linked to the first one. Belief in God is taken to diminish man, to be an alienation of traits proper to man and dubbing them God. What is wanted is to return man to himself, in absolute immanence and autonomy. But what has been the actual result of such atheism? Truth and justice and freedom are the watchwords, but what can they now mean? They become the products of the vagaries of history, contingent creations. What is today a meritorious act becomes on the morrow a crime. With the rejection of transcendence, human destiny becomes something in the future, to which individuals are sacrificed. The absolute atheist gives his life for something he can never himself enjoy. It is an almost mystical dedication to what has been called "the immanentization of the eschaton."

These two contradictions are essential if contemporary atheism is to be confronted. If it is, as Maritain argues, a religious phenomenon that mimics the self-sacrifice of the religious man, what initially seems wholly foreign and alien takes on the look of the truth distorted. Perhaps nowhere is Maritain's technique of looking for the lurking positive in positions that negate his own more effectively present than in his treatment of contemporary atheism.

What lifts off such pages is the author's dedication to the truth and his conviction that this is not some solitary occupation. It immediately puts one into relationship with the rest of mankind. The truth is a common good, to be shared; it is that for which we have been created. In kicking against the goad of truth, one pays tribute to it. Positive atheism is a longing for God despite itself. *Mon semblable, mon frère* is Maritain's attitude. He has been down that road himself and learned that it can turn out to be the road to Damascus.

6

When Maritain accepted appointment as the French ambassador to the Vatican, he agreed to serve for three years. Those years may have been the most heroic expression of his patriotism as a Frenchman. By all accounts he was a conscientious and effective diplomat. But France asked more of him. In November 1947, he attended the second general conference of UNESCO in Mexico City, as president of the French delegation. He spoke to the conference on the possibilities of cooperation in a divided world, and we can see another theme being struck to which he will return in the years just ahead.

Jacques returned to Rome by way of New York; and it was there, in a meeting with the president of Princeton University, Harold Dodds, that the next chapter of Maritain's life opened up. Dodds offered Maritain a resident professorship at Princeton with the specific wish that he would offer a course in moral philosophy inspired by his knowledge of Thomas Aquinas. It was an offer that, in the event, Maritain could not refuse. But neither at the moment could he accept it. This was something he must discuss with Raïssa and Vera. Moreover, his three-year commitment to serve as ambassador to the Vatican ran until the following May. He submitted his resignation and it was accepted. On June 1, he had a last audience as ambassador with Pope Pius XII. The little flock of three sailed from Naples a few weeks later: destination Princeton.

VESPERS
(1948–1960)

Chronology

1948   Resigns as ambassador and accepts appointment to Princeton.
        January. *Raison et raisons.*
        June. Jacques, Raïssa, and Vera embark for the United States.
        October. Begins teaching moral philosophy at Princeton. Lectures
        at Notre Dame, Chicago, and Hunter College.
        Special issue of *Revue Thomiste—Jacques Maritain, son oeuvre philosophique.*

1949   Spring. Trip to France.
        May 8. Conference on "The Significance of Contemporary Athe-
        ism."
        September. Maritains move into 26 Linden Lane, Princeton, N.J.,
        where they will live until 1960.

1950   August. Sojourn in France.

1951   *Man and the State.*
        Neuf leçons sur les notions premières de la philosophie morale.

1952   Introduction to Raïssa's book on Georges Rouault.

1953   *Creative Intuition in Art and Poetry.*
        Approaches to God.

1954   Coronary thrombosis attack. Begins editing his *Carnet de notes.*

1955   February. Death of Paul Claudel.
         Summer. Vacation in France.

1956   September. In *Civiltà Cattolica,* Father Messineo criticizes Maritain in "L'umanesimo integrale." Reply by Charles Journet in *Nova et vetera.* December 10. Public homage to Maritain in Paris by Centre Catholique des Intellectuels Français.

1957   *On the Philosophy of History.*
         Reflections on America.

1958   Jacques Maritain Center founded at University of Notre Dame, with Maritain in attendance.

1959   November. *Liturgy and Contemplation* by Jacques and Raïssa.
         December 31. Death of Vera.

1960   January. *Le philosophe dans la cité.*
         Responsibility of the Artist.
         June 30. Jacques and Raïssa return to France.
         November 4. Death of Raïssa.
         December. *Moral Philosophy.*

Man and the State

I

The next twelve years would be triumphant ones for Jacques Maritain, not quite proving the adage about prophets and their own country—in France a memorial volume of the *Revue Thomiste* would be dedicated to his work, and his achievement would be celebrated at a conference put on by the Institut Catholique. But in the New World he was feted and honored everywhere. He began teaching moral philosophy at Princeton in the fall of 1948, and there would emerge from this effort one of his largest books, *Moral Philosophy*. The Maritains moved into their Princeton home at 26 Linden Lane: it was a house they would never sell, bequeathing it to the University of Notre Dame.[1] From the house, they could walk the short distance to St. Paul's on Nassau Street to attend daily Mass. The campus was equally close. Jacques had reached retirement age when he began his Princeton career, but he would teach for five years. It was during this period that time began to take its inexorable toll. Jacques suffered a coronary in 1954; but it was Vera, the youngest of the three, who would succumb first, contracting breast cancer, having a mastectomy, and dying on the last day of 1959, December 31. A year later, Raïssa too was dead, and Jacques would enter the final period of his life.

But these years—call them the American Period—had to be among the most satisfying of Jacques's life. They came to love the United States—Jacques's *Reflections on America* is a veritable *billet doux*—but they remained thoroughly French and spent summers in their native land. Princeton let Jacques finish his class in April so the three could get away to Europe. The Institut Catholique held a special conference honoring Jacques. The Jacques Maritain Center at the University of Notre Dame was founded in 1958, and Jacques was there for the ceremony. His knack for making new friends and keeping old ones had not deserted him, and such friendships as that with Thomas Merton and, far more surprisingly, Saul Alinsky, can stand for many, many more with the less renowned. His intellectual work continued to exhibit its characteristic range and depth. His appointment at Princeton did not prevent him from lecturing at other institutions, and he became a regular presence at the universities of Chicago, Notre Dame, and Toronto. And there were prestigious lecture series that grew into books.

2

Jacques delivered the Walgreen Lectures at the University of Chicago in December 1949; they appeared as *Man and the State* in 1951 and can be seen as the culmination of his political philosophy. Criticism of Jacques's political views had never gone away; and toward the end of his ambassadorship to the Vatican, it flared up again when Julio de Meinvielle of Argentina published some letters he had received from Garrigou-Lagrange, commenting on Meinvielle's accusation that Maritain held many thoughts that had been condemned as heretical in the case of Lamennais. Long before, in 1937, Maritain had written a letter to the editor of *Criterio*, objecting to the manner as well as the substance of Meinvielle's criticism of him. The Argentine priest had called Maritain an "advocate of the Spanish Reds" and "suavely in favor of Communist Spain."[2] After the war, Meinvielle returned to the attack, publishing *From Lammenais to Maritain.*[3] Garrigou-Lagrange wrote to the author, objecting to the sensational title of his book, "since the deviation of which you speak is far from having the proportions of Lamennais', who became more and more mistaken about the very end of the Church. . . . that was his chief error and Jacques Maritain manifestly reproves that error."[4] Garrigou-Lagrange had added that Maritain did not, however, see where some of his "concessions" could logically lead, but "that many current events should increasingly show him the danger of these concessions."[5] On July 26, 1946, Meinvielle published this letter, along with two articles of his own in which he "examines the opinion of the Reverend Father Garrigou-Lagrange that Maritain's views do not coincide with Lamennais'." These led to an exchange of letters between Jacques and Garrigou-Lagrange, letters that Maritain published under the title "On a Form of Caesero-religious Fanaticism" in *Raison et raisons.*[6] When Garrigou-Lagrange was sent a copy of the book by Maritain, along with a copy of *Existence and the Existent*, the old controversy was reignited. Garrigou-Lagrange addressed Maritain as "Eminence," appropriate enough given the latter's ambassadorial status, but a little frosty between old friends. He wrote that he had a quibble about something Maritain had said about the permission of evil, in which he attributed Molina's position to Maritain; and on the Meinvielle matter, the Dominican held his ground. Indeed, he said he had consulted with Michael Browne, the Irish Dominican who was rector of the Angelicum. The theologians agreed that while Maritain did not deserve to be equated with Lamennais, his views were open to criticism. Maritain was no more inclined to concede a point than his friendly Dominican critic. There is no doubt that Garrigou-Lagrange wrote Maritain in the manner of one calling him to order, a teacher correcting a pupil. Maritain, at one point, suggested that his old friend had added loyalty to Franco to the Creed, repeating his view that it was a difference in politics, between the man of the Right that Garrigou-Lagrange was and the man of the Left that he was, and not a difference in theology. Read from the vantage point of the post–Vatican II Church, quarreling about religious liberty seems unreal in the light of *Dignitatis Humanae.*[7] One thing is clear: concepts and language that were once roundly condemned as false have been taken up by the Church. This is nowhere more obvious than in the case of human rights.

3

The Walgreen Lectures gave Maritain the opportunity to have another say on the matters that had so incited his critics. Maritain had been involved in the Universal Declaration of Human Rights issued by the United Nations in 1948; and at the UNESCO meeting in Mexico City, the question had arisen as to how there could be cooperation between societies based on radically different political theories. The prospect of overcoming such differences was bleak and, even if accomplished, such theoretical positions are insufficient. Historically, the conception of human rights would seem to have an intellectual provenance quite opposed to Christian faith. If the human individual is regarded as absolutely autonomous, if, in Rousseau's phrase, he can obey only himself, the Christian understanding of man and his destiny are rejected. In the postwar world, opposed ideologies were entrenched in societies and were backed up with power. How could communists and democrats agree on human rights?

Maritain is quick to agree that their theories are in conflict, but his diplomatic experience had brought home to him the fact that delegates representing the most diverse outlooks could agree on a list of human rights. Their ways of justifying those rights would be radically different, but, for all that, there was the fact of agreement on a practical level. Maritain speaks of human rights in this context as "practical conclusions," meaning that the theoretical justification of them will differ wildly, and yet it is the same rights that are justified. He is not suggesting that there is no true theory that alone justifies human rights. He makes it clear that, for him, the only adequate theoretical justification of human rights is the natural law theory to be found in Saint Thomas Aquinas[8] and of course in many of his predecessors. The eighteenth-century understanding of natural rights was fatally flawed. "Moreover, this philosophy of rights ended up, after Rousseau and Kant, by treating the individual as a god and making all the rights ascribed to him the absolute and unlimited rights of a god."[9] Despite this, Maritain suggests that this theory was, in effect, a degenerate form of a rights theory based on natural law. It "presupposed, no doubt, the long history of natural law evolved in ancient and mediaeval times; but it had its immediate origins in the artificial systematization and rationalist recasting to which this idea has been subjected since Grotius. . . ."[10]

Maritain provides a brilliantly succinct account of natural law and the way in which it grounds the rights of man. This is one account of human rights among others, but it is the true one. When this is coupled with the suggestion that modern talk of rights, modern theoretical justifications, are parasitic on classical natural law and, more importantly, on the influence of the Gospel, we begin to see what Maritain is suggesting. First, on the practical level, agreement can be reached on a list of human rights as long as we don't look into the diverse justifications of them. Second, inadequate theoretical justifications bear the stamp of what they sought to replace: the persistence of the recognition of rights is due to the influence of the Gospel even when it has been overtly rejected. Does this mean that Maritain can reflect on modern views and see them as a way back into a medieval or classical government? Not at all. History cannot be wished away; the sacral civilization of the Middle Ages cannot be reestablished. What Maritain is describing, it emerges, is a transitional period prior to the establishment of what he calls a new Christianity.

Man has two ultimate ends: one temporal and terrestrial, the other eternal and heavenly. The medieval system broke down when the relative autonomy of the terrestrial common good was realized. Modern political theories, preceding and following revolutionary events, have sought to pursue the terrestrial common good in total separation from man's supernatural end. The new society that Maritain intimates is based on a recovery of Christian faith. Far from ushering in a new version of a sacral society, Maritain argues, citing Cardinal Manning, that the religious faith of the majority of the citizens is the best guarantee of tolerance and pluralism. *Man and the State* thus provides a later version of the argument of *Integral Humanism.*

4

The Walgreen Lectures and the book that emerged from them represent Maritain's last major work in political philosophy. His eloquent justification of human rights by appeal to natural law and to what he calls its ontological and gnoseological aspects underscores the difficulty of the task he had set himself. By his own account, a large body of thought would reject his account. His justification of human rights is theoretically satisfying, but he does not expect universal agreement on that level. Where agreement can be had is on lists of rights. Of course a critic might say that what these rights *mean*—not their theoretical justification—varies so widely as to makes such lists equivocal. But Maritain will continue to appeal to practical realizations common to all.[11] But the force of his argument would seem to depend on the plausible suggestion that the eighteenth-century gave us secularized forms of Gospel-inspired truths about human beings. And this, in turn, would seem to be the basis for his hope for a new Christianity to follow on the secularized interval in which we still find ourselves.

It is noteworthy that, when Maritain speaks of the way in which ordinary folk lay hold of the precepts of natural law, he speaks of knowledge by inclination. Maritain's development of this notion animates both his moral and his aesthetic views.

CREATIVE INTUITION

Have you read Art and Scholasticism *by Jacques Maritain?*
—*Flannery O'Connor*

I

From the beginning of the meetings at Meudon, the *Cercles d'études thomistes* had included artists and writers and poets as well as philosophers. But then, Maritain's understanding of the role of Thomas by no means restricted it to the saint's influence on philosophers and theologians. Thomism provided an all-embracing cultural framework. Of course, to a great degree, Thomism in this sense is only implicit in the writings of Thomas. One might be inspired in various ways by Thomas in writing about modern science, but one could scarcely be mulling over what Thomas had to say about quantum physics. One needed first of all to assimilate Thomas's teaching and learn from the way he handled problems and then extend and apply that method into areas necessarily unknown to Thomas. When the Church recommended Thomas as our guide, it was not inviting us to become medievalists. Maritain's reflections on art and poetry are Thomistic in origin but of course go beyond anything Thomas himself wrote.

Written toward the end of World War I, *Art and Scholasticism* was a first sustained effort to show the relevance of Thomas in aesthetics. It is important to realize how original an effort this book represented. It was not so much a contribution to a genre as the creation of a genre. Of course, there were thousands of books on aesthetics, but there was nothing like *Art and Scholasticism*. The closest analogue to it must be sought perhaps in the books inspired by Aristotle's *Poetics*—a work that had not yet been translated into Latin before Thomas died, so he had not read it. If he had, if he had commented on it, Maritain's task would have been considerably easier. But if Thomas had not written on art and poetry, how could his thought be of interest in aesthetics?

It bears repeating that *Art and Scholasticism* begins in a deceptively pedestrian way. Having disarmed the writer by insisting that the Scholastic had no theory of art, Maritain proceeds to examine a series of doctrines that provide a framework for that unwritten treatise. The speculative order must be distinguished from the practical, and it is in the latter that such things as Thomas said about art fall. Making things, like doing things, performing moral actions, involves a thinking that is ordered to those ends. In the speculative use of the mind, thinking is ordered to the perfection of the mind, that is, to truth; but the practical use of the mind is ordered to directing some making or doing. How do these differ? Maritain puts before his reader the distinction between art and prudence that Thomas found in Aristotle, and not the Aristotle of the *Poetics*. Aristotle and Thomas habitually illustrate the meaning of art by considering the making of a pair of shoes or a house. The distinction between art and prudence is developed by Aristotle in the *Nicomachean Ethics* when he is talking of intellectual virtues, that is, the habits that enable the mind easily and infallibly to achieve its ends. Thus, Maritain devotes a chapter to art as an intellectual virtue, a chapter almost as much concerned with prudence as it is with art.

Prudence is an intellectual virtue that intrinsically depends on the moral virtues. Unless one's appetite is well disposed to the good of justice, say, the mind cannot swiftly and surely find the means to be just here and now. If one's heart is elsewhere than in justice, say in injustice, appetite will obscure and eclipse the effort to seek and choose the means to be just. But art does not depend for its excellent exercise on the moral quality of the artist. This contrast between prudence and art, faithfully reported by Maritain and never rejected by him, nonetheless inspired a host of original suggestions that have the look of trying to circumvent the distinction. But that is hardly the major problem Maritain now faces. How is he to extrapolate from texts that talk of art in terms of the carpenter and farmer in order to say things of the poet and painter and novelist?

2

The bridge for Maritain is a discussion of art and beauty. Bringing together asides on the nature of beauty found scattered through the writings of Thomas, Maritain develops a Thomisitc theory of beauty. Beauty, Thomas had written, is that which, when seen, pleases: *id quod visum placet.* Maritain broods over this text and then goes on to another in which Thomas had listed the elements of beauty. "Three things are required for beauty. First of all, integrity or perfection ... then right proportion or consonance. And finally clarity. . . ." It is out of such materials as these that Maritain develops his argument. Of course he was not the first to notice such texts in Aquinas; James Joyce makes use of them in *A Portrait of the Artist as a Young Man.* But Maritain finds in such texts the *rationes seminales* of a Thomistic aesthetic. As the little book progresses, it leaves behind the humble kind of making Aristotle and Thomas analyze when they speak of art. Maritain writes of the rules of art, of its purity, and finally of Christian art. The key concept of the *Poetics*—imitation—comes into play, and in subsequent editions other discussions were annexed and the notes expanded until the objective of the work was brought to full fruition.

Art and Scholasticism was not content to fashion an argument that would be persuasive to philosophers. As the meetings at Meudon and the series of works Maritain edited indicate, he meant to speak to working artists. And he did. The poets and writers of his circle, the painters who became his friends, responded to the vision of art Maritain constructed out of Thomistic materials. There were gaffes, of course, such as Maritain's intrusion into the composition of Bernanos's first novel, an intrusion accepted at the time and resented ever after. But this perhaps imprudent act must not be taken as definitive of Maritain's influence. It would be possible to trace the influence of *Art and Scholasticism* in such writers as Julian Green, Flannery O'Connor, Thomas Merton, Alan Tate, and Caroline Gordon—and doubtless in Robert Lowell as well. Flannery O'Connor found that Maritain liberated her from the notion that, as a writer, she was expressing herself. Of course what and who the artist is influences the outcome. "Maritain says that to produce a work of art requires the 'constant attention of the purified mind,' and the business of the purified mind in this case is to see that those elements of the personality that don't bear on the subject at hand are excluded. Stories don't lie when left to themselves."[12] To the same correspondent, she wrote, "I have sent you *Art and Scholasticism*. It's the book I cut my aesthetic teeth on, though I think that even some of the things he says get soft at times. He is a philosopher and not an artist but he does have great understanding of the nature of art, which he gets from St. Thomas."[13] Well, Maritain would have many other things to say about art. His second great aesthetic work, *Creative Intuition in Art and Poetry*, appeared in 1957.

3

As found in Thomas, "connatural" sometimes simply means proportioned to the nature of something, as when the essence of sensible reality is said to be the connatural object of the human mind. If ideas are formed against the background of sense experience, it is to express the nature of what is sensibly grasped. Another use of the term involves appetite as well as knowledge. The way in which sensible things are known by us differs from the way in which they exist: they exist as individuals, they are grasped universally. In being abstracted from individuating matter, things are made like the immaterial intellect. But if in our knowing, things become like the knower, desire is for things as they exist. Practical knowing is thus seen as an extension of knowing in the usual sort, theoretical knowing—beyond the realm of mere knowing to making or doing. The thing made is singular, actions too are singular. The practical use of intellect is thus drawn by a good beyond mere truth, and the desire for those goods essentially influences practical reason. Consider the implications of this in judgments of what is to be done.

Recall that when Thomas asks whether theology is a wisdom, he notes that wisdom is a matter of judging and, since there are two relevantly different kinds of judging, there are two kinds of wisdom. Take a case: You wonder what temperance demands of you in certain circumstances. You might ask the moral theologian to give you his judgment on the matter. His response will doubtless take the form of an argument, a discursive process that will conclude with what you ought to do. You might have asked someone whom you know to be temperate. Some theologians are temperate, but not all temperate people are theologians. The man you ask is not a theologian. You want him to put himself in your shoes and tell you how things look for one who lives a temperate life. The judgment of the theologian, Thomas calls cognitive, *per modum cognitionis*. The judgment of the virtuous man is not just cognitive, it is *per modum inclinationis*. Now it is this judgment through inclination that is sometimes called a judgment *per modum connaturalitatis*. In Saint Thomas, this judgment is peculiar to the virtue of prudence, which is distinguished from the virtue of art as doing is distinguished from making. While the appetite of the artisan is engaged when he is making, the good in question is the good of the artifact, not the good of the artisan as moral agent. Nonetheless, what Maritain proposes to do is to transfer the notion of connaturality, affective connaturality, to the realm of art. This is a central feature of *Creative Intuition in Art and Poetry*.

4

What enables Maritain to extend connaturality to the aesthetic realm is a distinction he makes at the very outset. "Art and poetry cannot do without one another. But the two words are far from being synonymous. By Art I mean the creative or producing, work-making activity of the human mind. By Poetry I mean, not the particular art which consists in writing verses, but a process both more general and more primary: that intercommunication between the inner being of things and the inner being of the human self which is a kind of divination (as was realized in ancient times: the Latin *vates* was both a poet and a diviner). Poetry, in this sense, is the secret life of each and all of the arts; another name for what Plato called *mousikè*."[14]

The making that is guided by the virtue of art presupposes a knowledge so conjoined to reality and the self that it can be likened to the appetitive harmony of the virtuous person with the good of virtue. That appetitive harmony is what makes possible judgments here and now as to means of achieving the end of virtue. On an analogy with this, Maritain proposes that poetic knowledge, a cognitive/appetitive harmony of self and world is what makes possible the artist's judgments in making. This transition has been prepared for by the analysis of beauty in *Art and Scholasticism*. *Id quod visum placet* was said to suggest both intuitive knowledge and joy. "The beautiful is that which gives joy, not every joy, but the joy of knowing; not the joy proper to the act of knowing, but a joy which goes above and beyond that act because of the object known. If a thing exalts and delights the soul by the very fact that it has been given to its intuition, it is good to apprehend, it is beautiful."[15] But if the beautiful is the object of understanding it also involves the senses insofar as they serve the intelligence. The senses are indispensable for us just because our intelligence is not intuitive in the manner of angelic intelligence. Discursive and abstractive, intelligence depends on sense, which possesses the intuitiveness necessary for the perception of beauty. "Thus man can no doubt enjoy purely intelligible beauty, but the beauty *connatural* to man is that which comes to delight intelligence by means of the senses and their intuition." This occurrence of "connatural" in *Art and Scholasticism* is an adumbration of what will subsequently be developed by Maritain and reach its fruition in *Creative Intuition in Art and Poetry.*

5

In the latter work, Maritain contrasts Indian and Chinese art with western art in terms of the emergence of the self. Oriental art, he says, never says "I." It is thanks to the influence of Christianity that the notions of person and personality are first given to the mind, out of the necessities of pondering the mystery of the Trinity, of three persons in one divine nature. This pondering brought about a new idea of man as well, the inner man.[16] Maritain suggests that a new self-consciousness took place in the artist, "a sudden beholding of the sublimity of the artist's calling and of the new power and ambition afforded to him by science, by anatomical knowledge, mathematics, perspective, and the discovery of three-dimensional representation in painting, which intoxicated with glory the great Italians of the *Rinascimento.*"[17] The external form was to be interpreted, not just copied. Here is the opening to Maritain's characteristic defense of the modern in art, particularly in painting. The primacy of poetry over art is the primacy of artistic subjectivity. Almost predictably, Maritain must speak of poetic knowledge as preconceptual or nonconceptual, yet intellectual.

God's creative knowledge presupposes nothing; it forms and makes its object. If human knowledge is to be called creative, it obviously cannot be so in the divine manner. Unlike God's, human creative knowledge must receive from things in order to take place. For all that, God's creative knowledge is the supreme analog of poetry. "And thus it implies an intellective act which is not formed by things but is, by its own essence, formative and forming. Well, it is too clear that the poet is a poor god. He does not know himself. And his creative insight miserably depends on the external world, and on the infinite heap of forms and beauties already made by men, and on the mass of things that generations have learned, and on the code of signs which is used by his fellow men and which he receives from a language he has not made. Yet, for all that, he is condemned to subdue to his own purpose all those extraneous elements and to manifest his own substance in his creation."[18]

6

At this point, it might be well to hear from the *advocatus diaboli*. A critic might say that Maritain is taking back, when he speaks of poetic knowledge, the criticism he made of Descartes in *The Dream of Descartes*. The Father of Modern Philosophy was said to have given an account of human knowledge that strikingly resembled the account Thomas Aquinas had given of angelic knowledge. The knowing subject had become the source and not the locus of knowledge, and knowledge was treated as something had prior to or independently of experience of the world. To this was opposed the refreshing realism of Saint Thomas, for whom to know was to become one with the object known, with extramental reality. However immaterial and spiritual the *mode* of such knowledge, *what* is first known is reality other than mind. Knowing could only be a reflective object of knowledge insofar as one was knowing something other than knowing. What to make of the champion of that realism and the Maritain who is modeling human knowledge on the divine creative knowledge?

It is just this set of questions that may be taken to guide Maritain in his efforts to give an account of poetic knowledge as creative and intuitive and as being essentially dependent on the subjectivity of the artist. But it is permitted to be surprised at what he says. Speaking of the artist, he writes, "His intuition, the creative intuition, is an obscure grasping of his own Self and of things in a knowledge through union or through connaturality which is born in the spiritual unconscious, and which fructifies only in the work."[19] By distinguishing poetry from art, Maritain has developed a kind of complement, if not rival, of metaphysics.

> Poetry is the heaven of the working reason. Poetry is a divination of the spiritual in the things of sense—which expresses itself in the things of sense, and in a delight of sense. Metaphysics also pursues a spiritual prey, but metaphysics is engaged in an abstract knowledge, while poetry quickens art. Metaphysics snatches at the spiritual in an idea, by the most abstract intellection; poetry reaches it in the flesh, by the very point of the sense sharpened through intelligence. Metaphysics enjoys its possession only in the retreats of the eternal regions, while poetry finds its own at every crossroad of the contingent and the singular. . . . Metaphysics gives chase to essences and definitions, poetry to any flash of existence glittering by the way, and any reflection of an invisible order.[20]

Such passages seem certainly to rank poetry above metaphysics, making up for the deficiencies in the latter. Nor can one ignore the pejorative use of abstraction and the conceptual. But something had happened before this in Maritain's understanding of metaphysics. He had begun to lay great stress on what he called the intuition of being. For this, we must now look again at the earlier work, *Existence and the Existent*.

The Intuition of Being

I

The goal of the philosopher is wisdom, and wisdom consists in knowing, understanding things in terms of their ultimate causes. There are many explanations of events, proximate, middle distant, remote; but ultimately the cause that explains everything is God. After a long trek through the various aspects of natural science—in the course of which he has achieved some intimation of the fact that *to be* is not synonymous with *to be material*, that physical being is not all there is—another science opens up before him. The science of being as being: being not as changeable, being not as quantified, but being as being. This is the subject matter of the ultimate philosophical inquiry, first philosophy, wisdom, metaphysics.

Maritain had written about, as well as engaged in, metaphysics from the beginning of his career. In the *Introduction to Philosophy*, he defines and locates metaphysics in the overall philosophical enterprise. In *The Degrees of Knowledge*, tracking the various inquiries that can lay claim to the title wisdom, he located metaphysics among sciences that are natural, that is, those that do not depend on religious belief or revelation, thus differing from wisdom in the sense of theology or the gift of the Holy Ghost. But a series of lectures he next gave provides the best point of comparison with *Existence and the Ex-*

istent. That work comes about a decade after *A Preface to Metaphysics, Seven Lectures on Being.*

2

Being is the subject of the highest science, and yet being would seem to be grasped in anything we know: what else is there besides being? In speaking of being as first grasped by the mind, that which no mind could fail to know since anything we know is being, Maritain invokes a phrase Cajetan uses to describe *ens primum cognitum:* it is being as concretized in a sensible nature: *ens concretum quidditati sensibili.* What the mind first knows is the nature of sensible realities; that is, we form ideas of the things we have encountered with our senses. It is not that we form an abstract notion of being; being is grasped as horse, bottle, Mama, etc. These things are there, they exist, they are beings. "It is something confiscally contained in this or that particular nature, for example, in the dog, the horse, the pebble, something clothed in this or that object and diversified by it."[21] So how does the being no one can fail to grasp differ from the subject of the ultimate philosophical science, metaphysics? It differs the way "being as being" differs from "being concretized in sensible nature." The former is an "*abstractum,* being, disengaged and isolated, at least so far as being can be taken in abstraction from more particularized objects. It is being disengaged and isolated from the sensible quiddity, being viewed as such and set apart in its pure intelligible values."[22] As a science or wisdom, metaphysics is a virtue, and Maritain likes to speak of the "metaphysical habitus" that is specified by being as being. His use invokes overtones of moral virtue as well as intellectual.[23]

Being "presents two aspects," essence and existence. Essence, what a thing is, is simply apprehended and expressed in a concept, ideally in a definition. There can be a concept of existence; but in the judgment, the second operation of the mind, existence is grasped as exercised; "X is." When being is said to be the object of intellect, the statement should not be understood as restricted to the first operation of the mind. "It is to existence itself that the intellect proceeds when it formulates within itself a judgment corresponding to what a thing is or is not outside the mind."[24] This creates a problem. Nothing is more contingent than existence as we grasp it. Things might so easily not have existed, and when they exist might so easily have existed otherwise than they do; and, alas, they will eventually cease to exist. How can a science—necessary knowledge—bear on such a contingency as existence?

> Therefore, where existence is contingent, simply posited as a fact, as is the case with all created being, it must, because of this defect in its object, be directly oriented only to possible existence. Which does not mean that it is restricted to a realm of pure essences. Its goal is still existence. It considers the essences as capable of actualisation, of being posited outside the mind. This is involved by the fact that the judgment is the perfection of knowledge of the act of intelligence. And this means that philosophy considers essences in so far as they require to issue forth and communicate themselves, to combine or separate in existence. In short, it considers them from the standpoint of the affluence and generosity of being. But this is not all. As the intellect "in a way leaving its proper sphere betakes itself by the instrumentality of the senses to corruptible things in which the universal is realized," so philosophy returns by the instrumentality of the senses to the actual existence of the object of thought which it contemplates.[25]

But this return to sensible existence is not to the object of metaphysics but to its mode of existence.[26] It it just here that Maritain, for the first time, compares Thomism and existentialism, here as he finds it in Kierkegaard. Thomism is an existential philosophy, speculatively, practically, and personally. In the last sense, existential means that one does not only know the truth but also lives it.[27]

And it is here too that Maritain speaks of an "infra-scientific knowledge" that is a matter of common sense. And common sense, he writes, "is, as it were, a rough sketch of metaphysics." The being that is the concern of metaphysics has a meaning for common sense, precisely because there is a commonsense understanding of God. In any case, the path to the grasp of being as being is intuition.

3

There are two sides to the question, two "lights." First, there is the mode of intellectual apprehension, the degree of immateriality of the object. This is the objective light. "At the same time proportionate to this objective light there is a subjective light perfecting the subjective activity of the intellect, by which the intellect itself is proportioned to a given object, fitted to apprehend it."[28] This is the habitus or virtue of metaphysics, and there is a mutual causality between it and the intuition of being. The metaphysical habitus comes to birth at the same time as its proper object is disclosed to it.

Maritain makes clear that he is not using intuition in the Scholastic sense of *intellectus*, which is the grasp of first principles. His use may seem akin to Bergson's, but is not. Maritain's intuition is intellectual, but he likens it to a mystical experience, since it occurs even in nonmetaphysicians. "There is a kind of sudden intuition which a soul may receive of her own existence, or of 'being' embodied in all things, however. It may even happen that to a particular soul this intellectual perception presents the semblance of a mystical grace" (47). He cites again a testimonial first given in *The Degrees of Knowledge:* "I have often experienced in a sudden intuition the reality of my being, the profound first principle which makes me exist outside nonentity. It is a powerful intuition whose violence has sometimes frightened me and which first revealed to me a metaphysical absolute."[29]

There are various paths to the intuition of being, and Maritain mentions three. The Bergsonian experience of duration is one; Heidegger's anguish at the contingency of being is another; and finally there is a moral path, suggested by Gabriel Marcel, in the experience of, say, fidelity. These in themselves are experiences and not yet the intuition of being. They present opportunities to take the decisive step, and if it is not taken we remain in the realm of psychology or ethics. The intuition of which Maritain speaks is confirmed by the rational analyses to be found in sober texts of Thomas Aquinas. Without the intuition of being, such analyses are barren; there must be both. By calling the intuition of being eidetic, Maritain is stressing the intelligible content at the highest degree of immateriality and spirituality. Modern existentialists remain at the level of experience, and it is noteworthy how Maritain describes their metaphysical inadequacy. "It discovers a singular reality or presence actually existing and acting—in any case a reality which the intellect does not grasp by an eidetic visualization in the transparence of an idea or concept. And it discovers it by a kind of affective connaturality."[30]

In *Existence and the Existent*, Maritain returns to the intuition of being and discusses it in a more pronounced separation from so-called existential philosophy. Being is now presented as an amalgam of apprehension and judgment, the grasp of essence as the potential to exist. Quoting Thomas, Maritain tells us that existence is the act of acts, even of forms, and this grounds the primacy of existence in Thomistic metaphysics. This is not to say of course that existence is the subject of metaphysics. When Maritain turns to the existent, to the subject of existence, the formal measure of existence— whatever exists is something or other—he reviews rapidly a host of tenets of Thomistic metaphysics, and the reader is likely to feel overwhelmed. But what no reader can fail to discern is the way in which Maritain, prodded particularly by Kierkegaard, unites after he distinguishes. This little book ends as a kind of précis of the vision of *The Degrees of Knowledge*, terminating in a discussion of philosophy and spirituality. This is the mark of Maritain's thought. He will lead the bewildered reader through almost shorthand discussions of subsistence, act, and potency—the transcendental properties of being—constantly referring to analogy in ways a tyro may find unhelpful, but in the crescendo, the reader will realize that the paths taken all lead finally to a unifying vision of the human task, to become holy.

MORAL PHILOSOPHY

I

Jacques Maritain had never been the kind of philosopher who settles into a single area and becomes expert at that, all but ignoring the other domains of philosophy. From the outset, his writings exhibit an incredible range and it becomes clear that he regards the full scope of philosophy as his responsibility. So he had written early of moral philosophy. Indeed, it will be remembered that one of the points of dispute at the famous Juvisy meeting on Christian philosophy had been Maritain's notion of "moral philosophy adequately considered." For all his admiration for Aristotle, he became convinced that Aristotelian ethics was not practical; it could not guide our lives because it operates with an inadequate notion of the very point of acting at all. Only as subalternated to moral theology, he reasoned, could moral philosophy become adequate.

The book that was the fruit of his teaching at Princeton, *Moral Philosophy*, is in many ways atypical for Maritain. In it he undertakes an account of the history of moral philosophy, beginning with the Greeks and culminating in an account of Kantian moral philosophy. It would be an understatement to say that Maritain is not a fan of Kant, and no mere negation could describe his estimate of Hegel. They, with Marx, represent the great delusion of modern moral philosophy. The book ends with a lengthy discussion of the crisis in moral philosophy and the chances of reorientation.

But if he was no stranger to moral philosophy, Maritain felt a little out of his depth when he began at Princeton. Given the practical nature of his recent life and the political and social themes of his writing, both pre- and post-war, this seems unnecessary diffidence. Still, there is a discussion in his letter to Charles Journet that catches the eye.

2

About the time that he was beginning to teach moral philosophy at Princeton, Maritain exchanged some letters with Charles Journet in which he proposes a surprising argument. The argument is prompted by the situation in which he finds himself where everyone, he tells Journet, is talking about birth control.

He first sets down the premise that sexual intercourse cannot frustrate natural ends and be morally legitimate, but (1) nevertheless it is not required that one have the *intention of procreating* (the wife might have had an operation rendering her sterile or she may be beyond childbearing age). (2) What is more, the *intention not to procreate* can be licitly present, as in the rhythm method, which the Church does not condemn. He concludes, "Therefore it is not the intention of the agent, the intention not to procreate, that renders birth control sinful. So what is it? It must be an alteration introduced into the act itself which turns it from its finality which is the *finis operis*, the end of the act, and not the *finis operantis*, the end of the agent." This latter is what he was referring to in the remarks about intention. The sin of Onan illustrates the frustration of the act.

With that as background, Maritain speculates. What if some day science invented a product, some pill you could swallow or some injection, that would make the woman sterile for a given period? Would spouses who used such a product in order not to procreate, when reason judges that this would not be wise, be guilty of a moral fault? He answers No! Why? "Their reason actively intervenes there where with the Ogino (rhythm) method it calculates only to take advantage of what nature herself does: it is impossible to see of what they would be guilty."[31] In short, there is a moral equivalence between marital acts that take place during a natural period of infertility and those that take place during a medically induced temporary infertility.

This is of course a bad argument since it deflects attention from the act of inducing infertility to acts performed once infertility has been induced. Journet's initial reaction to this letter of September 26, 1948, is favorable. But he mentions that all moralists would object that, if an injection renders a person sterile, this is mutilation and illicit. Journet quotes the famous moralist Merkelbach on the matter. He follows with citations from another, Catherein. But he adds that in putting the matter of such injections to his bishop, he was told that they might be legitimate. On the same day, October 6, Journet sends a long list of relevant biblical passages. That was on October 6. On October 21, he writes again, citing the encyclical *Casti Connubii* against seeking technical means to overcome the flesh. It is not until November 15 that Jacques replies, saying he is relieved that Journet does not think him a heretic for what he proposed. He knows that *Casti Connubii* sounds a different note. "But precisely if I am right (if *we* are right!) this question would provide one of those tragic examples where the Church defends a truth while blocking it with ways of thinking human experience has surpassed." Apparently unaffected by the points Journet has raised, Maritain writes, "The day the Church approves the future techniques of which we speak, it will have changed its doctrine in nothing, but the souls one has mobilized against any idea *whatsoever* of such a technique and on behalf of procreation uncontrolled by reason will understand nothing."[32]

Journet is now granted coauthorship of the suggestion, and none of the points he has made seem to have gotten through to Maritain. Of course Journet's arguments are all from authority; he never addresses as such the flaw in Maritain's proposal. On December 2, he again gently tells Maritain what moralists would make of his suggestion. Think of what is said about tubal ligation. But Journet adds that he himself has never been able to see an *essential* difference between inducing sterility and acting during naturally sterile periods; and he mentions a Zurich embryologist who, on the basis of Aristotle's and Thomas's theory of animation, argued for early-term abortion.

All in all, an inauspicious beginning for the Princeton Professor of Moral Philosophy. Of course, it would be absurd on the basis of these private exchanges between old friends to see an anticipation of the theological dissent that followed on the appearance of *Humanae Vitae* twenty years later. Maritain had made quite clear his loyalty to the Magisterium at the time of the condemnation of Action Française, and one can predict what his response to Paul VI's encyclical would have been: total acceptance. His letters to Journet of that period have still not been made public, but no reader of

The Peasant of the Garonne could imagine Jacques Maritain questioning, either privately or publicly, such a document as *Humanae Vitae.*

3

The vast interpretative survey of moral philosophy that grew into a huge book—in size second only to *The Degrees of Knowledge*—was regarded by Maritain, if only in retrospect, as valedictory. "It was at a time of life when the soul turns toward higher regions, a way for me to pay my respects to, and thus take leave of, the philosophers—in particular the modern philosophers, whose historical work it was once claimed I purely and simply rejected."[33] But the satisfaction this gave him, he characterizes as subjective. The real point of the book is to see in the historical unfolding of moral philosophy a melange of error and acquired truth. "And many essential truths are at the same stroke gathered in along the way, in a manner that is non-systematic but perhaps more stimulating for the mind, because they emerge from the long reflection that is pursued from age to age, with its advances and failures, and from the successive occasions that it offers for discussion. I think that in a general way such a procedure, turning to account, under a resolutely critical eye, a heritage of time-honored labors and disputes, could be carried out with advantage by the disciples of the *philosophia perennis* in the most varied fields."[34]

Given the role that Aristotle plays in the philosophy of Saint Thomas and the fact that Maritain is a quintessential Thomist, the treatment of Aristotle can, for our purposes, serve as a sufficient sounding in the vast ocean of this work. Any student of Aristotle must be impressed by the succinct and thorough presentation of Aristotelian moral philosophy. How can this moral philosophy be related to that of Aquinas? In an appendix to his first book, *Bergsonian Philosophy*, Maritain had offered a view on the nature of Thomas's commentaries on Aristotle and the nature of the Aristotelianism of Saint Thomas. In *Science and Wisdom*, he had put forward his notion of moral philosophy adequately considered. Here he returns to the inadequacy, as he sees it, of the notion of happiness Aristotle proposes and the definitive role it plays in his moral philosophy. Maritain finds in this a trace of utilitarianism.

All this amounts to saying that the equilibrium sought by Aristotle was not decisively attained. I fear, moreover, that a kind of vicious circle is implied in his procedure: the fact that virtue appears herein as essentially a *means* toward the good and beautiful life, the blessed life; and yet virtue is also an *integral part* of that blessed life, since without virtue there is no good and beautiful life—the means to the end (virtue) thus enters into the very notion and constitution of the end to which it is directed.[35]

Assuming that this is an insoluble problem for Aristotle, Maritain alludes to the ultimate and absolute end and beatitude of which Christianity speaks. Of course, Maritain is not suggesting that it was a philosophical flaw on Aristotle's part not to have anticipated Christianity and the supernatural order. Happiness for Aristotle is, so to speak, the subjective side of the Ultimate End—our pursuit and attainment of the end. But it is the terrestrial nature of human happiness in Aristotle, the good achievable by action in this life, that leads Maritain to object that it does not involve a reference to a transcendent common good. And this is a philosophical lack.

> But what Aristotle might have known, and did not, is the fact that in the natural order itself, the "monastic," as far as it considers the purely and simply final end of human life, identifies itself with a supra-political ethics. For even in the purely natural order (where there is no question of beatific vision) it is not the earthly city but God Who is the absolute end of man as of the whole universe. And even in the purely natural order there is for human persons, members of the city, a common good which is superior to that of the city, that is the common good of minds, the supra-temporal order of goods, of truths and of intangible laws which reveal themselves to the intellect–and which human life could not do without. The common good of the earthly city itself demands that the city recognize this supra-political common good, and that the persons who are members of the city direct themselves to it, thus transcending the political order of the city by what is eternal in man and in the things to which he is attached. One might say that it took the fracas of revelation and the scandal of grace coming to complete nature to make philosophy see these supreme data of the natural order, which it had been looking at all along, without realizing it.[36]

And so Maritain returns to the theme of Christian philosophy. It is not necessary to accept every jot and tittle of what he says about Aristotelian ethics—some would argue, for example, that contemplation in Aristotle is precisely turned to what transcends the city, however much the philosopher remains a citizen[37]—in order to see that the transcendent common good can, in its way, belong to a philosophical account. If it were indeed absent from Aristotle, that would be a philosophical flaw.

All in all, *Moral Philosophy* is a most impressive tour of the history of moral philosophy that is at once a narration and an appraisal. And it culminates in what could be taken as Maritain's farewell to philosophy. From now on, the center of gravity of his thinking becomes theological.

LITURGY AND CONTEMPLATION

Contemplata tradere.

The couple who had written *De la vie d'oraison* thirty-five years before wrote a complementary little work a year or so before the death of Raïssa on the subject of the liturgy. Written for the American review *Spiritual Life*, it was composed in French and appeared in Paris in 1959 with a preface by Charles Journet. Written on the eve of the Council, it adumbrated many of the points that would be made by Vatican II and was inspired by Pius XII's encyclical on liturgy, *Mediator Dei* (1947). Moreover, it paid explicit tribute to Dom Virgil Michel and the liturgical movement that emanated from St. John's Benedictine Abbey in Minnesota. The ideal is for liturgy to proceed from silence and love and to be achieved in silence and love. The many liturgical abuses, in practice and in theory, that have followed on Vatican II can claim no support from the Council. Jacques lived long enough to see a bit of that; and, of course, in *The Peasant of the Garonne*, he would write one of the most incisive and prescient analyses of what came to be called "the false spirit of Vatican II." More of that anon. For the nonce, let us read *Liturgy and Contemplation* as a powerful statement in old age of what had been the guiding hope of their lives.

The little book has three parts: the first devoted to defining liturgy, the second to contemplation, and a third that addresses the supposed opposition between the Church's liturgy and the Church's contemplation. *Obscurus fio dum brevis esse laboro,* Horace lamented: brevity is the foe of clarity. Never was this thought more decisively contradicted than by this short book. Journet's preface is equally brief and pointed. He had the inspiration to end with this passage from *The Primacy of the Spiritual.*

> Contemplation alone discovers the prize of charity. Without it one knows only by hearsay, with it one knows by experience. By love and in love, it makes us realize that God is love. Then a man allows God to do what he will with him, allows it out of love. Whatever lacks the flavor of love has no savor for him. Because of this love which consummates our life, only contemplation makes the universal real for us, makes the soul Catholic in spirit and in truth.

In *Moral Philosophy,* Maritain had made the point that, with Christianity, the inner or spiritual dimension of action takes primacy and is the soul of the external action. This inwardness is an openness to, not a turning away from, the real. Does the public worship of the Church draw us away from contemplation? It would be absurd to sacrifice contemplation to the liturgy or vice versa. Pius XII has stressed that there is neither opposition nor contradiction between the ascetic life and liturgical piety. Liturgy calls us to contemplation. As the worship of the Church—Christ's worshiping the Father as head of the Mystical Body—the emphasis in the New Law is on inwardness; it is the internal and invisible reality that is of greater importance. The Church's worship is external, of course—centrally the Mass and other liturgical activities like the Divine Office—but such acts must be offered in faith, hope, and charity. "One cannot worthily honor God if the soul is not tending to perfection," wrote Pius XII. To whatever degree, worshipers are called to a life of charity. "We do not mean that those who participate in the liturgical life of the Church must all be to some degree contemplatives and to have come under the sway of the gifts of the Holy Spirit. The indifferent, ignorant, negligent and weak are called to participate in the liturgy, but the aim is to draw, incite and instruct them in the direction of a participation in spirit and truth." For confirmation, the Maritains refer to Saint Gertrude but also to the Abbess of Solesmes's book *Prayer and the Spiritual Life.*

The liturgical cycle is based on the life of Christ, the mysteries of his abasement, redemption, and triumph. What is more, it is Christ himself who continues in the Church his "career of immense mercy." It would be wrong to think that participating in the liturgy is communal whereas contemplation is private and individual. To take part in the liturgy is to become part of the Church worshiping; to contemplate is to become part of the Church contemplating. In both cases, the individual person acts as part of the Mystical Body of Christ, and this is so even when the contemplative lives a hermetic life, far from the madding crowd. As a contemplative he participates in the contemplative life of the Church.

A further comparison of liturgy and contemplation is drawn from the fact that the liturgy—worship—is an act of religion, a moral virtue according to Thomas Aquinas, that attends to things other than God in order to relate them to God. Contemplation, on the other hand, is the life of the three theological virtues and the gifts of the Holy Spirit. Religion is ordered to the further end of the theological virtues and the gifts. What the liturgy "asks of the soul, and to which it incites, the liturgy of itself does not suffice to give. There is need of a personal ascetic effort, the personal practice of mental prayer, aspiration to personal union with God and personal docility to the Gifts of the Holy Spirit."[38]

Lest it may have escaped us, the Maritains make clear that it is infused contemplation they are speaking of. Contemplation is the goal and telos of philosophy, according to Aristotle, and its object is the divine. Contemplation in the Christian dispensation depends essentially on grace, on the theological virtues and the gifts. And what is it? "Contemplation is a silent prayer which comes about in recollection in the secret of the heart and is directly ordered to union with God."[39] Some souls that have made this ascent to God have received the further gift to write about it. Saint Teresa of Avila and Saint John of the Cross are cited, the latter writing both verse and prose about the stages of the spiritual life. Such contemplation is not an achievement; it is a gift. One can remove impediments to it, but either it is given or it is not, fueled by faith, hope, charity, and the gifts. Lallemant, a seventeenth-century spiritual writer, says that contemplation is the purest and most perfect instance of charity. Love is its beginning, its exercise, and its term.

There are different schools of spirituality, but the Maritains are not now concerned with their differences. Rather, it is the question as to whether or not all Christians are called to contemplation that interests them. Following Saint Bonaventure and Saint Thomas Aquinas, they hold that all Christians are so called, not necessarily in a proximate but at least in a remote manner. The reason for this is that the mystical life is the normal development of the grace of the theological virtues and gifts.[40] What are the signs that one has a proximate vocation to the mystical life? Tauler gives three: meditation becomes impracticable; the soul has no desire to fix the imagination on any interior or exterior object; the soul is content to be with God, fixing its loving attention on Him.

Contemplation may take typical or disguised forms, the latter when a person is in the active life. "Perhaps they will only be capable of reciting the rosary and mental prayer gives them a headache or puts them to sleep. Mysterious contemplation will not be in their conscious prayer, but perhaps rather in the way they regard the poor and suffering."[41] Prayer of the heart is described as "unconscious" because it takes place without reflection and can be continual in one's life. They quote Victorino Osende.

> One who practices unconscious prayer in all its fullness, and who thus attains to the state of continual prayer knows that his understanding is almost continually recollected in God and divine things, for his spirit draws him irresistibly there where his treasure is. That is why John of the Cross says, "In one who is pure, all things, high or humble . . . all the activities of sense and of the faculties are directed toward divine contemplation. Such a man . . . finds in everything a knowledge of God that is joyful, savory, chaste, pure, spiritual, light and loving."[42]

The dominant note of the spiritual life is the call to perfection. "Be perfect even as your heavenly Father is perfect." And perfection, Thomas Aquinas tells us, consists essentially in charity. "He who abides in love, abides in God, and God in him." Love of God and love of neighbor, the two laws of the New Covenant, pertain to perfection. The two laws of love are without measure. "The measure of the love of God," Saint Bernard writes, "is to be without measure." Christ's life shows us the path to such perfection, advancing toward God and the beatific vision by way of faith, hope, and love. Perfection thus is a way of life, ever increasing. To have charity is already to be on this path. The Maritains quote Saint Thomas. "Just as what falls under the precept can be accomplished in a variety of ways, one cannot sin against the precept by this alone that one does not accomplish it in the best way; it suffices for its not being transgressed that it be accomplished in one way or another."[43] This entails the exclusion of everything that impedes the movement of love toward God, not just mortal sin but whatever impedes the soul's desire to be carried entirely toward God. Contemplation is concerned directly and immediately with the love of God himself. "What else can we conclude from this if not that the precept of perfection as it were protects and sanctions the desire for contemplation? There is no true contemplation without progress toward perfection; on the other hand, there is nothing that better hastens the steps toward perfection and the accomplishment in us of the desire for perfection than contemplation."[44]

Is Christian perfection identical with the higher infused contemplation? The answer, the Maritains suggest, is simple. One never finds infused contemplation without perfection but one finds perfection without infused contemplation. For all that, in order to receive infused contemplation the soul must strive for Christian perfection; but this is to be on the way to infused contemplation, and one must conclude that such infused contemplation is to one degree or another the normal path of sanctity.

"Saint Thomas teaches that the gifts of the Holy Spirit are necessary for salvation because we are too weak of ourselves always to use as we ought even the theological virtues and the infused moral virtues."[45] The reference is to the question in which Thomas gives a schematic account of the gifts, *Summa theologiae*, IaIIae, q. 68. The acquired moral virtues are insufficient, of course, to direct us to our true and supernatural end. For this reason, there are infused moral virtues given by God so that we might achieve the beatific vision. How do the gifts differ from the virtues? Well, first of all, what are the gifts and what basis is there to speak of them at all? There are seven gifts, something taught by Scripture, Isaiah 11:2–3. "And the spirit of the Lord shall rest upon him: the spirit of wisdom and of understanding, the spirit of counsel and of fortitude, the spirit of knowledge and of godliness. And he shall be filled with the spirit of the fear of the Lord. He shall not judge according to the sight of the eyes, nor reprove according to the hearing of the ears." It is by means of the gifts that one crosses the threshold into infused contemplation.

The second part of this little book concludes by invoking a veritable litany of saints to corroborate what has been said. Seeking perfection is essentially linked to contemplation and since all are called to be perfect as their heavenly Father is perfect, all are called to contemplation. This can take many forms, masked in the active life, obvious in the contemplative life. A florilegium of texts from the saints makes clear that contemplation is the normal path for the Christian, the mystical life a universal call.

By way of summary, let us say that the principle of contemplation is the constant seeking after the greater and greater perfection of the soul, and that perfection consists essentially in charity; and that it is also on the love of God that contemplation lives. The most pure desire of God is therefore essential to it. The great contemplatives of all the ages, those of this reflex age as well as of the ages before it, desire God alone.[46]

Having put before the reader the ideal of Christian life, our authors consider certain false ideas that turn people away from contemplation. Some pit the liturgy, the public prayer of the Church, against contemplation, as if an either/or were involved. Only ignorance of what contemplation is as well as what the liturgy is can explain such a view. It manifests itself in a disdain for solitary prayer. The liturgy is said to move us spontaneously toward God, whereas mystical union is spoken of in terms of formulas and techniques. But ascetic and mystical knowledge aim at removing obstacles to the operation of the gifts of grace within us. Contemplation, especially infused contemplation, is not achieved by formula and technique. The beginner is struck by talk of technique when he begins to read the great mystics, the passage from the purgative to the unitive way. But it is the teaching of the Church and the consensus of the saints that there is no method, procedure, or rule by which mystical contemplation is acquired or which leads to it. All we can do is dispose ourselves to receive the gift it may please God to grant us.[47]

It is sometimes objected to contemplation that all its constitutive practices turn us in upon ourselves. Under the pretense of seeking mystical union, one abandons himself to introspection and a psychological fixation on one's own inner states. It is subjective. By contrast, liturgical spirituality is objective and disinterested, calling us and all creation to the praise of God. There is, of course, a constant danger of psychological fixation on oneself, and the masters of the ascetic and mystical life are the first to warn against it. "It is absurd to reproach mental prayer and interior recollection for the faults of a counterfeit. Given that infused contemplation only exists by the love of God sovereignly loved, and for this love, it is pure nonsense to accuse of a sort of transcendant egoism those to whom in reality it gives one supreme desire: *cupio dissolvi et esse cum Christo: I want to be dissolved and be in Christ.*"[48] To seek one's perfection does not imply an egoistic seeking of the self. It is for the sake of God's love, not for himself that the Christian seeks to become perfect. Only by vanquishing oneself and purging whatever in one impedes charity can one advance in the love of God.

Finally, there are those who say that Teresa of Avila and John of the Cross were the saints of the "reflex age" and doubtless wrote as they did because of the historical epoch that was theirs. However important they were for that past age, they are not what our age needs. We have already suffered too much from individual introspectiveness. Our need is for the social and communitarian.

This is to forget that the substance of spiritual life does not relate to time or history but to supratemporal truths. It is the same essential doctrine we find in John of the Cross that we find in the thirteenth century and in the Fathers. They all speak of the primacy of contemplation. "By what strange blindness is misunderstood the witness given by the saints and great spiritual writers all through the Christian centuries to that same experience of the depths of God whose states and degrees Saint Teresa and Saint John of the Cross have only described in a more analytic and more explicit fashion?"[49] We find in them and in Saint Francis de Sales more explicit and reflective consciousness of what takes place in the interior of the soul that has entered onto the contemplative way and has received a special gift of God to enlighten the entire Church. We owe an incomparable gratitude to them, not a dismissal, however courteously made. Of course, our time has different needs from theirs, but these do not consist in giving primacy to the social and communitarian. What our age requires is an understanding of the great masters of the mystical life.

The liturgy is essentially an aspiration beyond every natural communitarian fact. To divorce the liturgy from its orientation to contemplation is to rob it of its nature. The point of the liturgy is charity. We belong to a supernatural society, the principle of whose life is the blood of Christ and the gifts of the Holy Spirit. Why else are leaders of the liturgical renewal fervent defenders of the mystical life and contemplation?

The dignity of silence is opposed to the pseudoliturgical spirit. In some parishes, one is assailed by noise when he enters the church. Paradoxically, the "dialogue Mass," where the whole congregation responds to the celebrant along with the altar boys, is a powerful inducement to the inner life. Likewise, while the solemn high Mass is the most fulsome celebration of the Holy Sacrifice, "it would be foolish to pretend to condemn on that account low Masses—those low Masses said at dawn where in silence there descends upon the soul, with an unequaled sweetness, the rosary of feasts and the commemorations of each day."[50]

This final remark evokes the image of Maritain leaving his house on Linden Lane and going up to Nassau Street and St. Paul's, where each morning he attended Mass. Daily attendance at Mass, immersion in the liturgy, had characterized the lives of the "little flock" from the beginning. In this brief but profound little work that appeared toward the end of the

"Princeton period," we can detect behind the seemingly impersonal discussion of contemplation and the liturgy the lifelong quest of these godchildren of Léon Bloy. Soon after, Vera would be dead, and a year later, Raïssa, leaving Jacques the sole survivor. He would take with him into the final period of his life all the resources recalled in *Liturgy and Contemplation*. Such a book is not written out of the knowledge gained from books. The Maritains became increasingly well-versed in the great spiritual writers, and in their beloved Saint Teresa of Avila and Saint John of the Cross. But it could only have been from their own experience, as well, that they wrote such a book. *Amor transit in conditionem objecti.*

Compline

(1960–1973)

Chronology

1961   January. Trip to United States.
       March. Settles in Toulouse with the Petit Frères de Jésus.
       Grand prize for literature of the French Academy.
       Autumn. Visits United States.

1962   Private edition of Raïssa's journal.
       Cercle d'études Jacques et Raïssa Maritain established at Kolbsheim.
       Opening of Vatican II.

1963   June. Death of John XXIII, election of Paul VI.
       September. *Journal de Raïssa.*
       God and the Permission of Evil.

1965   Charles Journet created cardinal.
       February. *Carnet de notes.*
       September. Visits Paul VI at Castel Gandolfo.
       November. *Le mystère d'Israel.*
       December 8. Close of Vatican II. The pope presents Jacques with a
       message to intellectuals.

1966   April 21. Speech to UNESCO on the spiritual conditions of pro-
       gress and peace.
       Autumn. Last visit to United States.
       November 3. *The Peasant of the Garonne.* Touches off a controversy that
       lasts months.

1967   May. *On the Grace and Humanity of Jesus.*

1968   March 11. Last public lecture, at Dax, on Léon Bloy.

1970   Autumn. *On the Church of Christ.*
       October 15. Dons the habit of the Petit Frères de Jésus.

1971   Makes the vows of religion.
       Canticle of Canticles.

1973   April 28. Jacques Maritain dies at Toulouse.
       May 2. Burial at Kolbsheim with Raïssa.
       September. *Approches sans entraves.*

Custodi nos, Domine, ut pupillam oculi . . .

Jacques became professor emeritus at Princeton in 1952, but "the little flock" stayed on in the house on Linden Lane. It was there, in March 1954, that Jacques suffered a heart attack. Although Raïssa had been sickly and valetudinarian throughout their marriage, Jacques was the first to become seriously ill. But it was the sturdy and unflappable Vera who was struck next. She had a heart attack in 1956 and soon was diagnosed as having breast cancer. With treatment and surgery she lived on, dying on the last day of 1959. Jacques and Raïssa were in Paris in the summer of 1960 when Raïssa suffered a cerebral thrombosis. It had fallen to Jacques to tend Vera, and get her back and forth to doctors. Now he became Raïssa's nurse. But the ordeal was not prolonged. Raïssa, half his soul, departed this life on November 4, 1960. Jacques was on his own in the final chapter of his life. He was, he said, preparing to die.

THE JOURNALS

It was after his heart attack that Jacques formed the idea of writing his memoirs. This work was interrupted by the illnesses of the three, and *Carnet de notes* was not published until 1965. The opening chapters were written in 1954 and the rest later. In an introductory note to the *Carnet*, he tells us that it was in 1961, while walking in the garden at Kolbsheim, that he prayed for strength to read and transcribe the journals of Raïssa. The following year, a small private edition of Raïssa's journal was published and sent to selected friends. In 1963, an expanded version was published, with a preface by Father René Voillaume, spiritual head of the Little Brothers of Jesus. Jacques himself provides a precious *avertissement* to the book, dated in Toulouse. The two journals supplement the account of their lives Raïssa had given in the memoirs she had written in New York during World War II. Etienne Gilson had suggested the idea to her, and she responded with two books that have inspired many.

Julie Kernan tells us that the diaries and papers that make up Raïssa's Journal came to Jacques as an unexpected gift. They had been entrusted to Antoinette Grunelius and one day at her chateau near Kolbsheim, she turned them over to Jacques. On several large envelopes, Raïssa had written, "To keep, perhaps, for Jacques to look over." Early in their marriage, Jacques had toyed with the idea of writing his wife's biography. The diaries and papers brought back memories of their life together, but beyond the pleasures of nostalgia was the sense that Raïssa's story of her soul could be of help to others. His tendency increasingly was to efface himself before her memory, elevating her to the status of the principal member of the "little flock." To Thomas Merton he wrote, "You understand that I live now only for her, and by her. During these last years she has spoken to me at length from the other world."[1] Although Kernan writes that the recipients of the privately printed version urged Jacques to make it known to a wider public, some advised against publication. Jacques had written in his presentation of the journal of the vow he and Raïssa had taken to live as brother and sister. He accepted this "human prudence" as right, since the revelation might be misunderstood or give scandal and Raïssa's message not get through. Thomas Merton counseled against publication, and suggested that the book be available only to those who were as madly in love as she. Never one to take advice that did not coincide with his intentions, Jacques replied that what Merton had written was precisely an argument for publication. He described the effect he expected the journal to have on dispersed anonymous souls who, without such encouragement, might perish. He would publish the journal because to do so was "the kind of folly we practiced all our lives and without which we would have done nothing. The decision to publish would count as our last battle."[2] His soul had become more than half hers.[3]

Her husband's high regard for Raïssa and the fact that he speaks of her in the same breath as Saint John of the Cross and Thérèse of Lisieux might seem pardonable pious exaggeration. But Father René Voillaume of the Little Brothers of Jesus, in his introduction, speaks glowingly of the journal, himself suggesting a link between Raïssa's spiritual experience and that of Thérèse of Lisieux and Brother Charles of Jesus, the founder of the Little Brothers. Believing as he did in his wife's mystical experience, Jacques could well rank it above his intellectual work.

And what of himself? There is nothing in his *Note Book* remotely comparable to the fervent entries in Raïssa's diaries, which record the ups and downs of her inner life. He speaks of Vera as well as Raïssa as having reached the heights of contemplation. It is difficult to believe that the third member of the trio had not experienced what he recognized in others and wrote about so searchingly. In his case, his vocation as a philosopher is sustained by the prayer life to which he had vowed himself when the Thomistic Circles were formed. His suggestion that it was Raïssa's prayer that accounted for whatever is good in his philosophical work perhaps tells us indirectly that his own prayer too provided the grace and inspiration for his long lifetime work.

　　Raïssa's memoirs, her journal, and Jacques's *Note Book* put us in contact with the person Jacques Maritain was and the spiritual ambience that sustained and inspired his intellectual work.

Peasant of the Garonne

The Catholic Church is the only thing which spares man the degrading slavery of being a child of his times.

—*G. K. Chesterton*

When Pope John XXIII announced that he was convening an ecumenical council he surprised everyone. Historically, councils have disruptive effects, largely because they are called to settle some crisis in the Church and state their judgments in terms of *anathema sit*. But John XXIII said that there were no doctrinal problems facing the Church; what he had in mind was looking for ways to evangelize better, to find more effective ways of propagating the Good News. He called it *aggiornamento*. The first of four sessions began in 1962, and the council closed on December 8, 1965. Paul VI had been elected when John died after the first session. Already there were signs that, whatever the pope's aim in convening Vatican II, it had unleashed a movement to define the council in ways that had little to do with what was taking place in St. Peter's. Hundreds of interested parties gathered in Rome, interpreting what was taking place for the secular press. Among those often heard were the *periti*, or experts, who had been brought by their bishops to advise them. It soon became clear that there were those who saw in the council an opportunity to effect a radical revolution in the Church.

In Toulouse, in the valley of the Garonne, an aging Jacques Maritain watched warily what was going on. When he decided to speak out it was in a book that was the most controversial he had ever published, *The Peasant of the Garonne.* The title suggests a plain-speaker or, more negatively, one who puts his foot in his mouth. Maritain is alerting the reader to the fact that he intends to speak with uncharacteristic, even acerbic, frankness.

From the time of *The Letter on Independence*, Maritain had meditated on the Right/Left opposition, saying at the time that, while he was by natural disposition of the Left, he considered himself to be neither Left nor Right. What claims his attention now is the way in which this essentially political opposition has been introduced into religious discussions. Was the council Right or Left? Did the council jettison some truths and replace them with others? The attitude he opposes, Maritain describes quite simply as neo-modernism. It has been said that the errors condemned by Pope St. Pius X had continued in a suppressed form for decades, only to emerge at the time of the council as if modernism were vindicated by the call for *aggiornamento* and the opening of windows to the world.

The several relevant senses of "world" provide a recurrent theme of the book. On the one hand, the world, God's creation, is good. On the other hand, from a religious or mystical perspective, the world may either accept Christianity and be saved or oppose it and become inimical. It is in this last sense that the saints advised contempt of the world. Obviously, this does not mean contempt of creation, nor of the world as what Christ came to save. The worldliness, the secularism Maritain condemns involves what he calls a "kneeling to the world," as if the Church should be guided by secular values. He suggests that it is likely the case that what we are seeing is a necessary first phase, where the message of the council is distorted and falsified and only with time will its true import be felt. We can celebrate the council's ringing assertion of human freedom and of religious liberty, its condemnation of anti-Semitism, and its affirmation of the role of the laity. Indeed, it is only by means of the true spirit of the council that the false spirit can be described and opposed.

Maritain began this book during the month the council ended and worked on it throughout the spring of 1965. Reading the book now we can fail to appreciate how prophetic it was. Before anyone else, Maritain saw what was happening in the wake of the council. There is no question, of course, of his rejecting or questioning any of the sixteen documents that make up the conciliar teaching. But he saw—better, he recognized, having seen it before—the spirit animating those who were trying to turn the council to their own ends. The remedy is to be had in the true spirit, two aspects of which we can emphasize here. As a philosopher, Maritain was appalled by the epistemological relativism that was gaining ground. And, as a contemplative, he opposed a false activism and busyness.

During the years when the council was meeting, Maritain's apprehension grew. Julie Kernan writes of a meeting with Jacques on October 3, 1963, when they discussed a number of subjects. "Among them was his feeling that Catholic philosophers were turning away from the systematic Thomism that he taught, and that even among Thomists were appearing trends with which he could not agree in substance. As for the Church, he placed great hope in the renewal of spiritual life that should be brought about by the Second Vatican Council. . . ."[4] These two were among the most prominent subjects treated in *The Peasant of the Garonne.*

Maritain had been a foe of idealism all his philosophical life. A good part of his critique of Descartes had aimed at the Father of Modern Philosophy's making problematic our grasp of external reality. The rise of epistemology, the *soi-disant* problem of knowledge, is at the center of the modern philosophy Maritain rejected. In one form or another, in thinker following thinker, there were variations on the suggestion that we first know our ideas or knowing—later language—and next decide whether or not they are ideas of something outside the mind. In *The Peasant* this theme is struck early, with a reference to "epistemological time worship," having to do largely with the assumption that things that are true at one time cease to be true and are replaced by other, even contradictory truths. Of course "I am seated" can be true at eight o'clock and false at eight-thirty, but truths of the faith are not contingent truths in this way.

Man is made to know the truth; his intellect is a capacity to know the things that are. The first thing that we know is extramental reality and next, by reflection, we can think about thinking. Realism is thus diametrically opposed to Cartesianism and its many imitators. "*Unless one loves the truth, one is not a man.* And to love the truth is to love it above everything, because we know that Truth is God Himself."[5] We know God is truth right from the outset on the basis of faith—I am the way, the truth, and the life—but philosophically we move from truths about the world to the truth that God exists. The truths we accept on faith invite us to intellectual reflection, a reflection called theology; but theology presupposes philosophy. "In short, faith itself entails and requires a theology and a philosophy."[6] Maritain is speaking as a Thomist, but the truths he utters are not peculiar to a school. Of course theology has gone down different paths under the banner of *aggiornamento*, and Maritain refers to the book of Father Marc Oraison—he cannot forbear commenting sardonically on this surname, which means prayer—on the human mystery of sexuality. One of the most striking spectacles of postconciliar theology would be rhapsodizing about sexuality and the treatment of moral virtue as repressive and unhealthy. Here is a clear case of "kneeling to the world," accepting the neo-pagan pleasure principle. The result would be a distortion of human sexuality, of the family, and the acceptance of contraception and abortion. One can see in this how wrong it would be to interpret the exchange with Journet mentioned above as putting Maritain among those he criticizes here.

Ideas have consequences, in the famous phrase of Richard Weaver. Bad philosophy not only distorts our grasp of the world, it will have a deleterious effect on the faith. This is why the Church must interest itself in philosophy as well as theology—as most recently in John Paul II's *Fides et Ratio*.

But isn't there a plurality of philosophies? Must everyone be a Thomist? That there are many philosophies is not something *de iure*, Maritain writes, but merely *de facto*. But there are conditions for something being a philosophy worth taking into account. "But we must quickly remove all risk of misunderstanding. What do the words 'a *true* philosophy' or 'a *true* theology' mean? They signify that since its principles are true, and ordered in a manner which conforms to the real, such a (possible) philosophy or such a (possible) theology is thus equipped to advance from age to age (if those who profess it are not too lazy or complacent) toward a greater measure of truth."[7]

And now the author of *Antimoderne* is heard once more.

> Of all the thinkers—and great thinkers—whose lineage has its origin in Descartes, I contest neither the exceptional intelligence, nor the importance, nor the worth, nor, at times, the genius. In regard to them, I challenge only one thing, but that I challenge with might and main, and with the certainty of being right: namely their right to the name of philosopher (except, of course, for Bergson, and perhaps also Blondel). In dealing with these children of Descartes we must sweep away this name with the back of our hand. They are not philosophers; they are *ideosophers:* that is the only name which fits and by which it is proper to call them.[8]

It is the shared idealism of this Cartesian lineage that underlies Maritain's judgment. A philosophy that impugns extramental reality is no philosophy, but an ideosophy. He makes a great exception of Marxism which, whatever its flaws, and they are fundamental, is a philosophical doctrine because it takes extramental reality as basic. The problem is that it identifies it with matter.

Maritain places Husserl and phenomenology in the Cartesian lineage. Having recalled the elements of philosophical realism, Maritain writes, "These things Husserl did not see. A man of greatness and fundamental integrity, he deserved the gratitude and affection Edith Stein continued to feel for him while freeing herself from his influence. But like so many others, he was a victim of Descartes and Kant."[9] The second great *bête noire* of the book is Teilhard de Chardin, a then influential figure, now all but forgotten.

Maritain is half apologetic about the severity of his treatment of the mainline of modern philosophers, but it is refreshing to hear a spade called a spade, which is the mark of the peasant of the Garonne. Much of the trouble in postconciliar theology has been the assumption that the theologian could randomly pick a modern philosophy and interpret the faith in its light. But many of these philosophies are intentionally antithetical to the faith and to its basic presuppositions about the human mind. Maritain follows his criticisms with a splendid chapter on Thomas Aquinas.

But the heart of the book is not here. What Maritain takes the council to be is a call to inwardness, to the spiritual life, to contemplation. Thus we are not surprised when he turns to the themes of *Liturgy and Contemplation*, putting Raïssa in the center of his meditations. The liturgy of the sacraments or the common recitation of the canonical hours is the worship rendered by the mystical Body of Christ, head and members.[10] Having recalled things said about contemplation in earlier works, Maritain insists that contemplation is the common vocation of the Christian. Here, with obvious satisfaction, he quotes Raïssa.[11] "Saint Thérèse of Lisieux has shown that the soul can tend to the perfection of charity by a way in which the great signs that Saint John of the Cross and Saint Teresa of Avila have described do not appear. . . ."

In *The Peasant of the Garonne*, as throughout his career, it is clear that the pursuit of truth and clarity is not at the service merely of winning an argument or negatively appraising the efforts of others. As in few other thinkers, we are always conscious that a person is doing the thinking and that this person aspires to more than the perfection of the mind. From first to last, Maritain's philosophizing is embedded in the contemplative life. He calls *The Peasant* an old man's book, and it is true that in it he is a bit garrulous and repetitive; but it is a great book, the first to see and warn of what enormities would be perpetrated in the name of Vatican II.

LITTLE BROTHER OF JESUS

Returned to France, feeble, valetudinarian, yet still with years of life ahead of him, Maritain had the great good fortune of being offered a home with the Little Brothers of Jesus in Toulouse. He could share in the life of the community, teach, prepare for eternity. For all his hope and intention to lead an increasingly reclusive life, he was constantly drawn into wider affairs. And new books continued to appear. Summers he spent in Alsace, at Kolbsheim.

Father René Voillaume, a Little Brother of Jesus, had been a friend of the Maritains for years, and Jacques was a great admirer of his. We remember that he was asked to comment on the journal of Raïssa before publication. So this old connection, plus the presence of the Dominicans in Toulouse (and the grave of Thomas Aquinas), would have commended this move to Jacques. For the brothers, he was a great boon, providing seminars for them that blossomed into some of his last books. His themes were often explicitly theological—*The Grace and Humanity of Jesus, The Church of Christ*—and he followed the Second Vatican Council closely, viewing interpretations being made of it with alarm, as is indicated by *The Peasant of the Garonne.* He was consulted by Pope Paul VI before the pontiff issued his Credo of Paul VI.

In *The Peasant*, Maritain made much of himself as an old layman, but we have seen that he was a most unusual member of the laity. From the outset of their married life, he and Raïssa—and Vera—had followed a veritable religious rule in their daily life. And of course they were oblates of Saint Benedict. When to this is added the vow Jacques and Raïssa took early in their married life to live as brother and sister, he may seem even more remote from the lives most men and women lead. And then, as he neared his eighty-eighth year, Jacques Maritain himself became a Little Brother of Jesus, taking the vows of religion and becoming a full member of the community. The very simplicity of the community appealed to one who had long advocated *les moyens pauvres*, slender means, as the most effective. The Brothers built their own chapel and other buildings, and Jacques's quarters had always been simple and austere.

Perhaps Jacques sensed that many would be puzzled by this move. Taking the vow of chastity at eighty-eight might not seem demanding, but of course Jacques had taken it many years before. Writing to his dear friend Henry Bars, he asked for his prayers and said that he had always had it in his head to end his days under religious obedience. And he hoped his decision could be kept confidential.

Does Jacques Maritain's late entry into the religious life diminish the role we have been stressing in this presentation of his life? Is he any less a model for those lay believers whose calling it is to pursue the arts and sciences, philosophy, or theology? The *Cercles d'études*, it will be remembered, were not restricted to lay people, though the emphasis in the constitution is on the prayer life they must develop. The reason for this emphasis was that religious were already committed to a life of prayer. At the end, Jacques bridged the gap between the two and, I suggest, released his influence from too narrow an interpretation.

Models of behavior are complicated entities. The saints all imitate Jesus and no two of them are alike. And we lesser mortals take our cue from the saints as well, but not in order to replicate them exactly. Indeed, it is logically impossible to become the clone of anyone else. The life of Jacques Maritain can only be understood as the pursuit of sanctity through the life of study, of philosophy, and, in the end, theology. We can reflect on his life in its singularity and go on to imagine living our own life like that. Over the decades of his life, as often as not unwittingly, Jacques functioned in that way for many. It is the argument of this little book that he still can—and does.

In March 1973, Jacques, who had suffered a heart attack in Princeton, began to suffer pains in his limbs. For a time he used a wheelchair, but soon he was confined to his bed. On March 19, Holy Thursday, he received Holy Communion and the last rites. On Easter Sunday, he was able to attend Mass; it would be for the last time. On Saturday, April 28, he died. Did anyone think of those lines in the *Phaedo*? "Such was the end, Echecrates, of our friend; concerning whom I may truly say, that of all the men of his time whom I have known, he was the wisest and justest and best."

NUNC DIMITTIS

He was raised in a broken home, his mother a natural child who became one of France's first divorcées and reassumed her maiden name. His father had been his grandfather's secretary, was a wastrel, and ended a suicide. As a boy he was radicalized by a socialist servant and instructed in Christianity by a Protestant tutor. Jacques Maritain arrived at the Sorbonne with great talent, a thirst for truth, but little other than politics to slake it. When he met Raïssa Oumansov, he recognized immediately the *dimidium animae meae*, the other and complementary half of his soul. What would either have become without the other? It is impossible to imagine, so profoundly wed they were, even more profoundly after they vowed to live as brother and sister. A review, a book, the author—what could be more ordinary? Except when the reviewer is Maurice Maeterlinck, the book *The Woman Who Was Poor*, and the author Léon Bloy. Improbable as it may seem, this was the path the Maritains took to the Church. They became Catholics in a total and profound way, from the beginning determined to draw as close as possible to God in anticipation of eternal union with Him. Guided by Garrigou-Lagrange, Maritain became one of the two dominant laymen in the Thomistic Revival, the other being Etienne Gilson. A long and ambiguous connection with Action Française was ended with the papal condemnation of the movement. Jacques moved gradually leftward, following his natural disposition, and agitated against the Spanish Civil War, thereby alienating many fellow Catholics who did not understand that he sought to be on neither side. Visits to North America paved the way for a wartime exile in New York, from where his influence radiated over the continent. Raïssa's memoirs captivated a generation of American Catholics. After serving as his country's ambassador to the Vatican, Jacques returned to the United States, to Princeton, where he taught for some five years. Retirement and a heart attack resolved him to remain in Princeton. It was there that in 1959, Vera died; and the following year, on their annual visit to France, Raïssa fell ill and died. Alone, Jacques accepted an invitation from the Little Brothers of Jesus and moved to Toulouse. Summers he spent in Kolbsheim, where Raïssa was buried. In extreme old age, Jacques Maritain, the quintessential layman, took the vows of religion as a Little Brother of Jesus. After Raïssa's death he thought of himself as preparing for his own, but the more than a decade that remained was a time of great productivity. He died in 1973 and was buried in Kolbsheim with Raïssa.

Only God knows the real plot of any human story. Our estimates of one another are at best conjectural, based as they must be on signs and visible deeds. It is not the office of a biographer to canonize his subject, but who could fail to see the life of Jacques Maritain in any terms other than those of the quest for Christian perfection, for sanctity? This account of Maritain's life has made use of only a fraction of the mountains of material available. Many collections of his letters have been published and these are particularly precious, but there are many more in the archives at Kolbsheim awaiting future students of the life and work of Jacques Maritain. For all that, any account, even one based on every jot and tittle of information, would fall short of an adequate account of his life. As I bring this account to a close, I am deeply aware of its inadequacy.

What I hope to have given is some intimation of the role Jacques Maritain played for those of my generation. Of course, his influence continues to be felt, but to have read him first at the halfway point of the twentieth century was to read one of the main reasons for that golden period of Catholicism. What an incomparable blessing to be introduced to philosophy by a thinker who was both a superb philosopher and a paradigmatic Christian philosopher. How shallow by contrast seem the lives of the secular philosophers who were Maritain's contemporaries. The lives of Russell and Wittgenstein and Heidegger make melancholy reading; whatever insights one finds here and there in their work, there is absent any satisfying sense of the ultimate point of human life. The great questions, secularized, become trivial: markers in a game. How many modern or contemporary philosophers would one want to be alone with in an elevator, let alone in conversation for half an hour?

Such judgments may be severe, but they suggest the contrast with Jacques Maritain. First and foremost, one encounters a person of whom one can say: How I would like to be like that! For it is a question of *being* as much as or more than of knowing. Wasn't this the genius of Maritain's treatment of the question of Christian philosophy? Arguments are won or lost, critics obtuse or otherwise are constant; our grasp of truth even after a long lifetime brings the awareness of how little one knows. Thomas Aquinas, a year before he died, dismissed his writings, than which there are no better, as mere straw. Compared to what? To the mystical vision he had been granted. Still, he did not quite stop teaching. In 1274, when he was traveling north from Naples to attend the council to be held at Lyon, he fell ill and was taken to the Cistercian Abbey at Fossanova. There on his deathbed, at the request of the monks, he commented on the Song of Songs. So too, Jacques Maritain at the end of his life wrote a little book on the Song of Songs. Woe is me should I not think with Thomas, he had said, and it was a kind of motto. *Vae mihi si non thomistizavero.* He became a disciple worthy of his master. For both men, master and disciple, in the end, it was the true end of human life that occupied them.

Jacques Maritain continues to be the model of the Christian philosopher, of the Thomist, both by what he taught and by what he was. The Church's prayer in the office for the feast of Thomas Aquinas can apply, *toutes proportions gardées,* to Jacques Maritain as well.

> *Deus, qui Ecclesiam tuam beati Thomae Confessoris tui atque Doctoris mira eruditione clarificas, et sancta operatione fecundas: da nobis intellectu conspicere, et quae egit imitatione complere.*

NOTES

Notes to Matins

    1. Jean-Luc Barré, *Jacques et Raïssa Maritain: Les Mendiants du Ciel* (Paris: Stock, 1995).

    2. Jacques Maritain, *Carnet de notes* (Paris, 1965), p. 29. To be found also in *Jacques et Raïssa Maritain Oeuvres complètes* [hereafter *OC*], (Paris: Editions Saint-Paul, 1982–), XII. This edition, under the editorship of a team headed by René Mougel, comprises sixteen volumes.

    3. Raïssa Maritain, *We Have Been Friends Together* (New York: Longmans, Green and Co., 1942), p. 6, and *OC* XVI.

    4. Ibid., p. 50.

    5. Ibid.

    6. See Judith D. Suther, *Raïssa Maritain: Pilgrim, Poet, Exile* (New York: Fordham University Press, 1990), and Nora Possenti Ghiglia, *I Tre Maritain. La presenza di Vera nel mondo di Jacques e Raïssa* (Milan: Ancora, 2000).

    7. Ibid., p. 66.

    8. Ibid., p. 68.

    9. Henry Bars, *Maritain en notre temps* (Paris: Grasset, 1959).

    10. Ibid., p. 80.

    11. Maritain, *Carnet de notes*, p. 28.

    12. R. Maritain, *We Have Been Friends Together*, p. 87.

    13. *Quelques pages sur Léon Bloy, OC*, III, pp. 47–49.

    14. *The Life Of Jesus Christ and Biblical Revelations from the visions of Ven. Anne Catherine Emmerich as recorded in the journals of Clemens Brentano*, arranged and edited by Carl E. Schmoger, 4 vols. (Rockford: Tan Books, 1979).

    15. Jean-Joseph Surin, S.J. (1600–1665), visionary, exorcist at Ursuline convent of Loudon (on which Aldous Huxley based *The Devils of Loudon*), and author of *A Spiritual Catechism* and other works.

    16. R. Maritain, *We Have Been Friends Together*, p. 136.

    17. Ibid., p. 137.

18. Ibid., p. 138.

19. Ibid.

Notes to Lauds

1. R. Maritain, *We Have Been Friends Together*, p. 99.

2. Ibid., p. 115.

3. Blaise Pascal, *Oeuvres complètes*, preface d'Henri Gouhier, presentation et notes de Louis LaFuma (Paris: Editions du Seuil, 1963), pp. 550–51.

4. Ibid., p. 143.

5. Ibid., p. 145

6. See the following website: www.lasalettemissionaries.org.

7. J. Maritain, *Carnet de notes*, p. 117–18.

8. Ibid., p. 121. See Barré, *Jacques et Raïssa Maitain*, pp. 193–94.

9. J. Maritain, *Carnet de notes*, p. 48.

10. Ibid., p. 51.

11. R. Maritain, *We Have Been Friends Together*, p. 175.

12. This can be found in *OC* I, pp. 1112–26.

13. Ibid., p. 1115.

14. Maritain notes that this role is usually assigned to the Passionist Father, Cuthbert Dunne, and so it is in Richard Ellman's biography, *Oscar Wilde* (London: Penguin Books, 1985), pp. 549–50. Ellman has Dunne saying the Requiem Mass as well. Apparently the visiting card of the man, Robert Ross, who came to the Passionists has survived, but the message written on it does not close the door entirely on Clérissac. "Can I see one of the fathers about a very urgent case or can I hear of a priest elsewhere who can talk English to administer last sacraments to a dying man?" The account of Wilde's death by Ellman is graphic.

15. *OC* I, p. 1115.

16. Ibid., p. 1118.

17. Ibid., p. 1121.

18. Ibid. , pp. 1122–23.

19. Barré, *Jacques et Raïssa Maritain* (Paris: Stock, 1995), p. 131. Barré, taking his cue from Raïssa, seeks to explain elements of Maritain's life that are now politically incorrect as due to the sinister influence of his spiritual directors, in whose hands Jacques was supposedly mere putty. It is hard to imagine anyone less malleable than Jacques Maritain or a man less likely to take on another's political views against the grain. Barré's account is marred by such descriptive phrases as already mentioned, e.g., "leur austère protecteur" (p. 133). The apologia is clear when Barré, having noted the formation of Action Française and the *Nouvelle Revue Française* and the political and literary turmoil of the time, writes that "Jacques Maritain was a man too concentrated on his intimate route to take the least part yet in temporal de-

bates. And only the supremacy exercised on him by Clérissac led him to enlist under a banner to which nothing destined him to rally" (p. 136).

20. J. Maritain, *Carnet de notes*, p. 70.

21. Ibid., p. 103.

22. Ibid., pp. 110–11.

23. Ibid., p. 112.

24. An account of the Camelots can be found in R. L. Bruckberger, *Tu finiras sur l'echafaud* (Paris: Flammarion, 1978), pp. 245 ff.

25. Bernard Doering, *Jacques Maritain and the French Catholic Intellectuals* (Notre Dame, Ind.: University of Notre Dame Press, 1983), p. 17.

26. In informing Dom Delatte of the new publication, Maritain expressed reluctance at entering into a "worldly" (*mondain*) project, but took comfort from the fact that, for the first time, Thomistic philosophy could be presented to a wide public. "I hope to have the means, little by little, to express there more and more clearly the Catholic point of view. Moreover, it is the intention of Bainville and of the review to be covered by me on the Catholic side, given the more and more hostile attitide toward Action Française in French Catholic (and even Roman) circles ever since the Holy Father appears to want to resuscitate everything that Pius X destroyed." Memoir of Michel Cagin (Kolbsheim); in Barré, *Jacques et Raïssa Maritain*, p. 216. Maritain would be associated with the journal from April 1, 1920, until February 1, 1927. The close connection that was thus established between the politics of the Right and Thomism proved an impediment for many French philosophers. One of the deleterious effects of their reaction to the connection was the demonization of such figures as Garrigou-Lagrange.

27. Barré, *Jacques et Raïssa Maritain*, p. 146.

28. Ibid., p. 147.

29. "Clerical and lay, the leaders of the neo-Thomist revival, which was Catholicism's answer to its subversive exegetes, gravitated toward the Action Française. Unworldly men, great scholars like Billot or Father Thomas Pègues, saw only its single-minded opposition to the worldly forces of modernism. Catholic faculties were crowded with admirers of Maurras who, like the Abbé Maisonneuve at Toulouse, tended to consider his anti-liberal political ideas infallible. Of the Dominicans in particular, like Father Georges de Pascal, Jacques Vallée, and Garrigou-Lagrange—not forgetting Dom Besse, the master of novices at Notre-Dame-de-Ligugé—may be said what Raïssa Maritain has written about one of them, Father Humbert Clérissac: 'Father Clérissac passionately admired Maurras; in his disgust with the modern world, in his pure enthusiasm for the metaphysical notion of order, he trusted the [Action Française].'" Eugen Weber, *Action Française: Royalism and Reaction in Twentieth Century France* (Stanford: Stanford University Press, 1962), p. 220.

30. "And by 1937 Jacques Maritain, who had once been the coming theological sage of the Action Française, could address the International Congress of

Christian Workers on 'The Primacy of the Human'—not, as he might once have done, on the primacy of politics." Ibid., p. 255.

Notes to Prime

1. *Elements de philosophie, 1: Introduction; 2, Petite logique. OC* II. These appeared in English as *An Introduction to Philosophy*, trans. by E. I. Watkin (New York: Sheed and Ward, 1930); and *An Introduction to Logic* (New York: Sheed and Ward, 1937).

2. J. Maritain, *Carnet de notes*, p. 184.

3. In a letter of February 12, 1928, Edith Stein wrote, "It was through St. Thomas that I first came to realize that it is possible to regard scholarly work as a service of God. Immediately before, and a long time after my conversion, I thought living a religious life meant to abandon earthly things and to live only in the thought of the heavenly realities. Gradually I have learned to understand that in this world something else is demanded of us, and that even in the contemplative life the connection with this world must not be cut off. Only then did I make up my mind to take up scholarly work again. I even think that the more deeply a soul is drawn into God, the more it must also go out of itself in this sense, that is to say in the world, in order to carry the Divine life into it." Edith Stein, *Werke* VII, *Selbstbildnis in Briefen, 1916–1934* (Freiberg: Herder, 1976), pp. 54–55.

4. Tommaso Leccisotti, in *San Tommaso d'Aquino e Montecassino. Badia di Montecassino, 1965*, has clarified the status of oblates. It would not be accurate to say that Thomas was ever a professed Benedictine monk.

5. J. Maritain, *Carnet de notes*, p. 185.

6. John Henry Newman, *Letters and Diaries* XI, p. 279.

7. Claude Buffier, S.J., *Oeuvres philosophiques* (Paris: Charpentier, 1843).

8. See *OC* I (1906–1920), Annexe, pp. 889–1025.

9. Ibid., p. 893.

10. In April–May of 1914, Maritain began his discussion of the spirit of modern philosophy with a lecture on the Cartesian Reform. Cf. *OC* I, pp. 823–87.

Notes to Tierce

1. When Jacques's mother visited them in June, the two women got along. Geneviève told of a friend who was led to God by spiritism. Raïssa countered with the story that, when she was thirteen, in sleep, she heard a voice speaking in her left ear, a voice so strong it woke her and then impatiently said, "You're always asking what you should do. You have only to love God and serve him with all your heart." *Journal de Raïssa*, June 7, 1919, pp. 247–48.

2. See Barré, *Jacques et Maritain*, pp. 202–3, which relies on a March 1919 entry in Raïssa's journal.

3. For example, the entry that discusses intelligence and shame as signs of the spirituality of the soul (March 10, pp. 237–38).

4. Ibid., p. 237.

5. His *Introduction to Philosophy* was published in 1920 and *Formal Logic* in 1923.

6. A "transcendental" in this sense is the concept of a property which, like being, is not confined to one category but transcends the categorical divisions because, again like being, it is found, though differently, in a number of different categories. Not only substance is being, but also quantity, quality, and the like. The term "being," accordingly, is not said univocally of its various instances— substance and quantity are not being in the same sense—but, as Thomas put it, analogously or according to analogy. Maritain's point is that "beauty," too, is an analogous term.

7. *Summa theologiae*, Ia, q. 5, a. 4, ad 1m. Chapter 5 of *Art and Scholasticism* is devoted to the notion of beauty.

8. "This conception of the work [*oeuvre*] which depends on the whole spiritual and sensible being of the artist, and above all on the rectification of his appetite with respect to Beauty, and which bears on the *end* of the activity, is to art as the intention of the end of the moral virtues is to prudence." (N. 95)

9. *Paul Claudel/André Gide Correspondance 1899–1926*, Préface et notes par Robert Mallety, NRF (Paris: Gallimard, 1949).

10. Frédéric Lefèvre, "Une heure avec MM. Jacques Maritain et Henri Massis," *Les nouvelles littéraires*, 2eme année, n. 52 (13 Octobre 1923).

11. André Gide, *Journal 1889–1939* (Paris: Gallimard, 1951).

12. Quoted by Barré, *Jacques et Raïssa Maritain*, p. 265.

13. "Noël, visite chez Maritain à Meudon où je vois le jeune Juif converti par Copeau, Sachs, qui va entrer au séminaire (!!)." Paul Claudel, *Journal* I (Paris: Bibliothèque de la Pléiade, Gallimard, 1968), p. 699.

14. See Doering, *Jacques Maritain and the French Catholic Intellectuals*, p. 240.

15. Paul Claudel, *Journal* II, p. 645.

Notes to Sext

1. Georges Bernanos, *Combat pour la vérité: Correspondance inédite 1904–1934* (Paris: Plon, 1971), pp. 323–24.

2. *La philosophie chrétienne, Journées d'études de la Société Thomiste* (Juvisy: Editions du Cerf, 1933).

3. Ibid., p. 78.

4. Motte cites *Q. D. de veritate*, q. 14, a. 10: "Ab ipsa prima institutione natura humana est ordinata in finem beatitudinis—non quasi in finem debitum homini secundum naturam ejus, sed ex sola divina liberalitate."

5. *Summa theologiae*, Ia, q. 8, a. 4.

6. *Summa theologiae*, IaIIae, q. 2, a. 3: "Natura rationalis, in quantum cognoscit universalem boni et entis rationem, habet immediatum ordinem ad universale essendi principium; perfectio ergo rationalis creaturae non solum consistit in eo quod ei competit secundum suam naturam, sed in eo etiam quod ei attribuitur ex quadam supernaturali participatione divinae bonitatis." In a note to p. 82, Motte adds: "Il va de soi que la nature et l'existence même de ce secours surnaturel ne peuvent se déduire philosophiquement. Du moins sa possibilité est-elle certainement contenue dans la toute-puissance divine: Saint Thomas le prouve par l'absurde au moyen du fameux argument du désir naturel de connaître. (cf. *Bulletin Thomiste*, 1932, pp. 651–76) Il n'en faut pas davantage pour que le philosophe, dès là qu'il pose Dieu, réserve comme possible tout un ordre de participation surnaturelle du créé à l'incréé. Mais nous ne nous limitons pas ici au point de vue du philosophe."

7. *La philosophie chrétienne*, p. 82.

8. Ibid., p. 84.

9. *Summa contra gentiles*, I, 3.

10. *Summa theologiae*, IaIIae, q. 109, a. 1: "Intellectus humanus habet aliquam formam, scilicet ipsum lumen intelligibile, quod est de se sufficiens ad quaedam intelligibilia cognoscenda, ad ea scilicet in quorum notitiam per sensibilia possumus devenire."

11. *La philosophie chrétienne*, p. 93.

12. Ibid., p. 94.

13. Ibid., p. 98.

14. Ibid., p. 99.

15. Ibid., p. 103, note 1. "Au surplus la 'philosophie morale adéquatement prise' subalternée à la théologie, que M. Maritain place entre la théologie morale et la morale strictement philosophique (*De la philosophie chrétienne*, Paris, Desclée de Brouwer, 1933, pp. 108–66), semble difficile à concevoir, le schème classique de la subalternation pouvant malaisément chevaucher deux plans d'intelligibilité aussi distincts que celui de la foi et celui de la raison philosophique."

16. One of the more extended discussions of these matters is to be found in Jacques Maritain, *Science and Wisdom* (London: G. Bles, The Centenary Press, 1940).

17. Ibid., p. 162.

18. Ibid., p. 167.

19. "Si la foi seule peut nous fournir notre fin réele et nos réelles conditions existentiels—motifs invoqués par M. Maritain—c'est parce que la foi seule manifeste aussi notre lien réel, nos réels rapports avec notre Principe, tellement que toute systématisation, qu'elle soit théorique ou pratique, ne peut s'achever réellement, je veux dire avec une portée réelle et décisive, que par l'effort combiné de la philosophie et de la foi. Qu'on songe que, pour saint Thomas, la providence même ne se démontre pas en philosophie!" *La philosophie chrétienne*, p. 118.

20. Ibid., p. 120.

21. Jacques Maritain, *An Essay on Christian Philosophy* (New York: Pholosophical Library, 1955), p. 4.

22. Ibid., p. 8.

23. Ibid., p. 9.

24. Ibid., p. 17.

25. Ibid., p. 25.

26. Bernard Doering, ed. and trans., *The Collected Works of Jacques Maritain* 7 (Notre Dame, Ind.: University of Notre Dame Press, 1995), p. 264.

27. Ibid., p. 265.

28. Ibid., p. 266.

29. *Revue Thomiste* 84 (1984), pp. 663–64. Quoted by Serge-Thomas Bonino in "Historiographie de l'école thomiste: Le cas Gilson," in *Saint Thomas au XXe Siècle* (Paris, 1994).

30. *Deux approaches de l'être: Correspondence, 1923–1971/Etienne Gilson–Jacques Maritain*, ed. Géry Prouvost (Paris: J. Vrin, 1991).

31. See Laurence K. Shook, *Etienne Gilson* (Toronto: Pontifical Institute of Mediaeval Studies, 1984), p. 318.

32. Doering, ed., *The Collected Works of Jacques Maritain*, p. 20.

33. Prouvost, ed., *Etienne Gilson–Jacques Maritain Correspondence*, p. 275ff.

34. "Your severity with regard to Cajetan is expressed with a nuance and moderation that make me grateful to you. You know that my position with regard to the great commentators is not the same as Gilson's. They are far from being infallible and have often hardened our differences. I gladly recognize the serious deficiencies of Cajetan. But it remains my position that these great minds (and especially John of St. Thomas—from whom on occasion though I do not hesitate to separate myself) are like very precious optical instruments which enable us to *see much more clearly* certain depths of St. Thomas's thought even though other depths are given short shrift by them." Translation cited from Doering, *Jacques Maritain and the French Catholic Intellectuals*, p. 67.

35. "Unfortunately, on all the points on which he prides himself on improving, completing Thomas Aquinas, my own feeling is that he is distorting the true thought of the Angelic Doctor." Prouvost, *Etienne Gilson–Jacques Maritain Correspondence*, pp. 275–76, note.

36. See *Jacques Maritain and the Jews*, edited by Robert Royal, the proceedings of the American Maritain Association (Notre Dame, Ind.: University of Notre Dame Press, 1994).

37. Paul Claudel, *Oeuvres en prose* (Paris: Gallimard, 1965), pp. 1008–14.

38. See Dominique Millet-Gerard, *Claudel thomiste?* (Paris: Champion, 1999).

39. Claudel, *Journal* I, p. 924.

40. The poem was published as the preface to a book by M. Echtachill, *La persécution religieuse en Espagne* (Paris, 1937).

41. "Question sociale et questions sociales" first appeared in *Le Figaro Littéraires*, June 24, 1939. See Claudel, *Oeuvres en prose* (Paris: Bibliothèque de la Pléiade, 1965), p. 1326.

42. *Le Figaro*, July 8, 1939.

Notes to Nones

1. *A travers le désastre*, Avant-propos. *OC* VII, p. 343.

2. *OC* VII, p. 13 (*La crépuscule de la civilisation*).

3. One is surprised to find Maritain saying, in a note added in November 1941, "Now Russia is in the war against Nazism. Grafted thus into the western community. It is possible that profound inner changes will take place in it."

4. Jacques Maritain, *The Twilight of Civilization*, trans. Lionel Landry (London: Sheed and Ward, 1945), p. 43.

5. In C. S. Lewis, *The Weight of Glory and Other Addresses* (New York: Macmillan, 1949), p. 44.

6. See James V. Schall, *Maritain the Philosopher in Society* (New York: Rowman and Littlefield, 1998), pp. 181–99.

7. Translated from Maritain's French. See Thomas Aquinas, *Super evangelium S. Ioannis lectura* (Ed. Cai. Turin, 1952), Cap. XX, lect. 1, n. 2480.

8. Julie Kernan, *Our Friend, Jacques Maritain, A Personal Memoir* (New York, 1975), pp. 125–26.

9. Suther, *Raïssa Maritain, Pilgrim, Poet, Exile*, p. 127. See also Ghiglia, *I Tre Maritain*, p. 321ff.

10. One contretemps that was of particular interest in North America was occasioned by Charles DeKoninck's *De la primauté du bien commun contre les personalistes* (Quebec: Editions de l'Université Laval, 1943). DeKoninck was the youthful doyen of the Faculté de philosophie at l'Université Laval, whose early work had been markedly influenced by Maritain. In reviewing DeKoninck's book, Yves Simon agreed with the criticism that DeKoninck leveled but said that it would be pure calumny if it were thought to be applicable to Maritain. (There was no mention of Maritain, nor indeed of anyone else in DeKoninck's book, making his target difficult to identify.) I. Thomas Eschmann, on the other hand, claimed that the position DeKoninck criticized was indeed Maritain's, and he set out to defend it in a piece called *In Defense of Jacques Maritain*. DeKoninck responded with a lengthy *In Defence of St. Thomas Aquinas: A Reply to Father Eschmann's Attack on the Primacy of the Common Good* (Quebec: Editions l'Université Laval, 1945). Apart from his letters, Maritain's only reference to this controversy was a puzzling footnote in *The Person and the Common Good*, in which he thanked Eschmann for his defense and made no mention of Simon's demur.

11. Jacques Maritain, *Existence and the Existent* (New York: Pantheon, 1948), chap. 2, n. 12.

12. *Existence and the Existent* (New York: Image Books, 1956), pp. 148–49.

13. Ibid., p. 151.

14. *OC* IX, pp. 443–69.

15. I have in mind the veritable little treatise on atheism to be found in Part One of *Gaudium et Spes*, The Pastoral Constitution on the Church in the Modern World.

16. Ibid., p. 449.

Notes to Vespers

1. The house was occupied by the Louriés until Notre Dame took possession. It then functioned as a residence for Notre Dame professors on sabbatical until, without warning or consultation, the house was sold. This dismayed and astonished many, including Maritain's Princeton lawyer. In his will, Maritain had also left his heart to Notre Dame, but the French authorities prevented the transfer of this organ to South Bend. After the sale of the house, there was a mordant joke to the effect that it was a good thing the university hadn't received Maritain's heart, as the provost might have sold that as well.

2. See *OC* VI, pp. 1133–35.

3. Julio Meinvielle, *De Lamennais à Maritain,* segunda edicion corregida y notablemente aumentada (Buenos Aires: Ediciones Theoria, 1967).

4. See *OC* IX, pp. 1102ff.

5. Ibid., p. 1101, n. 1.

6. *Raison et raisons* is a collection of Maritain's essays put together by Charles Journet in 1948 to bring European readers up to date on Maritain's work. The text of this work appears in volume IX of the *Oeuvres complètes.* According to Maritain's instructions, this polemical piece is not part of it.

7. While the Council was still in session, Guy de Broglie, S.J., published *Le droit naturel à la liberté religieuse* (Paris: Beauchesne, 1964), addressing some of the controversy the document was generating. The controversy continues. See Romano Amerio, *Iota Unum. Studio delle variazioni della Chiesa cattolica nel secolo XX* (Milano: Riccardo Ricciardi, 1985), and Claude Barthe, *Quel avenir pour Vatican II?* (Paris: François-Xavier de Guibert, 1998).

8. ". . . which unfortunately was expressed in an insufficiently clarified vocabulary, so that its deepest features were soon overlooked and disregarded." Jacques Maritain, *Man and the State* (Chicago: University of Chicago Press), p. 85.

9. Ibid., p. 83.

10. Ibid., p. 82.

11. In *Fides et Ratio,* n. 4, John Paul II speaks of an "implicit philosophy," common to all, which provides a set of criteria for appraising philosophical systems.

12. Letter to 'A'. September 24, 1955. In Sally Fitzgerald, ed., *The Habit of Being* (New York: Farrar Straus, Giroux, 1979), p. 105.

13.   Ibid. p. 216 (April 20, 1957).

14.   Jacques Maritain, *Creative Intuition in Art and Poetry* (New York: Pantheon Books, 1953), p. 3.

15.   Jacques Maritain, *Art and Scholasticism and The Frontiers of Poetry*, trans. Joseph W. Evans (Notre Dame, Ind.: University of Notre Dame Press, 1974), p. 36.

16.   J. Maritain, *Creative Intuition*, p. 21.

17.   Ibid., p. 23.

18.   Ibid., p. 113.

19.   Ibid., p. 115.

20.   Ibid., pp. 235–36.

21.   Jacques Maritain, *A Preface to Metaphysics: Seven Lectures on Being* (New York: Sheed and Ward, 1939), p. 18.

22.   Ibid., p. 19.

23.   One thinks of the title Sally Fitzgerald gave to her edition of the letters of Flannery O'Connor: *The Habit of Being.*

24.   J. Maritain, *A Preface to Metaphysics*, p. 21.

25.   Ibid., p. 22. The internal quote is from Cajetan's commentary on the *Posterior Analytics.*

26.   Ibid., p. 23.

27.   Ibid., p. 24.

28.   Ibid., p. 45.

29.   Ibid., p. 47.

30.   Ibid., p. 60.

31.   *Journet-Maritain Correspondance* III, 1940–1949 (edition of the *Fondation du Cardinal Journet*. Edition Saint-Augustin, 1998), p. 698.

32.   Ibid., p. 716.

33.   Jacques Maritain, *Moral Philosophy: A Historical and Critical Survey of the Great Systems* (New York: Scribner, 1964), p. 448. The French version had appeared in Paris in 1960.

34.   Ibid.

35.   Ibid., p. 36.

36.   Ibid., p. 46. This passage may be said to write closure to the controversy over the common good to which *The Person and the Common Good* was a first response.

37.   Maritain, on this same page 46, seems to accept as good money the so-called errors of Aristotle having to do with free will and God's knowledge of his effects that Thomas Aquinas had argued were misinterpretations of Aristotle.

38.   Jacques et Raïssa Maritain, *Liturgie et contemplation* (Paris: Desclée de Brouwer, 1959), p. 28.

39.   Ibid., p. 33.

40.   Throughout this little book, the Maritains rely on the spiritual writings of Reginald Garrigou-Lagrange.

41.   Maritain et Maritain, *Liturgie et contemplation*, pp. 38–39.

42. Ibid., p. 41.

43. *Summa theologiae*, IIaIIae, q. 184, a. 3, ad 2.

44. Maritain et Maritain, *Liturgie et contemplation*, p. 46.

45. Ibid., p. 53.

46. Ibid., p. 60.

47. Ibid., p. 65.

48. Ibid., p. 69.

49. Ibid., p. 70.

50. Ibid., p. 87.

Notes to Compline

1. Quoted by Jean-Luc Barré, *Jacques et Raïssa Maritain*, p. 560.

2. To Thomas Merton. Cf. Barré, ibid., pp. 562–63.

3. "If there is any good in my philosophical work and in my books, the profound source and light should be sought in her prayer and the offering she made of herself to God." *OC* XV, p. 160.

4. Raïssa Maritain, *We Have Been Friends Together*, p. 171.

5. Jacques Maritain, *The Peasant of the Garonne: An Old Layman Questions Himself about the Present Time*, trans. Michael Cuddihy and Elizabeth Hughes (New York: Holt, Rinehart, and Winston, 1968), p. 85.

6. Ibid., pp. 85–86.

7. Ibid., p. 96

8. Ibid., 101–2.

9. Ibid., p. 105.

10. Ibid., p. 214. The reflections on the Mass in the following pages contain some of the best things he ever wrote.

11. Ibid., p. 234.

INDEX

RALPH McINERNY is Michael P. Grace Professor of Medieval Studies and director of the Jacques Maritain Center, University of Notre Dame. He is the author of numerous works in philosophy, literature, and journalism, including *Characters in Search of Their Author,* also published by the University of Notre Dame Press.